MULTILATERAL ENVIRONMENTAL AGREEMENTS

This book seeks to examine the genesis, development, and proliferation of multilateral environmental agreements (MEAs) – built-in lawmaking mechanisms and processes of institutionalization – and their ad hoc treaty-based status and the issue of the legal personality of their secretariats. It provides legal understanding of the location of MEA secretariats within an existing international host institution, as well as discussion of the issues of relationship agreements and interpretation of the commonly used language that triggers such relationships. It places under scrutiny the standard MEA phrase "providing a secretariat," delegation of authority by the host institution to the head of the convention secretariat, possible conflict areas, host country agreements, and the workings of relationship agreements. The book offers an authoritative account of the growing phenomenon in which an existing international institution provides a servicing base for an MEA that, in turn, triggers a chain of legal implications involving the secretariat, the host institution, and the host country.

Professor Bharat H. Desai holds the prestigious Jawaharlal Nehru Chair in International Environmental Law and is Professor of International Law, as well as Chairman of the Centre for International Legal Studies, at the School of International Studies of Jawaharlal Nehru University in New Delhi. As a Humboldt Fellow, he worked at the University of Bonn on the treatise *Institutionalizing International Environmental Law*. He is the author of *Creeping Institutionalization: Multilateral Environmental Agreements and Human Security*, an associate editor of the *Yearbook of International Environmental Law*, and Vice Chairman of the Foundation for Development of International Law in Asia.

Multilateral Environmental Agreements

LEGAL STATUS OF THE SECRETARIATS

Bharat H. Desai

Jawaharlal Nehru University

CAMBRIDGE
UNIVERSITY PRESS

CAMBRIDGE UNIVERSITY PRESS
Cambridge, New York, Melbourne, Madrid, Cape Town,
Singapore, São Paulo, Delhi, Mexico City

Cambridge University Press
32 Avenue of the Americas, New York, NY 10013-2473, USA

www.cambridge.org
Information on this title: www.cambridge.org/9780521883283

First published 2010
Reprinted 2011, 2012

A catalog record for this publication is available from the British Library.

Library of Congress Cataloging in Publication Data

Desai, Bharat.
Multilateral environmental agreements : legal status of the secretariats / Bharat
H. Desai.
p. cm.
Includes bibliographical references and index.
ISBN 978-0-521-88328-3 (hardback)
1. Environmental law, International. 2. Foreign trade regulation. 3. International
trade. 4. International labor activities. I. Title.
K3585.D479 2010
341.4–dc22 2009042398

ISBN 978-0-521-88328-3 Hardback

For

Jay and Sonal

Contents

Preface

This study is an off-shoot of the work (begun in 1998) by the author on the process of "institutionalization" in the field of international environmental law. This book seeks to take a closer view of the multilateral regulatory technique to address sector-specific environmental *problematique,* as well as of the legal status of the secretariats that "service" the institutionalized intergovernmental process. The work was spread over a period of some nine years, during which the author visited various secretariats of multilateral environmental agreements (MEAs) and held discussions with concerned *dramatis personae* in the field, both in person and through written communications.

The initial interest in the crucial aspect of legal status of the secretariats was triggered by interactions with Arnulf Müller-Helmbrecht, then Executive Secretary of the Convention on Migratory Species of Wild Animals (CMS), during my stay in Bonn. I was inspired by Ulf's sheer passion, knowledge of the field, legal acumen, and firsthand account of the pitched battles he fought to extract "legal due" for the secretariat of the CMS. The resultant insight provided the initial basis for a closer look into the mystical area of the legal status of convention secretariats from my perches at various times in the cities of Bonn, Geneva, and Heidelberg.

I express my gratitude to Alexander von Humboldt Stiftung who generously made possible my stays in Bonn, Geneva, and Heidelberg. I enjoyed the discussion sessions on multilateral institutional issues on the environment with Rudolf Dolzer at the Institute of International Law of the University of Bonn. They helped me to have an incisive understanding of the role of various actors, as well as the workings of regime-based institutions. I have had the benefit of staying in Heidelberg to work at the Max-Planck Institute of Public International Law. I thank Rudiger Wolfrum and Armin von Bogdandy for providing me with work facilities.

In the course of writing this book, I had the great pleasure of interacting with several heads and legal officers of convention secretariats, UNEP officials, and officials of other host institutions who generously shared their views and made available relevant documents. They include Barbara Ruis, Calestous Juma, Dan Ogolla, Daniel Navid, Elizabeth Mrema, Francesco Bandarin, Gerardo Gunera-Lazzaroni, Iwona Rummel-Bulska, Janos Pasztor, Jim Armstrong, John Donaldson, Katharina Kummer, Lyle Glowka, Marci Yeater, Martin Krebs, Michael Graber, Richard Kinley, and Robert Hepworth. I greatly appreciate the working space provided to me by the secretariats of the UNFCCC and CMS in Bonn and of the UNITAR at the International Environment House in Geneva.

I greatly appreciate the special gestures of Ralph Zacklin, former Assistant Secretary General of the UN Office of Legal Affairs, and Klaus Töpfer, former UNEP Executive Director – who both took time to send me detailed notes on their respective perspectives on the subject – as well as of Maritta Koch-Weser, former Director-General of the IUCN, who spared time in Gland for discussions on various issues.

In the wake of this book, I have benefited from the insight – through discussions in person or through written communications – and the works and experiences of several scholars and practitioners in the field. These include Alan Boyle, the late Alexander Kiss, Alexander Timoshenko, Bakare Kante, C. F. Amerasinghe, Daniel Navid, David Freestone, Donald Kaniaru, Edith Brown Weiss, Geir Ulfstein, Gerhard Löibl, Günter Handl, Francoise Burhenne, Jan Klabbers, Jose Alwarez, Jutta Brunnee, Nick Robinson, Niels Blokker, Oran Young, Peter Sand, Philippe Sands, Rahmatullah Khan, R. R. Churchill, and Wolfgang Burhenne.

My scholarly quest in this field has been nurtured by regular interactions with some of my brightest students, who provided a stimulating springboard for classroom discussions and widening horizons through their research works under my supervision.

Last, but not least, I am grateful to John Berger, Senior Editor at Cambridge University Press, who all along has shown immense patience, and who encouraged me to overcome the vicissitudes of life in order to complete this book.

January 29, 2010

desai@mail.jnu.ac.in

Introduction

There is an active link between development of law and the institutional mechanisms that emerge from it. In this context, the establishment of a multilateral regulatory approach in the field of environment is no exception.

The process of centralized legalization concerning sectoral environmental problems has almost been institutionalized, especially in the past three decades. Despite the fact that this multilateral lawmaking modus operandi has worked in a piecemeal, ad hoc, and sporadic manner, it has contributed in thickening the web of treaties[1] as the most important source of international environmental law. It has emerged as a "predominant method"[2] of regulating state behavior on a global *problematique.*

[1] As per the state practice, nomenclature of a multilateral instrument depends on the idiosyncrasies of the parties. As such, it is not necessary that the contracting parties need to use specific words. To decipher the nature of the instrument at which the states have arrived, one needs to look for the intention of the parties as well as the content of the instrument. In general, use of the words "treaty" or "agreement" is commonplace. The Vienna Convention on the Law of Treaties (1969) defines a "treaty" as "an international agreement concluded between States in written form and governed by international law, whether embodied in a single instrument or in two or more related instruments and whatever its particular designation" (see Article 2(a)); available at www.unog.ch/archives/vienna/vien_69.htm. Article 2(a) of the Vienna Convention on the Law of Treaties between States and International Organizations or between International Organizations (1986) also uses the same language; available at www.unog.ch/archives/vienna/vien_86.htm.

[2] "Developments in the Law: International Environmental Law," *Harvard Law Review*, vol. 104, no. 3, 1991, p. 1521.

Unlike the traditional method of resorting to development of a customary norm, states revert to treaties for the sake of, among other goals, convenience and certainty of the law, as warranted by the contingencies of a specific issue.

It appears that lawmaking on environmental issues is greatly facilitated through treaties because of scientific uncertainties and the sense of urgency involving environmental matters. As a result, multilateral environmental agreements (MEAs) have emerged as a unique technique, with flexibility, pragmatism, a built-in lawmaking mechanism, as well as a consensual approach to norm setting. MEAs are also regarded as part of a broader trend of an "increasingly more complex web of international treaties, conventions, and agreements."[3]

Treaty making on environmental issues has developed into a practice largely because of the inclination of states to resort to multilateralism[4] in addressing global problems. The states, ostensibly, claim to act in the "common"[5] interest when joining multilateral environmental negotiations. In view of the very nature of these negotiations and participation of a large majority[6] of the states, final outcome is achieved through the

[3] United Nations University, *Inter-Linkages: Synergies and Coordination between Multilateral Environmental Agreements* (Tokyo: UNU, 1999), pp. 5 and 8.

[4] It has been argued that opportunities for multilateralism "appear to abound," as they have in the "aftermath of both twentieth-century 'non-cold wars'"; see Michael G. Schechter, "International Institutions: Obstacles, Agents, or Conduits of Global Structural Change?" in Michael G. Schechter, *Innovation in Multilateralism* (Tokyo: UNU, 1999), p. 3.

[5] There is a general hypothesis that it is the *common interest* of states that propels them to negotiate an MEA. In general, however, the states are guided by their self-interest rather than any notion of common interest. In many of the cases, the move for an international legal instrument is pushed by a *trigger event*, for example, in the case of the ozone layer depletion or the climate change issue. The initiatives in both of these cases came in the wake of dire scientific findings, which forced international action.

[6] It is interesting that almost all of the MEAs negotiated in recent years have seen participation of an unprecedented number of states. For example, the 1985 Vienna Convention and 1987 Montreal Protocol on Substances that Deplete the Ozone Layer have been ratified by 195 states, see www.ozone.unep.org; the 1992 Framework Convention and the 1997 Kyoto Protocol on Climate Change have been ratified by 192 and 187

lowest common denominator. Still, the "sense"[7] of negotiating MEAs remains a matter of debate.

There has been remarkable growth in the sheer volume of multilateral environmental instruments in recent years. Although it has resulted in gradual "institutionalization"[8] of international environmental law, it has also led to increased fragmentation of the environmental agenda. In turn, it has triggered the problems of ensuring synergies, interlinkages, and the coordination of these multilateral instruments. From 1990 through 1994, more than fifty such international instruments, most of them multilateral (representing a 10–15% increase),[9] were adopted by the states. MEAs established in recent years are significantly diverse, and most of them underscore the multidimensional nature of environmental problems. There seems to be an increasing tendency among states, especially industrialized ones, to push for a global framework for more and more environmental issues. There is, however, much skepticism and even some opposition to this approach. This skepticism often makes multilateral environmental negotiations acrimonious and virtually a battlefield on such issues, reflecting political and economic interests of states, which often results in a stalemate. The subject matter of MEAs ranges from issues such as protection of a species (whale), flora and/or fauna in general (elephant or tiger), and cultural and/or natural heritage sites to regulation of trade of hazardous chemicals and/or

states, respectively, see www.unfccc.int; the 1994 United Nations Convention to Combat Desertification has been ratified by 193 states, see www.unccd.int; the 1992 Convention on Biological Diversity has been ratified by 191 states, and the 2000 Cartegena Protocol on Biosafety has been ratified by 156 states, see www.cbd.int (all as of August 17, 2009).

[7] On the issue of reasons for going into negotiations on MEAs, see the essay "To Treaty or Not to Treaty? A Survey of Practical Experience," in Peter H. Sand, *Transnational Environmental Law: Lessons in Global Change* (The Hague: Kluwer Law International, 1999), pp. 55–60.

[8] For an exhaustive treatment on the process of institutionalization, see Bharat H. Desai, *Institutionalizing International Environmental Law* (New York: Transnational Publishers, 2004).

[9] Alexandre Kiss and Dinah Shelton, *International Environmental Law: 1994 Supplement* (New York: Transnational, 1994), p. 1.

wastes, air pollution, and persistent organic pollutants; to more high profile issues like ozone depletion, climate change, and biological diversity. The MEAs on a host of these issues have in fact "changed over time, just as political, economic, social, and technological conditions have changed over time."[10]

In the history of international treaty making, the pace of development of MEAs has been unprecedented.[11] Such proliferation of intergovernmental instruments laying down obligations for the contracting states has created a unique situation and pressure for the participating states. This development has made a salutary contribution in 'engaging' the bulk of the members of the United Nations in the negotiations as well as in emerging normative framework. This has brought about a significant corpus of regulatory measures for the environmental behavior of states. At the same time, it has generated institutional mechanisms that serve as tools for these regulatory frameworks. Most of these institutional mechanisms have visibility in the public eye and are generally located at a 'seat' provided by the host country. As a logical corollary, this seat can be established by the MEA on its own or can be housed within an already existing international institution.

This book seeks to examine, among other aspects, the genesis, development, and proliferation of MEAs; their role as a technique to regulate state behavior, built-in lawmaking mechanisms, and process of "institutionalization"; their ad hoc and treaty-based status; issues of legal personality; and the status of the secretariats of the MEAs. Some legal aspects of the relationship that flow from the location of MEA secretariats within an existing international institution is also examined. A critical analysis reflects on the relevant issues in "relationship

[10] Edith Brown Weiss, "The Five International Treaties: A Living History," in Edith Brown Weiss and Harold K. Jacobson (Eds.), *Engaging Countries: Strengthening Compliance with International Environmental Accords* (Cambridge: MIT Press, 1998), p. 89.

[11] It is estimated that, since 1868, there have been approximately 502 international treaties and agreements concerning the environment, of which almost 300 have been entered into since 1972; see United Nations doc. UNEP/IGM/1/INF/1 of March 30, 2001, pp. 3–4.

agreements" – their context as well as interpretation of commonly used language that triggers such a relationship. The study examines an interpretation of the standard MEA clause on "providing a secretariat," a delegation of authority by the host institution to the head of the convention secretariat, possible conflict areas, the host country agreement, and the working of "relationship agreements." In view of the constraints of time and space, only a select number of MEAs are taken as illustrations to examine these issues as well as to unravel the growing phenomenon of existing international institutions (e.g., the United Nations Environment Programme [UNEP] and the International Union for Conservation of Nature [IUCN]), providing a "servicing base" for the MEAs. It triggers a chain of legal implications, including locations of the secretariats and their relationships with host countries and host institutions.

In the wake of this work, the author has collected three instruments on "relationship agreements" (Ramsar, CITES, and CBD) with the host institutions (IUCN and UNEP), as well as seven relevant headquarters agreements that govern the location of some of the MEA secretariats in host countries. It has been thought desirable to include these basic legal texts for ready reference material for scholars, practitioners, as well as international institutions. The fact that it took considerable amount of time and effort to obtain the original agreements testify to the need for inclusion of these texts in the book.

1 Institutionalizing Cooperation

Introduction

The word *institution* indicates "the act or an instance of instituting"; "an established law, practice or custom."[1] Thus, the process of instituting or establishing something results in an institution. In the national context, the process of institution building is much more smooth and orderly than at the international level, where sovereign states are the primary actors. In a national society, institutions emerge out of the needs of citizens at a given time. The practice of setting up an *organization* is just one such instance of establishing institutions. At the national level, governmental institutions derive their mandate as well as powers and competences from a statute enacted by the legislature. In the case of intergovernmental institutions, this is especially so as they derive their operational basis and *raison d'être* from an international instrument.

Organic Link

In general, the growth of law and the growth of institutions have been complementary to each other, and, in fact, do brook changes, keeping in view the needs of human society. Thomas Jefferson, one of the philosophers and architects of the American revolution, made a pertinent

[1] R.E. Allen (Ed.), *The Concise Oxford Dictionary* (Oxford: Clarendon, 1990), p. 614.

observation about the adaptability of institutions to societal requirements:

> [*L*]*aws and institutions must go hand in hand with the progress of the human mind.* As that becomes more developed, more enlightened, as new discoveries are made, new truths discovered and manners and opinions change, *with the change of circumstances, institutions must advance also to keep pace with the times.*[2] (emphasis added)

There seems to be an organic link between the development of law and the development of institutions – like an invisible umbilical cord. While institutions generally play a crucial role in triggering development of the law, they do so as institutional platforms on behalf of sovereign states. Such a role performed by the institutions could be the need of the hour as, increasingly, highly complex areas are being covered in the treaty-making venture. Institutions having a functional mandate in such areas are in the best position to take up such tasks, which require expertise, time, and continuous follow-up. In the past, one country could initiate the idea of a legal instrument and take responsibility for the entire process of treaty negotiations, including acting as a "depository" for the treaty.

This organic relationship applies especially to institutions set up at the international level. Unlike national law, the subjects of international law are primarily sovereign states. International law is unique in that its origin, sustenance, and development are essentially based on the *consent* of sovereign states. Because these states, with their national experience, determine the shape of international law, it is obvious that many of the concepts and national legal developments are reflected in it. Many times, international tribunals have derived inspiration from precedents and analogies[3] obtained at the national level. The growth of international

[2] Excerpt from Thomas Jefferson's letter to Samuel Kercheval, July 12, 1816; taken by the author from Thomas Jefferson Memorial, *Chamber Inscriptions*, Washington, DC.

[3] For a classical exposition on the subject of enrichment provided by private law analogies to international law, see H. Lauterpacht, *The Private Law Sources and Analogies of International Law: With Special Reference to International Arbitration* (London: Longmans, Green and Co., 1927); reprinted edition by Archon Books, 1970.

institutions is not immune to this process. This is amply demonstrated by the wide variety of ideas that have found reflection in the setting up of institutions at the international level, having had their roots in national experiences. This is a perfectly natural process. In this context, Lorimer observed:

> To me it has always appeared that our problem is to project into international life the institutions of which we have had experience in national life.[4]

At the international level, the function of institutions assumes importance not only for this but also for a host of other social, economic, and political purposes.[5]

Institutionalized Cooperation

In fact, the birth of an institutional form at the international level, for cooperation among states *inter se*, has been a remarkable development in view of the attendant surrender of state sovereignty for this purpose. It has been manifested in the efforts to "organize" cooperation among members of the international community. The concerted efforts for the purpose began sometime around the middle of the nineteenth century. The role of these institutions has been described thus by Brierly:

> These institutions operate by *organizing co-operation between the national governments and not by superseding or dictating to them*, and they are, therefore, probably not so much the beginnings of an international "government," though the term is often convenient, as

[4] J. Lorimer, *The Institutes of the Law of Nations* (1884), quoted in George Schwarzenberger and E.D. Brown, *A Manual of International Law*, 6th ed. (Milton: Professional Books, 1976), p. 192.

[5] For instance, Quincy Wright has remarked that: "Political institutions for the peaceful change of law are no less essential for a universal international system than legal institutions to maintain the law. The system of diplomacy, the United Nations and the Specialized Agencies were designed to supply this need that was formerly met in some measure by law and other uses of force"; see Quincy Wright, "The Foundations for a Universal International System" in R.P. Anand (Ed.), *Asian States and the Development of Universal International Law* (Delhi: Vikas, 1972), p. 164.

> a substitute for one. Their consideration, however, invites the same questions as those which arise in the study of any other legal system, and it is proper to ask how far and in what manner they perform for international law the functions which governmental institutions perform for the law of a state....[6] (emphasis added)

The rise of such institutions, assigned with specialized administrative functions, was essentially a product of the "compelling force of circumstances"[7] or "evident need"[8] arising from international intercourse as compared to other idealistic notions. The earliest version of such new institutions on the international scene came to be known as public international unions (PIU). These unions were set up basically on a functional basis for a variety of social and economic purposes and were administrative in nature.[9] Such international administrative unions emerged from the need to effectively administer certain natural resources (e.g., rivers, fisheries), deal with problems (e.g., opium), or regulate some common activities (e.g., post, telegraph, custom tariffs). In a way, they indicated the development of an "institutionalized international administrative law."[10]

[6] J.L. Brierly, *The Law of Nations: An Introduction to the International Law of Peace*, 4th ed. (Oxford: Clarendon Press, 1949), p. 86.

[7] Regarding the reason for this, Brierly has argued that "in one department of administration after another experience showed that government could not be even reasonably efficient if it continued to be organized on a purely national basis"; see note 6, p. 94 in Brierly.

[8] See D.W. Bowett, *The Law of International Institutions*, 4th ed. (London: Stevens & Sons, 1982), p. 1.

[9] These PIUs were designed specifically to administer several new areas, which became necessary in view of the technological innovations and the effect of such activities spanning continents or the globe. The earliest one was the International Telegraphic Union (1865). The PIUs set up were for postal communication (1874), protection of industrial property rights (1883), protection of copyrights (1886), international traffic of goods by rail (1890), publication of customs tariffs (1890), prevention of the spreading of disease (1892), abolition of sugar premiums (1902), agricultural interests (1905), radiotelegraphy (1906), fight against the abuse of opium (1909), and international commercial statistics (1913). For concise information on the issue, see, generally, Rüdiger Wolfrum, "International Administrative Unions" in Rudolf Berhardt (Ed.), *Encyclopedia of Public International Law*, Vol. 5 (Amsterdam: North-Holland, 1983), pp. 42–49.

[10] See Wolfrum, *ibid*, p. 43.

The gradual movement toward international administrative cooperation among states sometimes did not necessarily result in an institutional organ. It took the shape of an "agreement to co-ordinate national laws or to introduce uniform methods into the national administration."[11] There does not seem to be any consensus regarding distinguishing international administrative unions from international organizations. It has been suggested that the criteria for such may be along the lines of "administrative and technical" functions (indicating an international administrative union) as compared to "political and military" functions (characterizing international organizations), or considering institutional organs that exercise "executive" functions as international administrative unions.[12]

State entities, both as subjects and as makers of international law, have carved out the system of international institutions to serve their own interests. As creations of states, these institutions are as good as states want them to be. The practice, in place since the early twentieth century, reveals a preference for more concrete organizational forms of institutions. The evolution of international organization is a manifestation of the desire of states for a more durable structure – an association of states – to fulfill certain objectives.

It is no wonder that the twentieth century witnessed a remarkable effort to *organize* international relations among states. It shows progressive growth in the process of institutionalization, as dictated by the needs and interests of states at a given time. This evolution from PIUs to general international organizations also underscores multiplicity in institutional structures, as required by complexities of international society that arise from technological developments and the emergence of various global *problematiques*. That progressive development paved the way

[11] Brierly, note 6, p. 95. Such instances of "co-ordination" at the national level include the Convention for the Protection of Submarine Cables (1884) and the Automobile Convention (1904).

[12] See Wolfrum, note 9, p. 42. According to Wolfrum, however, "administrative unions may develop into political organizations or at least assume some political functions. Therefore, the classification is justified not from an accurate legal viewpoint but simply for its convenience for the purposes of presentation," *ibid*, p. 43.

for specialized or functional organizations that perform various roles in various organized areas of international life.

The practice of such functional international organizations, which began during the League of Nations period, took firm root almost immediately after the United Nations (UN) came into being. A whole range of these functional organizations have been specifically brought into relationship with the UN. As such, they are popularly known as *specialized agencies*. Each of these agencies has a "relationship agreement" with the UN in accordance with Articles 57 and 63 of its Charter.

Institutions and Organizations

Some writers have used the words "institutions" and "organizations." interchangeably. In general, it is advisable to underscore that an international organization is just one form of an international institution, but not *vice versa*. In fact, international organizations are structured and organized forms of international cooperation and are the most conspicuous form of international institutions. It is argued by some that institutions play the role of "defining social practices" (through rules of the game or codes of conduct), whereas organizations are "actors in social practices."[13] In general, an international institution may be regarded as an international organization that is based on an agreement under international law between states to cooperate for a specific purpose, and has a distinct legal capacity from member states.[14]

[13] While underscoring this subtle difference between institutions and organizations, however, Oran R. Young has argued: "(T)he purpose of drawing a distinction between institutions and organizations is not to argue that one is more important than the other but to open up a large and important research agenda focusing on the relationship between institutions and organizations"; see Oran R. Young, *International Governance: Protecting the Environment in a Stateless Society* (Ithaca: Cornell University Press, 1994), pp. 3 and 4.

[14] For instance, to qualify as international organizations, international institutions are required, per the *Encyclopaedia of Public International Law*, to fulfill certain basic requirements as "an association of states established by and based upon a *treaty*,

Accordingly, an organization implies institution.[15] This growing "institutionalization" of interstate relations has resulted in the gradual *verticalization* of international law. As such, the new institutional forms have effectively acted as *stabilizers* and *stimulators*, not only in international relations but also for the "development of international law intended for their legal regulation."[16] Notwithstanding the fine distinction brought out by scholars, for the purpose of the present study, I have used the terms "international institutions" and "international organizations" interchangeably to avoid any confusion. This study has sought to understand the process of institution building with a special focus on the

which pursues common aims and which has its own special organs to fulfill particular functions within the organization"; see Rudolf L. Bindschedler, "International Organizations, General Aspects" in Rudolf Bernhardt (Ed.), *Encyclopaedia of Public International Law*, Vol. 2 (Amsterdam: North-Holland, 1995), p. 1289. Schermers and Blokker's *magnum opus* on the subject of international institutional law is even more specific in prescribing criteria for international organizations, which are defined as "forms of cooperation founded on an international agreement creating at least one organ with a will of its own, established under international law"; see Henry G. Schermers and Niels M. Blokker, *International Institutional Law: Unity Within Diversity*, 3rd ed. (The Hague: Martinus Nijhoff, 1995), p. 23. It seems that this definition provides essential elements with which one may be able to remove "grains from the chaff" regarding designating international institutions as international organizations. What it basically requires is a distinct legal personality of the institution from the member states based on an international agreement regulated by international law. It entails an advanced form of institutionalized cooperation among states, excluding even an organ of an organization. Inis Claude, Jr., has also regarded international organization as a *process* and international organizations as *institutions*; see Inis L. Claude, Jr., *Swords into Plowshares: The Problems and Progress of International Organization*, 4th ed. (New York: Random House, 1971), p. 4. In fact, Claude has, in the introduction to his book, pertinently observed: "This is a book about international organization . . . It is written in the conviction that international organizations, *as institutions*, have a double significance: they are important, though not decisively important, factors in contemporary world affairs; and they are significant expressions of, and contributors to, the process of international organization, which may ultimately prove to be the most significant dynamic element in the developing reality of international relations."

15 J.L. Brierly, *The Outlook for International Law* (Oxford: Clarendon Press, 1944), p. 91.

16 Hanna Bokor-Szego, *The Role of the United Nations in International Legislation* (Budapest: 1978), pp. 9–11; quoted in R.P. Anand, "International Organizations and the Functioning of International Law," *Indian Journal of International Law*, vol. 24, 1984, p. 53.

role and status of the secretariats within the framework of multilateral environmental treaty making.

Institution-Building Process

The world has also entered a new era of cooperation and coexistence compared with previous efforts at mere coordination. As a result, "interdependence" has become one of the "cornerstones of the new law of nations."[17] It mainly emanates from the felt belief of states that they cannot live in isolation. States, as members of the international community, consider it necessary to depend on each other on a regular basis, as well as in times of need. This need for interdependence has also necessitated the coming together of states in common international institutional forums. It has been pointed out that "it would be difficult to name a single area of human activity in our times which is not creating interdependence."[18] Most states have been willing to do it, as a necessity, despite the fact that it has caused considerable inroads into state sovereignty. Every state, big or small, has found to its advantage joining such international institutions, primarily for the furtherance of its own national interests.[19]

Thus, "interdependence" has in a way forced states to come together on common institutional platforms. An assumption of the international organizational forums is one important facet in their quest for the attainment of common objectives, which may not be possible within the confines of state jurisdictions. Therefore, the growing trend of international institutional development indicates:

[17] Philip C. Jessup, *A Modern Law of Nations* (New York: 1949), p. 40.

[18] Karl Zemanek, "Interdependence," in Rudolf Bernhardt (Ed.), *Encyclopedia of Public International Law*, Vol. 2 (Amsterdam: North-Holland, 1995), p. 1023.

[19] As U.S. President Dwight Eisenhower once stated: "No single free nation can live alone in the world... If you are going to try to develop a coalition... you have got to compromise"; see *The New York Times*, May 29, 1953, p. 4; quoted in Daniel S. Cheever and H. Field Haviland, Jr., *Organizing for Peace: International Organization in World Affairs* (London: Stevens & Sons, 1954), p. 2.

> smooth transition from loose cooperation between states to structured cooperation within an international organization, just as there is a smooth transition between some international organizations and sovereign states. Thus a *sliding scale of institutionalization* of international cooperation can be identified.[20] (emphasis added)

The gradual development from simple international institutions such as consuls and ambassadors to international unions (private as well as public) to conferences[21] for the settlement of special political questions of the day to general international organizations[22] amply demonstrates that

[20] Henry G. Schermers and Niels M. Blokker, *International Institutional Law: Unity Within Diversity*, 3rd ed. (The Hague: Martinus Nijhoff, 1995), p. 22.

[21] The technique of *conferencing* used to be employed especially by the European powers to resolve particular political problems of that time. It was generally regarded as having legislative character but did preserve the "forms of mere mediation between supposedly sovereign states." Such conferencing was particularly put to use effectively as a means of preventing wars. For example, the Conference of London (1831) established the independence of Belgium; the Conference of London (1867) established the independence of Luxemburg; the Congress of Berlin (1878) dealt with the affairs of Turkey and the Balkan states. The Hague Conferences for the Pacific Settlement of International Disputes in 1899 and 1907 also fall into this category. J.L. Brierly has regarded the formation of the League of Nations, which emerged from the Peace Treaty of Versailles (1919), as a "standing conference system"; see Brierly, note 6, pp. 88 and 90.

[22] There are different views regarding the initiation of the term *international organization*. The British jurist Lorimer is generally credited with this in an address (1867) before the Royal Academy in Edinburgh. For a discussion on this issue, see, generally, Pitman B. Potter, "Origin of the Term International Organization," *AJIL*, vol. 39, 1945, pp. 803–806. In this context, however, Potter appears to exclude the use of ideas and terms prevelant in other parts of the world, which may have conveyed the same or even broader meaning. For instance, the ancient Indian notion of *vasudhaiv kutumbakam* (the world as a family) is relevant in this context. Potter's preference for the term *international organization* not only indicates mere convenience regarding the usage of particular words in English, which came into usage by sheer chance rather than design, as well as either refusal to take cognizance of or ignorance about ideas prevalent in well-developed systems of law in other parts of the world. The issue that merits attention is that one need not judge an issue through such competition in the use of a particular phrase, which, because of some historical reasons, has come to be widely accepted. The *content* of the idea needs to be regarded as more important than mere usage of particular words. If this approach is followed, then we would be enlightened with similar and even much more encompassing ideas prevalent since time immemorial in other civilizations as well.

the *sliding scale* is moving in an upward direction, which also confirms vertical expansion of international law.

The development of international institutional cooperation has rested on the bedrock of a fine balance between the quest of states to keep sovereignty as intact as possible and the growing need for interdependence for practical purposes. The advent of international institutions has basically reflected the proliferation of interstate cooperation on a wide range of social, economic, and political issues. It reflects the desire of states to cooperate, and institutional platforms facilitate the process. It appears that, in the absence of international institutions, sovereign states would find it difficult to access other mechanisms to "pool their resources"[23] to grapple with a *problematique*. In the wake of the changing needs of the international community, institution-building processes have made some dent in the notion of absolute sovereignty of the states.

The process has witnessed the emergence of new forms of institutional cooperation to cope with administrative requirements, propelled by scientific inventions on the one hand and resolutions of political issues on the other hand. It is interesting that the momentum has continued by learning from experiences and even by setting up new international institutions to replace old ones. The developments in the direction of general organization of states – the UN – have been most remarkable. The ambit of the international institutional cooperation under it reflects the desire of states to cover a wide range of human activities. Such a general international organization reflects a "mirror of the conditions existing in the international society of States."[24]

The institution-building process has witnessed a quantum leap in the post–UN Charter period. Most institution building has centered on thickening the web of multilateral treaties. Thus, institutions have become both products of the giant state-centric treaty-making machine, as well as contributors to the enterprise. As a corollary, there has been

[23] Jose E. Alvarez, "The New Treaty Makers," *Boston College International and Comparative Law Review*, vol. xxv, no. 2, 2002, pp. 213–234, at 219.

[24] Jochen A. Frowein, "United Nations," in Rudolf Berhardt (Ed.), *Encyclopedia of Public International Law*, Vol. 5 (Amsterdam: North-Holland, 1983), p. 280.

phenomenal growth in international institutions. This is especially the case in the multilateral regulatory processes concerning environmental issues. Environment-related global conferencing and multilateralism is a classic example of need-based responses of the states to address specific problems. In this organic and continuous treaty-making exercise, states have sought to create and, in turn, to rely on institutional mechanisms to serve specific purposes. In their advent and proliferation, multilateral environmental agreements (MEAs) are a reflection of the functional approach at work, as well as of the craving of states for institutions as facilitators, catalysts, and inevitable cooperative frameworks.

Conclusion

In a rapidly changing global environment, sovereign states have come to rely on international institutions to promote interstate cooperation on a wide range of issues. The process of institutionalizing cooperation has been based on the bedrock of "shared sovereignties." It has emerged as the need of the hour and as one of the best tools to address global challenges in their various manifestations. Thus, it seems that institutionalized cooperation has emerged as a functional necessity. It has provided a tool for states to grapple with problems as they arise. The process does have its own limitations and weaknesses and faces the challenge of growing institutional fragmentation. Nonetheless, the marathon task of bringing together a large number of states on common institutional platforms has given fillip to the basic rule of the game – sovereign equality of states – and to the emergence of consensual decision making in contrast to obsessive reliance on either weighted voting or brute majorities. It has resulted in far-reaching implications for the quality and content of lawmaking and equity and transparency in problem-solving techniques, as well as the proliferation of international institutions as a response to emerging challenges.

It is noteworthy that states have engaged in a constructive process of "codification." They need to work out multilateral treaties on even routine issues of international cooperation, in addition to dealing with common problems (described more recently as "common concerns"). The process has ushered in an intricate mosaic of treaties at bilateral, regional, and global levels. Thus, treaties seem now to have become cornerstones of multilateral regulatory enterprise as well as institutionalized forms of international cooperation and coexistence. In essence, the treaty making has come to be amply reflected in the marathon, multilateral environmental regulatory process in recent years.

2 Multilateral Environmental Regulation

Introduction

Multilateral treaty making has emerged as one of the important sources of international law. It does not appear to be sheer coincidence that the International Court of Justice (ICJ), while dealing with a "dispute" submitted to it, is expected to apply "international conventions."[1] The Statute of ICJ has not laid down any order in which the Court is expected to apply various sources of international law. **Still, placing an international convention at the top of the list of sources available to the court is a testament to the value and emergence of treaties as the most important source.** It is also no less significant that the United Nations (UN) Charter has sought to give "respect for the obligations arising from treaties," a pride of place in the preamble itself, and has placed onus on its plenary organ (the General Assembly) to encourage the progressive development of international law and its "codification."[2] Thus, based on this

[1] Article 38 (1) of the Statute of the ICJ provides: "The Court, whose function is to decide in accordance with international law such disputes as are submitted to it, shall apply: a. *international conventions, whether general or particular, establishing rules expressly recognized by the contesting states*; b. international custom, as evidence of a general practice accepted as law; c. the general principles of law recognized by civilized nations; d. subject to the provisions of Article 59, judicial decisions and the teachings of the most highly qualified publicists of the various nations, as subsidiary means for the determination of rules of law" (emphasis added); see the Statute at www.icj-cij .org.

[2] See the Preamble and Article 13 of the UN Charter (1945) at www.un.org.

crucial mandate, the General Assembly established the International Law Commission (as a subsidiary organ of the Assembly).[3]

During the initial decades after the UN came into being, there was a flurry of movement to codify a host of established customary principles of international law. It did unleash an era of codification and laid roots for the giant treaty-making machine for the future. It seems that the UN system itself (for instance, "specialized agencies" like the International Labour Organization [ILO] and the International Maritime Organization [IMO]) regularly churned out conventions that met the needs of their member states to regulate specific areas (like occupational health and safety, maritime safety, and pollution). They have in fact unleashed a "gigantic treaty network"[4] that covers many crucial areas of human activities. Interestingly, in the past three decades or so, the baton for triggering the treaty-making process seems to have been "**passed**" as the process is no longer exclusively preserved by the ILC. The states seem to have tacitly allowed functional international organizations and a host of other intergovernmental actors on the international scene to engage in treaty-making enterprises. The web of international law seems to be gradually *thickening* largely due to proliferation of treaties for regulating state activities in various spheres of international life. **The speed at which the number of pages of the official register[5] of the UN – *UN Treaty Series* – is increasing provides classic testimony to this vibrant process**.

[3] The General Assembly adopted resolution 174 (II) on November 21, 1947 that established the International Law Commission (ILC) and approved its Statute. The ILC formally came into being in 1948 with a mandate to work for "the progressive development and codification of international law," in accordance with article 13(1)(a) of the Charter of the UN. The ILC comprises 34 members, elected for 5-year-period (quinquennium) sessions; see www.un.org/law/ilc.

[4] Roy Lee, "Multilateral Treaty-Making and Negotiation Technique: An Appraisal," in Bin Chang and Edward Brown (Eds.), *Contemporary Problems of International Law: Essays in Honour of Georg Schwartzenberger on His Eightieth Birthday* (1998); quoted in Jose E. Alvarez, "The New Treaty Makers," *Boston College International and Comparative Law Review*, vol. XXV, no. 2, 2002, pp. 213–34 at 218.

[5] The UN Charter provides a mechanism for "registration" of treaties: "1. Every treaty and every international agreement entered into by any Member of the United Nations after the present Charter comes into force shall as soon as possible be registered with the Secretariat and published by it. 2. No party to any such treaty or international

Rapid Growth

In the post–UN Charter period, there has been both vertical and horizontal expansion in the body of international law. It has branched out into different specialized areas that require specific normative frameworks to grapple with their respective challenges (such as human rights, trade matters, refugees, humanitarian issues, criminal matters, terrorism, and environmental issues). Despite such "branching out," **the basic legal underpinning for regulating state behavior in these various global *problematiques* are drawn from the main body of international law.**

The crystallization of rules and principles concerning environmental protection and natural resources conservation has now been placed under the rubric of "international environmental law." The employment of new tools and techniques characterizes the lawmaking process in this rapidly expanding branch of international law. In view of the commonalities of interests for the 'common concerns' and workability of the lowest-common-denominator approach, state sovereignty does not seem to pose an insurmountable problem. Depending on the level of consensus that emerges from negotiations, the states are willing to "share" their sovereign decision making to deal with a specific problem area within a global framework.

In view of the very nature of present-day environmental challenges, legal responses have started affecting the day-to-day lives of people across the globe, as they are no longer confined only to matters of high state affairs. This expansion of international environmental law may be regarded as pervasive as:

> International Environmental Law links individuals and their local governments into a worldwide network. This system is not often perceived locally, because each country's own legislation and institutions are assigned the job of applying the shared environmental rules.

agreement which has not been registered in accordance with the provisions of paragraph 1 of this Article may invoke that treaty or agreement before any organ of the United Nations"; see Article 102 of the UN Charter at www.un.org.

> However, when one considers how the weather transports air pollution, how species migrate, how trade of a food product like coffee can carry pesticide residues, how tourists, business staff, or visitors move daily around the world, it is evident that each country needs to undertake roughly equivalent environmental protection measures. Law is the mechanism for defining and applying those services.[6]

The remarkable growth of the body of international environmental law is contributed to mainly by multilateral treaties. Alongside the growth of treaties, there has been panoramic expansion in the "soft law" instruments, which often, in due course, also contribute to the development of treaty-based law. Still, in general, states have shown treaties as a clear favorite in the norm-setting exercise because modern environmental treaties seek to accommodate competing interests and often carry a 'soft belly' to provide latitude to the states in their obligations.

Multilateral environmental agreements (MEAs) arrived at in recent years have great diversity. Most of them underscore the multidimensional nature of environmental problems. For instance, the *Millennium Ecosystem Assessment* (2005) focused on the links between ecosystems (defined as dynamic complexes of plant, animal, and microorganism communities and the nonliving environment interacting as functional units) and human well-being (including basic materials for a good life, health, good social relations, security, freedom of choice, and action).[7] It seems that our ever-growing developmental quest (especially for raw materials, food, fresh water, and energy) has "substantially reduced nature's ability to continue providing the services we need in our daily

[6] See Nicholas A. Robinson, *Agenda 21: Earth's Action Plan*, IUCN Environmental Policy & Law Paper No. 27 (New York: Oceana, 1993), p. xiv.

[7] The Millennium Ecosystem Assessment dealt with the full range of ecosystems – from those relatively undisturbed, such as natural forests, to landscapes with mixed patterns of human use, to ecosystems intensively managed and modified by humans, such as agricultural land and urban areas. It has examined how changes in ecosystem services influence human well-being; see Millennium Ecosystem Assessment, *Ecosystems and Human Well-being: a Report of the Millennium Ecosystem Assessment* (Washington, DC: Island Press, 2005), Synthesis at p. v. Also see www.millenniumassessment.org.

lives."[8] It is interesting that there is an increasing tendency among states, especially industrialized ones, to push for a global framework for more and more environmental issues. Due to sharp differences in ways of understanding "historic" contributions to global environmental problems (e.g., climate change and ozone layer depletion), multilateral environmental negotiations often turn out to be acrimonious and virtually battlefields.

The subject matter of MEAs ranges from issues such as protection of a species (whale), flora, and fauna, in general (Convention on International Trade in Endangered Species; CITES), or cultural and heritage sites, to regulation of trade in hazardous chemicals and wastes, to air pollution and persistent organic pollutants, to more remote issues such as ozone depletion, climate change, and biological diversity. The core MEAs have come to be categorized into five main groups: the biodiversity-related conventions, the atmospheric conventions, the land conventions, the chemicals and hazardous wastes conventions, and the regional seas conventions and related agreements.

The trigger events or responsible factors that gradually give rise to these MEAs could be different in each of these groups as is the case of diverse interests, objectives, and priorities laid down in them by the states' parties. It is interesting that the content, format, phraseology used, built-in lawmaking mechanisms formulated, institutional devices designed, as well as funding patterns also show considerable variations among the MEAs. As a part of an organic process with lessons learned, MEAs on a host of these issues have in fact "changed over time, just as political, economic, social, and technological conditions have changed over time."[9] The growth in the field of international environmental law

[8] Philippe Rekacewicz, "Introduction," in *Planet in Peril: an Atlas of Current Threats to People and the Environment* (Arendal and Paris: UNEP/GRID, Le Monde diplomatique, 2006), p. 6.

[9] Edith Brown Weiss, "The Five International Treaties: A Living History," in Edith Brown Weiss and Harold K. Jacobson (Eds.), *Engaging Countries: Strengthening Compliance with International Environmental Accords* (Cambridge: MIT Press, 1998), p. 89.

could be mainly assigned to circumstances and responsible factors during the pre-Stockholm period, to the contribution of the 1972 Stockholm Conference, and to the 1992 Rio Earth Summit that brought mega-global conferencing techniques to the fore.

Pre-Stockholm: Limited Concerns

In the pre-Stockholm period, treaty-making efforts were primarily guided by limited concerns such as the regulation of marine pollution, nuclear energy issues, or conservation of a particular species such as the whale.[10] In this early era, the principles of "unfettered national sovereignty over natural resources and absolute freedom of the seas beyond the three-mile territorial limit"[11] provided the guiding force to emerging international environmental law. The inherent perception of the architects of earliest international, as opposed to global, regulatory efforts was in fact mainly directed toward the use of living and nonliving resources and not toward environmental protection. Most of the efforts were, basically, of *utilitarian* character. For example, the Convention for the Protection of Birds Useful to Agriculture (1902) sought to address those birds that were regarded "useful" to agriculture at the time, as compared to certain "non-useful birds" (such as eagles and falcons), which have come to be protected today. Thus, the negotiators as well as the drafters of the treaty at that time essentially took into account "short term utility, the immediate usefulness of protected species,"[12] as dictated by the prevailing societal needs.

[10] Some of the early international conventions in this direction were, for instance, the International Convention for the Regulation of Whaling (1946), the International Convention for the Prevention of Pollution of the Sea by Oil (1954), the Convention on Third Party Liability in the Field of Nuclear Energy (1960) and its Supplementary Convention (1963), and the Convention Relating to Intervention on the High Seas in Cases of Oil Pollution Casualties (1969).

[11] Edith Brown Weiss, "Global Environmental Change and International Law: The Introductory Framework," in Edith Brown Weiss (Ed.), *Environmental Change and International Law* (Tokyo: United Nations University Press, 1992), p. 7.

[12] Alexandre Kiss and Dinah Shelton, *International Environmental Law*, 2nd ed. (New York: Transnational Publishers, 2000), p. 56.

Most of the efforts, however, were concentrated at the regional level to address some environmental problems specific to a region.[13] Such efforts were confined only among the few states that had economic interests in the exploitation of a particular species and hence the need for their regulation. The United States – Great Britain treaty (1911) for the preservation and protection of Fur Seals falls into this category. Significantly, some of these early regulatory efforts comprised innovative tools and techniques such as the fixing of national quotas or annual catch limits as well as the regulation of international trade in objects produced from seal hunting (adopted later in the 1973 CITES). Similarly, many of the international treaties, especially in Europe, concerning shared international rivers and lakes, such as the Rhine (1963), the Mosel (1956), as well as lakes Constance (1960) and Leman (1962), specifically contained provisions for prevention of water pollution.[14] These European measures were largely propelled by the need to ensure the smooth flow of navigational routes or to maintain a certain standard of quality of the waters of rivers and lakes.

In view of an essentially *utilitarian* approach at work, the legal responses for regulation of state behavior in this era were sporadic and catered to specific needs (mainly economic), especially at the regional level. It was not until the 1970s that the issue of protecting the environment entered the global stage in a big way. Some major developments set the tone and motivated states to come out with concrete measures to prevent a worsening global environmental scenario. It gradually started being understood, especially in the highly industrialized states, that the human impact on the environment, through endless quantitative growth, "necessitates a readjustment of current perspectives on ecological issues and a redefinition of our conventional views."[15] A sense of caution and

[13] For instance, the Convention Relative to the Preservation of Fauna and Flora in their Natural State (1933) applied only to the then-colonized African continent and the Convention on Nature Protection and Wildlife Preservation in the Western Hemisphere (1940).

[14] See Kiss and Shelton, n. 12, p. 35.

[15] Nazli Choucri, "Population, Resources and Technology: Political Implications of the Environmental Crisis," in David A. Kay and Eugene B. Skolnikoff (Eds.), *World*

finiteness regarding human progress on the planet earth was injected by several important reports and scholarly writings. In this context, it was gradually realized that the rise of the industrial state, and with it science and technology, has led us to overlook these conditions of finitude and fragility. This ominous reality underscored that:

> We are living now in the first stages of a planetary crisis. It is the first such known crisis in the history of the planet... The crisis is of planetary scope because the danger is not confined to any part of the planet; the patterns of behaviour that generate the crisis are created by the scale of production and life-style in the most advanced industrial societies. An adequate response eventually requires a new pattern of organization and coordination that needs to encompass the entire planet.[16]

The concerns of individual scholars regarding an impending crisis looming large on the horizon for humankind drew attention and led to organized efforts to examine the issue in greater detail.

In this context, the issue of inherent limitations of human developmental efforts came to the fore following a study done for the Club of Rome.[17] The Club of Rome, through its seminal project on the "Predicament of Mankind," sought to examine commonality in seemingly divergent parts of what it described as "world *problematique*." It viewed this predicament as follows:

> It is the predicament of mankind that man can perceive the *problematique*, yet, despite his considerable knowledge and skills, he does not understand the origins, significance, and interrelationships of its many components and thus is unable to devise effective responses.

Eco-Crisis: International Organizations in Response (Madison, WI: University of Wisconsin Press, 1972), p. 9.

[16] Richard A. Falk, *This Endangered Planet: Prospects and Proposals for Human Survival* (New York: Vintage Books, 1972), pp. 9–10.

[17] Donella H. Meadows, et al., *The Limits to Growth: A Report for the Club of Rome's Project on the Predicament of Mankind* (New York: Potomac, 1972); hereinafter *The Limits to Growth.*

> This failure occurs, in large part because *we continue to examine single items in the problematique without understanding that the whole is more than the sum of its parts*, that change in one element means change in the others.[18] (emphasis added)

The Club of Rome underscored bleak prospects for the future of humankind on the earth if the pace of environmental deterioration continues unabated. It was Sweden, however, that took the initiative and mooted the idea in 1968 for the holding of a global conference for a threadbare discussion on issues surrounding the human environmental future.

Stockholm: UN Environment Programme as a Catalyst

Thus the Stockholm Conference (June 1972) that came to be convened by the UN General Assembly launched a formal process of institutionalization of international environmental cooperation. It became a major landmark in providing a sound trajectory as far as international environmental policy and law were concerned. The Stockholm Declaration comprised 26 principles that, in addition to the general concern for environment, also were cognizant of developmental concerns of developing countries. The most notable component of it was Principle 21, which put forward a two-part statement that:

> States have, in accordance with the Charter of the United Nations and the principles of international law, the sovereign right to exploit their own resources pursuant to their own environmental policies, and the responsibility to ensure that activities within their jurisdiction or control do not cause damage to the environment of other States or of areas beyond the limits of national jurisdiction.

This principle, which was explored earlier by international tribunals in one form or another, was placed on a more sound footing by the Stockholm Declaration. It contributed to the emergence of an important norm in customary international law. Widely regarded as a declaratory norm at

[18] See *The Limits to Growth*, *ibid.*, p. xi.

the time, the principle was a fine balancing act between two apparently competing components, which in fact could be regarded as two sides of the same coin. It, in turn, uplifted the hitherto limited application of the norm, rooted in case law, to that of one of the important declaratory principles for the exploitation of natural resources and developmental activities within national jurisdiction. The laying down of this salutary *threshold* has become a landmark in the development of international environmental law. The responsibility of states, however, was kept vague, especially regarding the "level of damage" that would necessitate the crossing of the threshold. The fact remains that not *all* damage to other states or the global commons is actionable. In this context it has been pertinently observed:

> To say that a State has no right to injure the environment of another seems quixotic in the face of the great variety of trans-border environmental harms that occur every day. Many result from ordinary economic and social activity; others occur by accident, often unrelated to fault. No one expects that all these injurious activities can be eliminated by general legal fiat, but there is little doubt that international legal restraints can be an important part of the response.[19]

It seems that the inherent vagueness in this general norm was subject to further fine-tuning to be done by the states in determining specific criteria for judging the resultant damage. This was reflected in Principle 22, which called on states to "develop further the international law regarding liability and compensation for the victims of pollution and other environmental damage" caused by activities within the jurisdiction or control of

[19] Arguing that not every detrimental effect resulting from environmental factors falls within the scope of the concept of *environmental harm*, Schachter prescribed four conditions necessary for the purpose: (i) the harm must result from human activity, (ii) the harm must result from a physical consequence of the causal human activity, (iii) the physical effects cross national boundaries, and (iv) the harm must be significant or substantial; see Oscar Schachter, "The Emergence of International Environmental Law," *Journal of International Affairs*, vol. 44, 1991, pp. 463–4.

states in areas beyond their jurisdiction. It implied that, in view of the very nature of environmental issues as well as strong concerns for development on the part of a large number of states, the issue of fixing liability and compensation could best be left to the political will of the states. The Stockholm Declaration, being a soft instrument, was not an appropriate vehicle for such specificity and detail. It is interesting that these two principles were singled out in terms of their normative significance by a General Assembly resolution[20] that ruled out any adverse effect on their content by virtue of any resolution adopted by the Assembly as a follow-up to the Stockholm Conference. Therefore, it is no exaggeration to state that these principles could even be regarded as the "starting point of international environmental law."[21]

Rio's Contribution

The UN General Assembly officially recognized the report of the World Commission on Environment and Development (WCED).[22] As a follow-up to it, the Assembly subsequently decided to convene[23] the UN Conference on Environment and Development (UNCED) in Brazil. It was expected to be of the highest possible level of participation, which earned

[20] This significant resolution of the General Assembly [2996(XXVII) of December 15, 1972] stated: "The General Assembly,

Recalling principles 21 and 22 of the Declaration of the United Nations Conference on the Human Environment concerning the international responsibility of States in regard to the environment,
Bearing in mind that those principles lay down the basic rules governing this matter,
Declares that no resolution adopted at the twenty-seventh session of the General Assembly can affect principles 21 and 22 of the Declaration of the United Nations Conference on the Human Environment"; see *GAOR*, vol. 27, supp. 30, 1972, p. 42.

[21] Oscar Schachter, *International Law in Theory and Practice* (Dordrecht: Martinus Nijhoff, 1991), p. 363.

[22] The General Assembly resolution 42/187 of December 11, 1987; UN *Doc.A/42/427, annex.*

[23] The General Assembly resolution 44/228 of December 22, 1989; UN *GAOR* Supp. 49, p. 151; UN *Doc.A/44/49*, 1989 (hereinafter the UNCED resolution).

the UNCED the nomenclature of the *Earth Summit.* The primary objective of the conference was to:

> (E)laborate strategies and measures to halt and reverse the effects of environmental degradation in the context of increased national and international efforts to promote sustainable and environmentally sound development in all countries.[24]

The enabling resolution of the General Assembly set up a Preparatory Committee (Prep COM) to address an ambitious agenda. In view of the sheer magnitude and size of this international environmental event, it was variously described by writers as a "many-ringed circus,"[25] "the foundation of a new global partnership,"[26] and "an attempt at environmental planning on the Grand Scale."[27]

The UNCED itself was the largest intergovernmental conference. It was unprecedented in the history of international environmental cooperation, the international lawmaking process, as well as global environmental diplomacy. One of the important mandates given to the UNCED was:

> To promote the further development of international environmental law, taking into account the declaration of the United Nations Conference on the Human Environment, as well as the special needs and concerns of the developing countries, and to examine in this context the feasibility of elaborating general rights and obligations of States, as appropriate, in the field of the environment, and taking into account relevant existing international legal instruments.[28]

[24] *Ibid.*, Part I, para 3.

[25] See Stanley P. Johnson, "Did We Really Save the Earth at Rio?" in *The Earth Summit: The United Nations Conference on Environment and Development (UNCED)* (London: Graham & Trotman/Martinus Nijhoff, 1993), p. 3.

[26] See the Statement of Maurice F. Strong, UNCED Secretary-General, at the opening of the UNCED, Rio de Janeiro, on June 3, 1992, reproduced in S.P. Johnson, *ibid.*, p. 519.

[27] David Freestone, "The Road from Rio: International Environmental Law after the Earth Summit," *Journal of Environmental Law*, vol. 6, no. 2, 1994, p. 193.

[28] See n. 23, the UNCED resolution, Part I, para 15(d).

In a way, the Rio Earth Summit provided a somber reminder of the apocalyptic predictions about the future of our fragile planet, which propelled the coming together of more than 100 heads of states or governments and representatives of 176 countries, in addition to thousands of non-governmental organizations and environmental activists on the global stage. As the largest-ever collection of *sovereignties* at the summit level, the Rio conference provided an ideal opportunity for introspection and a belated effort to lay down a *threshold* of human "need" as compared to "greed."

The preparatory process for the UNCED was launched as a sequel to the mandate given by the General Assembly. The Assembly provided detailed guidelines for the purpose, especially regarding UNCED's structure, time schedule, participation of other organs, organizations, and programs of the UN system, and of its funding. The UN Environment Programme (UNEP) – as the principal UN environmental program to date – was neither entrusted with the task of organizing the mega-event nor assigned with any major responsibility in the matter. The original initiative for convening the UNCED (as a follow-up to the report of the World Commission on Environment and Development), had come from the UNEP Governing Council (GC).[29] A special Prep COM, serviced by an ad hoc secretariat, was entrusted with the preparatory task for the UNCED. The Prep COM had an ambitious task cut out for it, to be attained within a period of approximately 2 years.[30] The Prep COM,

[29] The UNEP GC resolution 15/3 of May 25, 1989; see *GAOR*, 44th Session, Supp. No. 25 (A/44/25), annex.

[30] The Prep COM held four meetings, each lasting 4 or 5 weeks. The ProComm meetings were attended by most of the member states of the UN, UN specialized agencies, other intergovernmental institutions, non-governmental organizations, as well as a host of other "interest groups" on environmental and developmental issues. The first session of the Prep COM was held in Nairobi in August 1990, and the second and third sessions were held in Geneva in March and August 1991. The final session was held in New York in April 1992; this final session prepared the final documentation for the UNCED (beginning in the first week of June 1992). For a detailed account of the Pre COM as well as glimpses of the main event (UNCED at Rio), see, generally, Stanley P. Johnson, n. 25.

despite time constraints, was expected to impart a "strong impetus and direction"[31] for the development of a variety of international legal instruments that were proposed.

An assessment of the contribution made by the UNCED may be perceived in various ways, depending on what one expected of it. From the perspective of its contribution to the development of international environmental law, however, it may be seen in terms of immediate results obtained as well as the UNCED's impact on the norm-setting process. The UNCED itself may be regarded as one of the most remarkable events in the history of multilateral environmental negotiations. It may even seem to be an unparalleled situation for the coming together of such a large number of states to address global problems, which came to be regarded as "common concerns of humankind."

Just prior to the UNCED, and simultaneously with the Prep COM, preparations had started to bring about concrete results concerning international legal instruments on the problems of climate change as well as biological diversity. Both these instruments were concluded before the UNCED commenced. In fact, assigning the task of negotiations to a specially constituted Intergovernmental Negotiating Committee (INC), to prepare draft text of agreements on both issues, greatly helped in accelerating the process. The conclusion of negotiations and reaching of a consensus within a span of less than 2 years was indeed significant. When the two multilateral agreements (i.e., UN Framework Convention on Climate Change [UNFCCC][32] as well as Convention on Biological Diversity [CBD][33]) opened for signature at the UNCED, more than 150 states put their signatures to them. One may attribute success in reaching these "framework" agreements mainly to the need for urgent action, states' inclination to go for "precautionary measures," convergence of

[31] The *Introductory Statement* of the UNCED Secretary-General, Maurice Strong, at the opening of the First Session of the Prep COM on August 6, 1990; see UN Doc.A/Conf.151/PC/5/Add.1.

[32] See *ILM*, vol. 31, 1992, pp. 851–73.

[33] See *ILM*, vol. 31, 1992, pp. 822–41.

competing interests of the negotiating states, and workability of the politically convenient lowest common denominator through consensus.

In terms of content, both of these agreements (UNFCCC and CBD) carried some soft obligations couched in a hard treaty form. In view of the intrinsic scientific uncertainty on both the issues as well as inadequate assessments at the national level on them, however, the instruments had to be designed as *frameworks* that required follow-up actions by the parties. For instance, the UNFCCC has used formulations in laying down general commitments that call on the parties to "*formulate, develop, and cooperate*" or prescribe "*reporting*" requirements.[34] Similarly, the CBD lays down obligations for the parties that are to be carried out "*as far as possible, and as appropriate*, or *in accordance with its particular conditions and capabilities.*"[35] The fact that an overwhelming majority of states appended their signatures to both of these agreements immediately showed that they felt it was politically convenient to go for the carefully crafted consensus.

In the heat of the moment, most of the states wanted to be seen on the right side. Both of these "hard" legal instruments, comprising vague and exhoratory obligations, brought together a complex array of actors within the ambit of the process of crafting of respective regimes. The very nature of the issues at stake required the states to face political as well as economic problems in addressing them. The MEAs on climate change and biological diversity provided an opportunity to lay the groundwork for built-in lawmaking mechanism, linked to the emergence of concrete scientific evidence (regarding anthropogenic influence on climate change), by the respective Conference of Parties (COP). Thus crafting of these treaties in the shape of work-in-progress imparted the much-needed flexibility to the nascent regimes. Moreover, incorporation of some form of calculated ambiguity as well as the emerging principles of international environmental law in these agreements underscored the

[34] See Article 4 (1) of the UNFCCC.
[35] See Articles 5, 6, 7, 8, 9, 10, 11, and 14 of the CBD.

growing acceptability of judging the *threshold* of environmental behaviors of states.

There is still no consensus, however, regarding the legal status of some of these principles. Mere incorporation of such principles in a multilateral agreement may not necessarily elevate them to the status of an established norm of international environmental law. Still, they do provide evidence of their existence as well as the willingness of states to guide their respective actions on the basis of such emerging normativity. It is an interesting facet of intergovernmental negotiations that states are willing to allow incorporation of something even in the formative stage of law *as law*. In that sense it does create a mirage that also guides sovereign states in the multilateral environmental regulation. In such cases, what needs to be deciphered is the *content* rather than the *form*. As noted earlier, the *soft* character of some of these principles depicts the political dilemma of the states. It takes consistent adherence in *actual practice* on the part of states, as well as the acceptance of the principle as an obligation, and confers legitimacy on such soft norms as *hard* obligations. Thus the principles could also be regarded as *legal soft law* in a transitional stage.

Common Concerns

The premise that some of the global environmental problems need global solutions has brought about change in the perception of these issues as *common concerns of humankind*. The efforts by Malta[36] in this connection, however, to have the General Assembly declare conservation

[36] The General Assembly had considered the agenda item proposed by the Government of Malta on "Conservation of climate as part of the common heritage of mankind" and adopted the resolution *Protection of Global Climate for Present and Future Generations of Mankind* on December 6, 1988. The General Assembly resolution 43/53 (1988) was adopted without vote. Similar resolutions have been adopted by the Assembly as: 54/222 of December 22, 1999; 61/201 of December 20, 2006; 62/86 of December 10, 2007, and 63/32 of November 26, 2008; see http://www.un.org/Depts/dhl/res (as of August 8, 2009).

of climate as the *common heritage* of mankind[37] did not succeed. The Assembly instead recognized the issue of climate change as a *common concern* of humankind. The echo of this salutary declaratory statement was reflected in two global conventions on climate change[38] and biological diversity,[39] adopted at the 1992 Rio Earth Summit. In a sense, the notion of *common concern* caters to the requirements of international community interest (as opposed to limited national interest) in a common resource. It lays down a *prima facie* basis for common action regarding a regulatory framework on those issues that cannot be addressed in a bilateral context or by a limited number of states. As Alexandre Kiss has observed:

> In principle, the proclamation that safeguarding the global environment or one of its components is a matter of common concern for the whole of mankind would mean that it can no longer be considered as solely within the domestic jurisdiction of States, due to its global importance and consequences for all . . . the States, under the jurisdiction of which environmental components are to be found and the conservation of which constitutes a common concern of mankind, should be considered as trustees charged with their conservation.[40]

[37] Article 136 of the UN Convention on Law of the Sea (UNCLOS) provided that: "The Area and its resources are the common heritage of mankind." Article 1(1) of the UNCLOS states that *Area* "means the sea-bed and the ocean floor and subsoil thereof, beyond the limits of national jurisdiction." As per Article 140, the activities in the Area were to be carried out for the benefit of mankind as a whole, irrespective of the geographical location of states. The International Sea-Bed Authority was to provide for the equitable sharing of financial and other economic benefits derived from activities in the Area through appropriate mechanisms. The idea of common heritage of mankind was mooted in a Maltese proposal by Arvid Pardo. The UNCLOS came into force, after a period of 12 years, on November 16, 1994.

[38] The very first paragraph of the *Preamble* to the Framework Convention on Climate Change states: "*Acknowledging* that change in the Earth's climate and its adverse effects are a common concern of humankind"; see *ILM*, vol. 31, 1992, p. 849.

[39] The *Preamble* to the CBD states: "*Affirming* that the conservation of biological diversity is a common concern of humankind"; see *ILM*, vol. 31, 1992, p. 822.

[40] Alexandre Kiss, "The Common Concern of Mankind," *Environmental Policy and Law*, vol. 27, no. 4, 1997, p. 247.

It appears that negotiators now consciously avoid the term "common heritage," which incidentally came to be applied with reference to the exploitation of the resources of the deep seabed. The idea of regarding a resource as a common heritage implies the duty to preserve it for future generations. "Common concern" can be regarded as forming part of common heritage. An explicit reference to the term "common heritage" appears to have been avoided as it met with controversy in the case of the UNCLOS. Following the 1994 Agreement on the Implementation of this Convention, Part XI (on the common heritage of mankind) has been explicitly targeted, and, it is widely felt to have almost been emasculated (i.e., bereft of its original purpose).

It is interesting that the subtle change in emphasis from "common heritage" to "common interest" to "common concern" at various stages appears to have been made to accommodate conflicting interests of the negotiating states. It does, however, underscore the nature of the issues sought to be dealt with, the need for approaches beyond the confines of national or bilateral domains, as well as the conflicting demands it places on various international actors. The common concerns are to be addressed within a multilateral framework, on the basis of common but differentiated responsibilities on the part of the contracting states to a global convention (e.g., the UNFCCC). The advent and usage of this new phrase in the legal parlance has wide ramifications in terms of the growing centralization of multilateral environmental lawmaking enterprise. As a corollary to it, issues of *ethics* and *equity* hold the key to some of the "common concerns" being addressed within the framework of multilateral environmental negotiations.

Montevideo Mandate

One of the important mandates that the UNEP carved out for itself was to act as a *catalyst* in the development of international environmental law. Initially, when the UNEP embarked on efforts in this direction, it prepared a set of fifteen draft principles on the conduct of states in the field of environment regarding conservation and harmonious utilization of natural resources shared by two or more states.[41] These principles emerged in the wake of a request by the UN General Assembly[42] to lay down appropriate international standards in the matter. The Charter of Economic Rights and Duties of States adopted by the General Assembly also incorporated a similar principle.[43] These draft principles were adopted by the UNEP GC but, for inexplicable reasons, were not subsequently considered by the General Assembly. The explanatory note to the draft makes it clear that it did not seek to refer to a "specific legal obligation under international law, or the absence of such obligation," and did not intend to express an opinion (as far as they do not reflect already existing rules of general international law) as to whether these principles "should be incorporated in the body of general international law."[44]

[41] UNEP Principles on Conservation and Harmonious Utilization of Natural Resources Shared by Two or More States (1978); for the text, see *ILM*, vol. 17, 1978, pp. 1097–9.

[42] See the UN General Assembly resolution 3129 (XXVIII), 1973.

[43] Article 3 of the Charter of Economic Rights and Duties of States annexed to the UN General Assembly resolution 3281(XXIX) of December 12, 1974, provided:

> "In the exploitation of natural resources shared by two or more countries, each state must cooperate on the basis of a system of information and prior consultation in order to achieve optimum use of such resources without causing damage to the legitimate interests of others"; see *ILM*, vol. 14, 1974, p. 251.

[44] The *Explanatory Note* to the Draft Principles of Conduct read as:

> "The draft principles of conduct, in this note have been drawn up for the guidance of States in the field of the environment with respect to the conservation and harmonious utilization of natural resources shared by two or more States. The principles refer to such conduct of individual States as is considered conducive to the attainment of the said objective in a manner which does not adversely affect the environment. Moreover, the principles aim to encourage States sharing a natural resource, to co-operate in the field of the environment.
>
> An attempt has been made to avoid language which might create the impression of intending to refer to, as the case may be, either a specific legal obligation under international law, or to the absence of such obligation.
>
> The language used throughout does not seek to prejudice whether or to what extent the conduct envisaged in the principles is already prescribed by existing rules of general

In the background of this initial effort, for formulation of some general principles of international environmental law, the UNEP GC adopted an ambitious plan for the development and periodic review of environmental law, which was prepared at an ad hoc Meeting of Senior Government Officials Expert in Environmental Law at Montevideo (the Montevideo Programme).[45] This program was adopted by the UNEP GC[46] and became an ambitious exercise in laying down a framework, method, and program for the development of environmental law. It recognized the importance of codification and progressive development of environmental law to promote international cooperation, mutual understanding, and friendly relations among states, apart from serving as an essential instrument for proper environmental management and improvement of quality of life.

The first phase of the Montevideo Programme led UNEP to focus on framing as well as adopting a series of guidelines, rules, and principles that prescribed a general framework for the behavior of states on a host of issues such as land-based sources of marine pollution, protection of the ozone layer, and the transport, handling, and disposal of toxic substances. Some other areas covered under the Programme included the problems of international environmental cooperation in emergencies, coastal

international law. Neither does the formulation intend to express an opinion as to whether or to what extent and in what manner the principles – as far as they do not reflect already existing rules of general international law – should be incorporated in the body of general international law"; see *ILM*, vol. 17, 1978, pp. 1097–8.

[45] The Ad Hoc Meeting of Senior Government Officials Expert in Environmental Law took place in Montevideo from October 28 through November 6, 1981, to establish a framework, method, and program for the development and periodic review of environmental law and to contribute to the preparation and implementation of the environmental law component of the system-wide medium-term environment program. See *Report of the Ad Hoc Meeting of Senior Government Officials Experts in Environmental Law*, UNEP/GC 10/5/Add.2, Annex, Ch. 11 (1981). Also see *Yearbook of the United Nations*, vol. 35, 1981, pp. 839–40 and *Yearbook of the United Nations*, vol. 36, 1982, p. 1030.

[46] The UNEP GC resolution 10/21 of May 31, 1982, adopted the experts' program and endorsed their conclusions and recommendations; see UNEP GC report A/37/25, May 31, 1982.

zone management, soil conservation, transboundary air pollution, international trade in potentially harmful chemicals, protection from pollution of inland waterways, legal and administrative mechanisms for prevention and redress of pollution damage, and methods of environmental impact assessment.[47] It, in turn, contributed to the development of both "soft" and "hard" instruments.

The UNEP was able to crystallize a normative framework through the first phase (1981–1992) of the Montevideo Programme, to regulate the conduct of the states. The significance of this mandate under the Montevideo Programme was that soft-law instruments became precursors to hard obligations. Expert Working Groups prepare drafts of most of these instruments through painstaking work. An interesting facet of such drafts is the use of vague language, which is politically convenient to the states. They are not legally binding (nonlegal soft law) and have, at best, an educative value. Such soft instruments have turned out to have a subtle influence, and often provide a basis for crafting hard instruments. As a result, a number of multilateral environmental agreements have taken shape on issues such as depletion of the ozone layer (1985 and 1987)[48] and transboundary movements of hazardous wastes and their disposal (1989).[49] They also have served as a basis for developing conventions on climate change (1992)[50] and biological diversity (1992).[51]

[47] Mostafa K. Tolba and Iwona Rummel-Bulska, *Global Environmental Diplomacy: Negotiating Environmental Agreements for the World 1973–1992* (Cambridge, MA: MIT Press, 1998), p. 6.

[48] Convention for the Protection of the Ozone Layer (Vienna, 1985) and Protocol on Substances that Deplete the Ozone Layer (Montreal, 1987), both entered into force on September 22, 1988, and January 1, 1989; see *ILM*, vol. 26, 1987, p. 1529 and *ILM*, vol. 26, 1987, p. 1550. For Amendments and Adjustments to the Montreal Protocol, see *ILM*, vol. 30, 1991, pp. 539 and 541 and *ILM*, vol. 32, 1993, p. 874.

[49] Convention on the Control of Transboundary Movements of Hazardous Wastes and Their Disposal (Basel, 1989), entered into force on May 24, 1992; see *ILM*, vol. 28, 1989, p. 657.

[50] United Nations Framework Convention on Climate Change (Rio de Janeiro, 1992) entered into force on March 21, 1994; see *ILM*, vol. 31, 1992, p. 849.

[51] Convention on Biological Diversity (Rio de Janeiro, 1992) entered into force on December 29, 1993; see *ILM*, vol. 31, 1992, p. 822.

In light of the experience of the first phase of the Montevideo Programme, the UNEP carried out an exercise to strengthen it. At two review sessions of the Meeting of Senior Government Officials Expert in Environmental Law, a second phase of the Montevideo Programme was adopted.[52] In the second phase, the Montevideo Programme further addressed emerging environmental challenges and to develop relevant legal regimes. It was adopted[53] by the UNEP GC as a broad strategy for the activities of the UNEP in the field of environmental law for the 1990s. The GC in its decision (17/25 of May 21, 1993) underscored the role of the UNEP for the:

> Continued progressive development of international environmental law as a means of wider adherence to and more efficient implementation of international environmental conventions, as well as future negotiating process for legal instruments in the field of sustainable development.

The Montevideo Programme II identified nineteen[54] principal areas for the development of environmental law, each of which contained the objectives, strategies, and activities to be carried out under it. The

[52] UNEP organized two sessions of the Meeting of Senior Government Officials Expert in Environmental Law for the Review of the Montevideo Programme that took place in Rio de Janeiro (October/November 1991) and in Nairobi (September 1992). The sessions were attended by government experts from more than eighty developing and developed countries as well as observers from relevant international organizations; see UNEP, *Programme for the Development and Periodic Review of Environmental Law for the 1990s* (Nairobi: UNEP, June 1993), pp. 1–17 (hereinafter, Montevideo Programme II). Also see *Yearbook of the United Nations*, vol. 47, 1993, pp. 820–1.

[53] See *Yearbook of the United Nations*, vol. 47, 1993, pp. 820–1. Also see UNEP GC decision 17/25 of May 21, 1993; see UN *Doc.A/17/25*.

[54] The Montevideo Programme II comprised the following nineteen elements:

> (A) enhancing the capacity of states to participate effectively in the development and implementation of environmental law; (B) implementation of international legal instruments in the field of the environment; (C) adequacy of existing international instruments; (D) dispute avoidance and settlement; (E) legal and administrative mechanisms for the prevention and redress of pollution and other environmental damage; (F) environmental impact assessment; (G) environmental awareness, education, information, and public participation; (H) concepts or principles significant for the future of environmental law; (I) protection of the

program, in general, sought to ensure full participation of all the states in the development and effective implementation of environmental law and policy, implementation of relevant international legal instruments, and evaluation of the adequacy of these instruments for the respective problem areas, apart from specific environmental issues. It also recognized new areas which will necessitate international legal responses, such as environmental protection of areas beyond the limits of national jurisdiction, biotechnology, liability and compensation, environment and trade, environmental implications of international agreements not directly relating to environment, human settlements, and transfer of technology and technical cooperation.[55]

To align UNEP's priorities with those of the governments, midterm review of the Montevideo Programme provided an opportunity for taking stock to ensure the effectiveness of UNEP's role in multilateral environmental lawmaking process. As such, the midterm review[56] (1996) provided a series of suggestions. The UNEP GC launched a process in 1999 for the third phase of the Montevideo Programme. It called for convening a Meeting of Senior Government Experts in Environmental Law in the year 2000, for the "preparation of a new programme for the development and periodic review of environmental law."[57] This decision

stratospheric ozone layer; (J) transboundary air pollution control; (K) conservation, management, and sustainable development of soils and forests; (L) transport, handling, and disposal of hazardous wastes; (M) international trade in potentially harmful chemicals; (N) environmental protection and integrated management, development, and use of inland water resources; (O) marine pollution from land-based sources; (P) management of coastal areas; (Q) protection of marine environment and the law of the sea; (R) international cooperation in environmental emergencies; and (S) additional subjects for possible consideration during present decade; see UNEP, Montevideo Programme II.

[55] *Ibid.*, p. 17.

[56] See *Report of the Meeting of Senior Government Officials Expert in Environmental Law for the Mid-Term Review of the Programme for the Development and Periodic Review of Environmental Law for the 1990s*, Nairobi, December 2–6, 1996; UNEP/Env.Law/3/3 of December 10, 1996.

[57] UNEP GC Decision 20/3 of February 3, 1999 on "Programme for the Development and Periodic Review of Environmental Law beyond the year 2000"; see 20th GC Decisions at http://www.unep.org/Documents.

authorized the Executive Director of UNEP to use the Programme II as strategic guidance for the work of UNEP in the field of environmental law until the GC adopted a new program. As a follow-up to this renewed mandate, the Executive Director convened the Meeting of Senior Government Officials Expert in Environmental Law in October 2000.[58] The deliberations at the meeting were facilitated by two documents,[59] namely, possible components of a program and implementation of the program for the 1990s. Following extensive debate and elaboration on twenty proposed subject areas, the meeting adopted[60] a *draft* Montevideo Programme III for presentation in February 2001 to the twenty-first session[61] of the UNEP GC, which also served as second session of the Global Ministerial Environment Forum (GMEF). It was adopted[62] by the twenty-first session of the GC and provided a road map to the UNEP for the development of environmental law in the next decade.

[58] The meeting to prepare a Programme for the Development and Periodic Review of Environmental Law for the First Decade of the Twenty-First Century was held at UN Offices in Nairobi, October 23–27, 2000.

[59] See the documents (i) "Possible Components of a Programme for the Development and Periodic Review of Environmental Law for the First Decade of the Twenty-First Century" (UNEP/Env.Law/4/2) as well as (ii) "Implementation of the Programme for the Development and Periodic Review of Environmental Law for the 1990s" (UNEP/Env.Law/4/3).

[60] The *draft* Montevideo Programme III encompasses various elements aiming to enhance the effectiveness of environmental law, apart from addressing sectoral environmental issues of current concern; see UNEP/Env.Law/4/4 of October 21, 2000. Also see *Environmental Policy and Law*, vol. 30, no. 6, 2000, p. 268.

[61] See Report of the Executive Director on *Policy Responses of the United Nations Environment Programme to Tackle Emerging Environmental Problems in Sustainable Development*; Items 4 (b) and 5 of the provisional agenda for the Twenty-First Session of the GC of UNEP/Global Ministerial Environment Forum, Nairobi, February 5–9, 2001; Doc.UNEP/GC.21/3, December 18, 2000, p. 6, para 9.

[62] The twenty-first session of the UNEP GC adopted the "Programme for the Development and Periodic Review of Environmental Law for the First Decade of the Twenty-first Century" as the broad strategy for the activities of UNEP in the field of environmental law. The GC requested the Executive Director to implement the Program, within available resources and program of work of UNEP. It also called for close collaboration with states, conferences of the parties and secretariats of MEAs, other international organizations, nonstate actors and persons; see the GC Decision 21/23 of February 9, 2001; available at http://www.unep.org/gc.

As a part of this organic process, the work on the next phase of the program was launched in 2007. It coincided with the cycle of development of the 2010–2011 program of work of the UNEP and against the backdrop of the UNEP Medium-Term Strategy for the period 2010–2013. The UNEP secretariat prepared a draft outline of a fourth Programme for the Development and Periodic Review of Environmental Law, which was submitted to an open-ended consultative meeting of government officials and experts on the Montevideo Programme.[63] The draft of the Montevideo Programme IV was finalized at the conclusion of the Meeting of the Senior Government Officials Expert in Environmental Law in Nairobi on October 3, 2008.[64] The representatives agreed on the text of the draft program, comprising the twenty-seven areas.[65] It

[63] The meeting took place in Nairobi on November 26–30, 2007 (UNEP/Env.Law/MTV4/IG/1/2). At that meeting, government officials from fifty-seven states and representatives of eight intergovernmental and non-governmental organizations reviewed the draft outline and provided their observations and suggestions thereon (UNEP/Env.Law/MTV4/IG/1/4).

[64] The Meeting of Senior Government Officials Expert in Environmental Law to prepare a fourth Programme for the Development and Periodic Review of Environmental Law (Montevideo Programme) was convened by UNEP in Nairobi from September 29 through October 3, 2008. It was attended by representatives from the following countries: Antigua and Barbuda, Argentina, Austria, Bahamas, Bangladesh, Belize, Bhutan, Bolivia, Brazil, Burkina Faso, Burundi, Canada, Central African Republic, Chad, Chile, China, Colombia, Comoros, Congo, Côte d'Ivoire, Cuba, Czech Republic, Democratic Republic of the Congo, Djibouti, Dominican Republic, Ecuador, Egypt, El Salvador, Eritrea, Ethiopia, Fiji, Finland, France, Gambia, Germany, Ghana, Grenada, Guatemala, Guinea, Haiti, Honduras, India, Indonesia, Iran (Islamic Republic of), Japan, Kenya, Kiribati, Kyrgyzstan, Lao People's Democratic Republic, Madagascar, Malawi, Malaysia, Maldives, Mali, Mauritius, Mexico, Mongolia, Morocco, Mozambique, Myanmar, Nepal, Netherlands, Nicaragua, Niger, Oman, Pakistan, Panama, Paraguay, Peru, Russian Federation, Rwanda, Samoa, Saudi Arabia, Senegal, Serbia, Somalia, Sri Lanka, Sudan, Suriname, Swaziland, Switzerland, Syrian Arab Republic, Timor-Leste, Togo, Turkey, Uganda, United Kingdom of Great Britain and Northern Ireland, United Republic of Tanzania, United States of America, Uruguay, Venezuela (Bolivarian Republic of), Zimbabwe; see http://www.unep.org/GC/GC25/working-docs.asp (as of August 8, 2009).

[65] Fourth Programme for the Development and Periodic Review of Environmental Law, Report by the Executive Director, Twenty-fifth session of the GC/Global Ministerial Environment Forum, Nairobi, February 16–20, 2009; see Doc. UNEP/GC.25/11, October 28, 2008.

contains most of the items contained in Programme III. Programme IV stands apart, however, because it covers (i) climate change, (ii) poverty, (iii) access to drinking water and sanitation, (iv) ecosystem protection, (v) environmental emergencies and natural disasters, (vi) new technologies, and (vii) synergies among MEAs.[66] It was duly adopted by the Twenty-Fifth session of the UNEP GC as a "broad strategy for the international community and the United Nations Environment Programme in formulating the activities in the field of environmental law for the decade commencing in 2010."[67] UNEP's Medium-Term Strategy 2010–2013 also reflects some aspects of the goals of the Montevideo Programme IV.[68]

It appears that the Montevideo Programme has emerged as a major pillar for UNEP's contribution to the international environmental lawmaking process. It has guided the development and implementation of UNEP's international environmental law program, in response to the environmental challenges of each decade.[69] In fact, it has facilitated an interesting interplay between scientific processes and public policy making and its expression through environmental law. In the course of the three decades of the Montevideo Programme implementation, both the range and the content of UNEP's role in multilateral environmental lawmaking have undergone significant changes. In view of increasing

[66] Report of the meeting of Senior Government Officials Expert in Environmental Law to prepare a fourth Program for the Development and Periodic Review of Environmental Law (Montevideo Program IV), Nairobi, September 29 through October 3, 2008; see UNEP/Env.Law/MTV4/IG/2/2, October 22, 2008, pp. 10–28; available at http://unep.org/law/About_prog/montevideo_progIV.asp (as of August 8, 2009). The agreed text of the draft program as contained in the annex to the report of the meeting (UNEP/Env.Law/MTV4/IG/2/2) was reproduced in document UNEP/GC.25/INF/15 for the consideration of the Twenty-fifth Session of the UNEP GC/Global Ministerial Environment Forum held in Nairobi, February 16–20, 2009.

[67] See Decision 25/11 of the UNEP GC/Global Ministerial Environment Forum, February 16–20, 2009; available at http://www.unep.org/GC/GC25/working-docs.asp (as of August 8, 2009).

[68] UN Medium-term Strategy 2010–2013, p. 4; available at http://unep.org/Documents.Multilingual/Default.asp?DocumentID=43 (as of August 8, 2009).

[69] See UNEP Annual Report 2008 (Nairobi: UNEP, 2009), p. 44; available at http://unep.org/Documents.Multilingual/Default.asp?DocumentID=43 (as of August 8, 2009).

technicalities of the sectoral environmental issues in the negotiations for multilateral agreements, however, it makes sense that UNEP collaborates with other "specialized agencies" of the UN. For instance, on the issue of chemicals, the Food and Agriculture Organization (FAO) has joined UNEP in the negotiations for a global Convention on Prior Informed Consent Procedure (PIC) for Certain Hazardous Chemicals and Pesticides in International Trade (Rotterdam, 1998).[70] Both UNEP and FAO now jointly provide a secretariat[71] for this convention.

With the entry of other high-profile actors, especially within the UN system in this cherished domain, UNEP now faces good competition. It has, in turn, to some extent affected UNEP's ability to set the global environmental agenda. The Montevideo Programme, however, still provides the *raison d'être* for UNEP's role as the "environmental voice" of the UN.

Conclusion

The era of multilateral environmental regulatory technique has heralded the coming together of sovereign states to address specific challenges. The emergence of treaty making as almost a fine art and special negotiating craft to address some of the "common concerns" reflects its unrivaled edge over other methods of lawmaking in the field of international law. To go for a treaty or not to address a specific sectoral environmental problem still remains the prerogative of the states that are primary subjects of international law. An instrument that is crafted by the states has to be tested both on the criteria of the intention of the negotiating states

[70] The PIC Convention for Certain Hazardous Chemicals and Pesticides in International Trade was adopted at Rotterdam on September 10, 1998. It seeks to curtail the $1.5 trillion trade in hazardous pesticides and chemicals; see UNEP, *Annual Report 1998* (Nairobi: UNEP, 1998), pp. 7 and 21. For text of the Rotterdam PIC Convention, see UNEP/FAO/PIC/CONF.5 of September 17, 1998. Also see http://www.irptc/pic/incs/dipcom/finale.htm#convention.

[71] See UNEP GC Decision SS.V/5 of May 22, 1998, as well as Decision 20/22 of February 4, 1999 at: http://www.unep.org/Documents.

as well as on its content. The rules of the game governing treaty-making practice are now placed on the concrete footing of the 1969 Vienna Convention on the Law of Treaties.

It goes without saying that treaties have placed regulatory frameworks in different areas of international law on a sound footing. There could be disadvantages to a treaty, especially if the contracting parties take an unduly long time to bring it legally into force. The methodology of treaty-making followed in different areas and tools and techniques adopted to address specific problems could and in fact do vary. There is no denying, however, that treaties have brought certainty to the applicable law in the given area. They also have been responsible, in general, for promoting institutionalized international cooperation. The multilateral environmental cooperation is the best example of this practice. It has not only led to the proliferation of MEAs; these agreements themselves have been turned into *sui generis* lawmaking machines through regular and institutionalized multilateral intergovernmental negotiations. The participation of an overwhelming number of sovereign states in this marathon process seems to provide a testimony to the apparent working of the regulatory technique.

3 Nature and Character of Environmental Agreements

Introduction

As discussed in the previous chapter, the twentieth century witnessed unprecedented growth in the making of treaties, not only as codification exercises for existing customary state practices, but also as regulation of numerous subjects that confront the states. An important outcome of intergovernmental institutionalized cooperation in environmental matters has been the growth of a unique body of treaty-based and other rules. The advent of such environmental agreements seems to carry the "genes" and imprint of the maker/initiator. The methodology of treaty making in this field stands apart from that in other areas of international law as it reflects the changing needs of sovereign states in an increasingly complex world. It has also heralded qualitative and quantitative change in the character of international environmental law. This phenomenon of multilateral environmental agreements (MEAs) needs much closer legal scrutiny regarding its nature and character, the uniqueness and content of MEAs, and the lawmaking approach followed in marathon global environmental conferences.

Proliferation of Agreements

MEAs have emerged as the "predominant legal method for addressing environmental problems that cross national boundaries."[1] The pace at which the multilateral instruments concerning environmental issues are growing remains unprecedented. From the earliest reported multilateral treaty concerning the environment in 1868, approximately 502 international treaties and other agreements have taken shape. Of these, 302 (a staggering number, almost 60 percent) have been entered into since the 1972 Stockholm Conference.[2] In a way, these developments reflect a strong sense of multilateralism at work to address some of the common concerns that sovereign states consider necessary to regulate through these instruments. There are, however, some issue-specific common elements and differences in the treaty making resorted to in some of the sectors (see Table 1 for a comparison of twenty select MEAs). In fact, during the four-year period (1990–1994) coinciding with the 1992 Rio Earth Summit, more than fifty such international instruments – most of them multilateral[3] – came to be adopted by the states.

As discussed earlier, many factors have been responsible for the increasing resort to the methodology of MEAs by the sovereign states as well as institutional actors (e.g., United Nations Environment Programme [UNEP]) that often initiate the process for such an instrument. One of the standard features of these instruments is that negotiations on them take place in a backdrop of urgency, and often the instrument is expected to be ready within a certain time frame. It was seen in the cases of both the United Nations Framework Convention on Climate Change

[1] "Developments in the Law: International Environmental Law," *Harvard Law Review*, vol. 104, no. 3, 1991, p. 1521.

[2] United Nations Environment Programme (UNEP), "Multilateral Environmental Agreements: A Summary," Open-Ended Intergovernmental Group of Ministers or Their Representatives on International Environmental Governance (First meeting, New York, April 18, 2001); UNEP/IGM/1/INF/1 of March 30, 2001, p. 3.

[3] Alexandre Kiss and Dinah Shelton, *International Environmental Law: 1994 Supplement* (New York: Transnational, 1994), p. 1.

Table 1. *Comparative Status of Select MEAs (as of August 18, 2009)*

MEAs	Year	Entry into Force	Parties Ratification	Host Institution	Seat	Decision-Making Organ	Issues Covered
Convention on Wetlands of International Importance	1971	12/21/1975	159	IUCN	Gland	COP	Conservation and wise use of wetlands, primarily as habitat for the waterbird
Convention for the Protection of World Cultural and Natural Heritage	1972	12/17/1975	186	UNESCO	Paris	General Assembly of States Parties	Protection and conservation of cultural and natural heritage
Convention for the Prevention of Marine Pollution by Dumping of Wastes	1972	8/30/1975	72	IMO	London	Consultative Meeting of the Parties	All sources of pollution of the marine environment, especially dumping of waste
Protocol to the Convention on the Prevention of Marine Pollution by Dumping of Wastes	1996	3/24/2006	96	IMO	London	Meetings of the Parties	All sources of pollution of the marine environment, especially dumping of waste
Convention on International Trade in Endangered Species	1973	7/1/1975	175	UNEP	Geneva	COP	International trade in endangered species of wild fauna and flora

(*continued*)

Table 1 *(continued)*

MEAs	Year	Entry into Force	Parties Ratification	Host Institution	Seat	Decision-Making Organ	Issues Covered
CMS	1979	11/1/1983	112	UNEP	Bonn	COP	Conservation & management [wise use] of migratory species of wild animals and their habitats
Agreement for the Conservation of Bats in Europe (EUROBATS)	1991	1/16/1994	32	UNEP co-located with CMS	Bonn	MOP	Conservation of bats, especially threats from habitat degradation, disturbance of roosting sites, and certain pesticides
Agreement for the Conservation of Small Cetaceans of the Baltic and North Sea [ASCOBANS]	1992	3/29/1994	13	UNEP co-located with CMS	Bonn	MOP	To achieve and maintain a favorable conservation status for small cetaceans
Agreement on the Conservation of African-Eurasian Migratory Waterbirds [AEWA]	1995	11/1/1999	65	UNEP co-located with CMS	Bonn	MOP	To maintain favorable conservation status for migratory waterbirds, especially endangered species

Convention on Substances That Deplete the Ozone Layer [Vienna]	1985	9/2291988	195	UNEP	Nairobi	COP	Atmospheric ozone layer above the planetary boundary layer
Protocol on Substances That Deplete the Ozone Layer [Montreal]	1987	1/1/1989	195 London (192) Copenhagen (189) Montreal (175) Beijing (156)	UNEP	Nairobi	COP	Atmospheric ozone layer above the planetary boundary layer
Convention on Transboundary Movements of Hazardous Wastes and their Disposal [Basel]	1989	5/5/1992	172	UNEP	Geneva	COP	Transboundary movements of hazardous wastes and their disposal
Ban Amendment	1995	Not in Force	65				Prohibiting exports of hazardous wastes from countries listed in a proposed new annex to the Convention (that are members of the EU, OECD, Liechtenstein) to all other Parties to the Convention

(*continued*)

Table 1 (*continued*)

MEAs	Year	Entry into Force	Parties Ratification	Host Institution	Seat	Decision-Making Organ	Issues Covered
Protocol on Liability and Compensation for Damage Resulting from Transboundary Movements of Hazardous Wastes and their Disposal [Basel]	1999	Not in Force	9	UNEP	Geneva	MOP	Comprehensive regime for liability and for adequate and prompt compensation for damage
UNFCCC	1992	3/21/1994	192	UN	Bonn	COP	Changes in the earth's climate system due to anthropogenic interference
Protocol to the UNFCCC [Kyoto]	1997	2/16/2005	187	UN	Bonn	MOP	Quantified emission limitation and reduction commitments for Annex I Parties
CBD	1992	12/29/1993	191	UNEP	Montreal	COP	Biological diversity and biological resources
Protocol on Biosafety to the CBD [Cartagena]	2000	9/11/2003	156	UNEP	Montreal	MOP	Transboundary movement, transit, handling, and use of living modified organisms

UN Convention to Combat Desertification	1994	12/26/1996	193	UN	Bonn	COP	Combating desertification and mitigating the effects of drought, particularly in Africa
Rotterdam Convention on the Prior Informed Consent Procedure for Certain Hazardous Chemicals and Pesticides in International Trade	1998	2/24/2004	128	UNEP and FAO	Geneva and Rome	COP	Promote shared responsibility and cooperative effort among the parties in the international trade of certain hazardous chemicals, to protect human health and the environment from potential harm and to contribute to their environmentally sound use
Stockholm Convention on Persistent Organic Pollutants	2001	5/17/2004	164	UNEP	Geneva	COP	Protect human health and the environment from persistent organic pollutants

COP: Conference of the Parties
EU: European Union
FAO: Food and Agriculture Organization
IMO: International Maritime Organization
IUCN: International Union for Conservation of Nature
MOP: Meeting of the Parties
UNESCO: United Nations Educational, Scientific and Cultural Organization

(UNFCCC) and the Convention on Biological Diversity (CBD), which were expected to be ready (within a period of some 16 months) for adoption at the 1992 Rio Earth Summit. In such eventuality, MEAs suit the negotiating states most because the final text, by established practice, generally, emerges as a framework only. Such accommodation, built-in flexibility, and step-by-step strengthening of the instrument are the major hallmarks responsible for the proliferation of MEAs.

It has now been widely accepted that lawmaking and institution-building processes have gone hand in hand. Therefore, a need-based organic increase in international institutions in the environmental field has given fillip to the growth of treaties in this field. In fact, it has been argued by some that the "proliferation of treaties is aided and abetted by the concomitant rise in intergovernmental organizations"[4] (or institutions). Thus the practice and behavior of the maker, in turn, could also affect the "patterns"[5] of treaty making being put into place.

Regulating State Behavior

The emergence of international law as a guardian of the global environment and the commons (e.g., outer space, Antarctica) also reflects its capacity to adapt and change with the new challenges and changing requirements of international society. The process has experienced different phases in the evolution of a distinct branch of international

[4] Jose E. Alvarez, "The New Treaty Makers," *Boston College International and Comparative Law Review*, vol. XXV, no. 2, 2002, pp. 213–34 at 217.

[5] Alvarez has argued that most of the multilateral treaties in existence today are products of four kinds of organizational patterns: (i) international organization-sponsored (e.g., UN) treaty-making conferences (e.g., law of treaties, diplomatic immunities, and privileges or international criminal court); (ii) expert treaty-making bodies (e.g., international law commission and functional agencies for civil aviation, atomic energy, intellectual property, maritime); (iii) managerial forms of treaty making (e.g., in areas like trade, environment, human rights); and (iv) institutional mechanisms for treaty making with "strings attached" (e.g., constitutionally sanctioned treaty making by organizations like the International Labour Organization [ILO]); see *ibid.*, pp. 220–2.

environmental law. Amid various scattered and piecemeal efforts in this direction, the growing trend of centralization of lawmaking on environmental issues is most discernible. The trend appears to be a reflection of that of a *functional* approach to specific problems. In the environmental context, the functional approach takes the form of sectoral treaties (e.g., climate change, desertification, biodiversity). Alongside such "hard" instruments, it is interesting that the "soft law" instruments (e.g., conference statements and declarations), described as a "Trojan horse of the ecologists" (*trojanische Pferd der Ökologistern*),[6] have also played a pivotal role in the growing legalization of global environmental issues. Often such soft normativity is a precursor to the hard instrument on the subject. The 1972 UN Conference on the Human Environment (UNCHE) may be said to have set the ball rolling for multilateralism on global environmental issues. The inherent logic in centralized international lawmaking on environmental issues appears to be that many of them necessitate a global, as distinguished from international, framework.

The process of centralized legalization has taken various forms. Unlike the development of traditional international law, the pace of lawmaking in this sphere has been relatively fast. Furthermore, it is more in the direction of conventional (treaty) law than customary law. It is interesting that most of the international legal developments in the field of environmental protection have taken place outside the precincts of the UN's International Law Commission (ILC),[7] which was assigned the

[6] Winfried Lang, "Die Verrechtlichung des internationalen Umweltschutzes: Vom "soft law" zum "hard law," *Archiv des Völkerrechts*, vol. 22, 1984, pp. 282–305 at 303.

[7] The ILC was set up by the UN General Assembly in 1947. Its thirty-four members are elected by the General Assembly for a term of 5 years. They serve as legal experts in their individual capacities. The ILC has, over a period spanning more than five decades, done commendable work in promoting progressive development and codification of international law. Some of its principal achievements include The Statute of the International Criminal Court (1998); The Convention on the Non-navigational Uses of International Watercourses (1997); The Convention on the Law of Treaties between States and International Organizations or between International Organizations (1986); The Convention on the Succession of States in Respect of State Property,

task of progressive development and codification of international law. In the absence of a central lawmaking institution in the environmental field, this task has generally fallen on the General Assembly of the UN. The General Assembly has in fact played a crucial role in terms of convening global conferences that, in turn, have contributed significantly to the increasing centralized legalization on environmental issues. The 1972 UNCHE, the 1992 UN Conference on Environment and Development (UNCED), as well as the 2002 WSSD (World Summit on Sustainable Development, Johannesburg) have been major milestones in triggering and nurturing this marathon process.

The multilateral regulatory approach concerning environmental issues has come to be institutionalized as a systematic way of attaining intergovernmental cooperation. This multilateral lawmaking method has, however, been used in a rather piecemeal, ad hoc, and sporadic manner. The basic underpinning for this form of regulation is provided by the quest for institutionalized forms of international cooperation. The advent of the multilateral regulatory approach in the field of environmental issues is no exception. The recent pace of development of MEAs has been unprecedented[8] in the history of international treaty making. Such proliferation of intergovernmental instruments, laying down obligations for the contracting states, has created a unique situation for, and pressure on, the participating states.

MEAs have drawn attention to issues for global consideration (that were until recently dealt with at the national level) and also have decisively brought about change in the lawmaking approach. The innovative

Archives and Debts (1983); The Convention on the Prevention and Punishment of Crimes against Internationally Protected Persons, including Diplomatic Agents (1973); The Convention on the Law of the Treaties (1969); the Convention on Diplomatic Relations (1961) and on Consular Relations (1963) and the four Conventions on the Law of the Sea, adopted at the First UN Law of the Sea Conference (1958); see http://www.un.org/law/ilc/.

[8] It is estimated that, since 1868, there have been approximately 502 international treaties and agreements concerning the environment, out of which almost 300 have been entered into since 1972; see UN doc. UNEP/IGM/1/INF/1 of March 30, 2001, pp. 3–4.

methodology used to regulate sector-specific environmental issues has been able to encourage participation from an unprecedented number of sovereign states. This innovative process of engaging the bulk of the state members of the UN in multilateral environmental regulation has implications for the normative standards, the nature of issues addressed, as well as criteria for reaching consensual agreement especially through framework instruments. It could not but have had profound implications for multilateralism at work in the field of international law as well as institutionalized patterns of intergovernmental environmental cooperation.

The current process of lawmaking has brought about a significant body of "codified" normative frameworks for regulating the environmental behavior of sovereign states. It could have been partly triggered by the perceived inadequacies of the traditional rules of customary international law to grapple with the simmering environmental challenge. At the same time, it has generated institutional mechanisms that serve as tools for the regulatory frameworks. Although the growing trend of environmental treaty making does not undermine the historical contribution of customary law, it was initially argued that "general international law (or customary law) contains no rules or standards related to the protection of the environment as such"; therefore, the customary law "provides limited means of social engineering."[9]

Such a view in a way ignored the state practice developed through the normative contribution of the landmark award in the *Train Smelter*[10]

[9] While contending such "limitations" of the traditional customary methods of norm setting, Brownlie has underscored the relevance of three trends: (i) the rules of state responsibility; (ii) "territorial" sovereignty of states that permits use and enjoyment of resources subject to the rules of state responsibility; and (iii) the old concept of "freedom of the sea" provided for elements of reasonable user and non-exhaustive enjoyment; see Ian Brownlie, "A Survey of International Customary Rules of Environmental Protection," in Ludwik A. Teclaff and Albert E. Utton (Eds.), *International Environmental Law* (New York: Praeger, 1974), pp. 1–11 at 1.

[10] Train Smelter arbitration (*United States v. Canada*), 3 *Reports of International Arbitral Awards* (1938 and 1941), p. 1905.

arbitration as well as the International Court of Justice (ICJ) judgment in the *Corfu Channel*[11] case (every state has a duty not to knowingly allow its territory to be used for acts contrary to the rights of other states). Subsequently, that perception came to be radically altered, when it came to be emphatically acknowledged that the "legal underpinnings of the protection of the environment continue to be the institutions of general international law."[12] The recent decisions of the ICJ in the *Nauru*[13] case, the *Nuclear Weapons*[14] advisory opinion, as well as the *Gabcikovo/Nagymaros*[15] project case emphatically sought to put the record straight (general obligations of states to ensure that activities within their jurisdiction and control respect the environment of other states or areas beyond the limits of national jurisdiction) in terms of the relevance and contribution of the rules of general international law to address such environment-related disputes.

The thickening web of treaties[16] in a wide array of areas reflects the growing practice among states to use them as a primary source of

[11] Corfu Channel case (U.K. v. Albania), *ICJ Reports* (1949), p. 4.

[12] Ian Brownlie, who had argued in a published article in 1974 (see n. 2) about so-called "inadequacy" and relevance of general international law in environmental matters, came to acknowledge (in 1998) that it *did* provide such basic legal underpinning for environment protection. Even as a "generalist," Brownlie felt the necessity of incorporation, for the first time, in his textbook on international law (in a six-page chapter on "legal aspects of the protection of the environment"); see Ian Brownlie, *Principles of Public International Law*, 5th ed. (Oxford: Clarendon Press, 1998), Chapter XIII, pp. 283–8.

[13] Case Concerning Phosphate Lands in Nauru (Nauru v. Australia), *ICJ Reports* (1992), p. 240

[14] Advisory Opinion on Legality of the Threat or Use of Nuclear Weapons, *ICJ Reports* (1996), p. 226

[15] Gabcikovo/Nagymaros Project case (Hungary v. Slovakia), *ICJ Reports* (1997).

[16] As per state practice, the wording of a multilateral instrument depends on the idiosyncrasies of the parties. As such, it is not necessary that the contracting parties need to use specific words. To decipher the nature of the instrument that the states have adopted, one needs to look at the intention of the parties as well as the content of the instrument. In general, use of the words "treaty" or "agreement" is commonplace. The Vienna Convention on the Law of Treaties (1969) defines [see Article 2(a)] a "treaty" as "an international agreement concluded between States in written form and governed by international law, whether embodied in a single instrument or in two

lawmaking. It has contributed to gradually bringing about contours of the normative threshold as well as has led to the step-by-step institutionalization of international environmental law itself. In view of the various advantages of such codification and unprecedented treaty-making ventures, multilateral treaties have been used as the most effective and the "predominant method"[17] for regulating state behavior on a global *problematique*.

Instead of using the traditional method of resorting to the development of customary norms, states resort to treaties for the sake of, among other things, convenience, certainty of the law, and requirements of the contingencies of a specific issue. It appears that lawmaking on environmental issues is greatly facilitated by treaties due to a sense of urgency involved in the matter as well as to scientific uncertainties intrinsically embedded in the issues. Moreover, states have found that it is possible to have treaties as frameworks, which, in turn, could be shaped with the availability of scientific evidence, the convergence of interests of the respective contacting parties, as well as the atmospherics and posturing (e.g., the huge participation of states, civil society groups, media) dictated by circumstances of the specific treaty-making exercise. Thus, by their very nature, such skeleton (framework) treaties require built-in lawmaking mechanisms to facilitate gradual tightening up of the specific treaty. As a corollary, the whole treaty operates as a 'process,' necessitating the engagement of the contracting parties at regular intervals and efforts to arrive at convergence/balancing of interests to build up regimes (i.e., regulatory process involving soft and hard instruments).

or more related instruments and whatever its particular designation"; for text of the 1969 Vienna Convention, see *ILM*, vol. 8, 1969, p. 679; *UNTS*, vol. 58, 1980. Also see, http://untreaty.un.org/ilc/texts/instruments/english/conventions/1_1_1969.pdf and www.unog.ch/archives/vienna/vien_69.htm. Article 2(a) of the Vienna Convention on the Law of Treaties between States and International organizations or between International Organizations (1986) also uses the same language; available at www.unog.ch/archives/vienna/vien_86.htm.

17 "Developments in the Law: International Environmental Law," *Harvard Law Review*, vol. 104, no. 3, 1991, p. 1521.

As a result of such a marathon enterprise, MEAs have emerged as a unique technique or regulatory method containing flexibility, pragmatism, built-in lawmaking mechanisms, as well as a consensual approach to norm setting. They manifest increasing state-centric institutionalized cooperation that contributes to the broader trend of an "increasingly more complex web of international treaties, conventions, and agreements."[18] This vibrant process is in no less measure pushed, contributed to, and taken forward by growing participation of civil society groups and other actors. It has almost become routine to witness inherently state-centric treaty-making exercise being baked in the fire that is kept alive often by a growing cacophony of participation by civil society groups that could sometimes degenerate into lawmaking on the street (through protests, demonstrations, seize of the conference venue, etc.). Notwithstanding that, the role and contribution of such "observers" have become an integral and inevitable part of the treaty-making process.

Salient Characteristics

MEAs have emerged as one of the best examples of institutionalized intergovernmental cooperation to address specific environmental issues. In a way, this form of governance is *sui generis* as it has all the trappings of an international organization without formally being one. As a matter of fact, these forms of governance cater to the requirement for ad hoc bodies flowing from multilateral treaties akin to functional international organizations. The legal instrument in question provides the backbone for the institutionalized cooperative mechanism. Their existence is determined by the political will of the contracting states and is tailored to the need to address a specific global *problematique*. Through their various institutionalized forms (e.g., plenary political bodies, subsidiary scientific and technical bodies, funding mechanisms, and compliance committees), MEAs have established *processes of cooperation* to address new and complex challenges as they arise.

[18] United Nations University (UNU), *Inter-Linkages: Synergies and Coordination between Multilateral Environmental Agreements* (Tokyo: UNU, 1999), pp. 5 and 8.

As treaty-based bodies, MEAs primarily seek to put into place ad hoc and autonomous arrangements that are tailored to address a sectoral global environmental issue. In view of the very nature of this problem-specific institutional arrangement, an MEA is expected to be "wound up" as and when its desired objectives are met. Its autonomous nature is determined by the instrument in question as well as by the political will of the contracting states as reflected in the decisions (arrived at through the lowest common denominator) of the Conference (or Meeting) of the Parties of the MEA. Many questions arise regarding the origin, initiation, process, and workability of these treaty-based regimes. The lawmaking process is characterized by special features that includes the role of a "trigger event" that forces states to consider possible legalization on an environmental problem, an institutional catalyst that initiates a preparatory process for crystallization of a regulatory framework, a negotiating process to arrive at the consensual text of the instrument, a subsequent lawmaking process to flesh out the gaps or inherent ambiguities, their regulatory contribution, inherent complexities, flexibility, large participation of states, role of nonstate actors, and issues of implementation and compliance.

It seems evident that treaty making on environmental issues has developed into a sustained practice and a fine art, largely due to an inclination of the states to resort to multilateralism[19] to address some of the *common concerns of humankind*. The states, ostensibly, claim to act in the "common interest"[20] while joining multilateral environmental negotiations. Still, in view of the very nature of these negotiations and

[19] It has been argued that opportunities for multilateralism "appear to abound," as they have in the "aftermath of both twentieth-century 'non-cold wars'"; see Michael G. Schechter, "International Institutions: Obstacles, Agents, or Conduits of Global Structural Change?" in Michael G. Schechter, *Innovation in Multilateralism* (Tokyo: UNU, 1999), p. 3.

[20] There is a general hypothesis that it is the *common interest* of states that propels them to negotiate an MEA. In general, however, states are guided by their self-interest rather than any notion of common interest. In many of the cases, move for an international legal instrument is pushed by a *trigger event* (e.g., in case of the ozone layer depletion or the climate change issue). The initiatives in both these cases came in the wake of dire scientific findings, which forced international action.

participation of a large majority[21] of the states, a final outcome is achieved through the notion of *slowest boat in the race* (lowest common denominator).

In some circles, it still remains a matter of debate regarding the "sense"[22] of negotiating MEAs, possibly due to the intricate nature of negotiations, scientific uncertainty plaguing the negotiations (as well as the negotiated final text of the instrument), and the long period of time for the treaty to enter into force. Enforcement of and compliance with such treaties intrinsically remain problems. Notwithstanding these teething troubles, in fact the very weaknesses are the strengths of MEAs. It is no mean achievement that most of the global MEAs have been joined by a staggering number of sovereign states. (Most of the global treaties – such as those regarding wetlands, cultural and natural heritage, endangered species, ozone layer depletion, transboundary movements of hazardous wastes, climate change, biological diversity, desertification, hazardous chemicals and pesticides in international trade, and persistent organic pollutants – have more than 100 state parties to them.) Such interest and participation by sovereign states could possibly be due to much needed built-in latitude and political convenience to address issues that have basic underpinnings in the crucial socioeconomic and developmental priorities of the states.

The nature and character of MEAs crafted by the states have witnessed a sea of change over the years. Many of the traditional

[21] It is interesting that almost all of the MEAs negotiated in recent years have seen participation of an unprecedented number of states. For example, the 1992 UNFCCC has been ratified by 192 parties (including the European Economic Community); The Kyoto Protocol has been ratified by 187 states; see www.unfccc.int (as of August 17, 2009). Similarly the 1994 United Nations Convention to Combat Desertification (UNCCD) has been ratified by 193 states; see www.unccd.int (as of August 17, 2009). The 1992 Convention on Biological Diversity (CBD) has been ratified by 191 states, and the 2000 Cartagena Protocol on Biosafety has been ratified by 156 states; see www.cbd.int (as of August 17, 2009).

[22] On the issue of reasons for going into negotiations on MEAs, see the essay "To Treaty or Not to Treaty? A Survey of Practical Experience," in Peter H. Sand, *Transnational Environmental Law: Lessons in Global Change* (The Hague: Kluwer Law International, 1999), pp. 55–60.

multilateral agreements among the states, especially those concerning the sharing of common transboundary resources such as waters, included provisions prohibiting the fouling or pollution of waters as well as affixed state responsibility for such purposes. Issues of mainly regional concern (e.g., acid rain and air pollution as well as protection of flora and fauna) later followed it. The range of issues, however, needing to be addressed within the framework of multilateral agreements in the past three decades or so is quite remarkable. It appears that states are gradually leaning more toward specialized multilateral regulatory agreements as a mode of grappling with global environmental problems. The range, content, and complexity of these MEAs surpass lawmaking endeavors in other spheres of international law. The considerable "proliferation"[23] of such MEAs in recent years underscores this state practice that seems have come to stay.

Sui Generis Treaties

This *sui generis* lawmaking process has started making inroads into the cherished domain of sovereign jurisdiction of the states. The increasing need for international cooperation has propelled states to come together on common platforms, including institutional ones. The notion of "sharing of sovereignties" by the states on *common concerns* is gradually gaining ground. The subject matter of MEAs ranges from issues such as protection of a species (whale), flora, and fauna, in general (Convention

[23] It is understood that, of an estimated 500 international conventions related to the environment, almost 300 have been negotiated since the 1972 UNCHE. MEAs can be generally put into three categories: (i) core environmental conventions and related agreements of global significance, which have been closely associated with UNEP (in terms of initiative for negotiation, development, and/or activities); (ii) global conventions relevant to the environment, including regional conventions of global significance, which have been negotiated independently of UNEP; and (iii) other MEAs, which are restricted by scope and geographical range. For further details on MEAs, see UNEP, "International Environmental Governance: Multilateral Environmental Agreements," First Meeting of the Open-ended Intergovernmental Group of Ministers or their Representatives on International Environmental Governance, New York, April 18, 2001, Doc. UNEP/IGM/1/INF/3 of April 6, 2001.

on International Trade in Endangered Species [CITES]), or cultural and heritage sites to regulation of trade of hazardous chemicals and wastes, to air pollution and persistent organic pollutants; to more remote issues like ozone depletion, climate change, and biological diversity. MEAs on a host of these issues have in fact "changed over time, just as political, economic, social, and technological conditions have changed over time."[24]

If one examines the growing mosaic of international environmental law, one cannot but feel the absence of a central lawmaking institution, which can give a coherent shape and direction to the development of law. The lawmaking process hitherto has been distinctly characterized by ad hoc, piecemeal, and need-based responses. The remarkable growth of sectoral environmental regulatory framework testifies to this. As a result, there has been considerable proliferation in sector-specific rules and principles in areas ranging from atmosphere (e.g., air pollution, ozone, climate change), to transboundary movements of substances (e.g., hazardous wastes, chemicals, persistent organic pollutants, living modified organisms), to conservation of living resources (endangered species, migratory species, wetlands, biological diversity, etc.). There is, however, a noticeable dearth of general norms for application to all the environmental issues. Many of the earlier MEAs were designed largely as a result of the perceived need to take conservation or protection measures. The main thrust of these sectoral regulatory measures, except for certain exceptional cases, has been primarily anthropocentric (i.e., to protect long term human *utilitarian* interest in a species or natural resource).

Most of these hard instruments do not end up as a one-time process as they do not adopt a comprehensive approach in negotiating an MEA. This situation was witnessed especially during the marathon negotiations on the UN Convention on Law of the Sea (1973–1982), resulting in the

[24] Edith Brown Weiss, "The Five International Treaties: A Living History," in Edith Brown Weiss and Harold K. Jacobson (Eds.), *Engaging Countries: Strengthening Compliance with International Environmental Accords* (Cambridge: MIT Press, 1998), p. 89.

"Constitution for the Oceans."[25] It imparted lessons regarding the placement of all the issues into a single basket for threadbare negotiations and arriving at a consensual text. In the context of environmental issues, the negotiating process is faced with the requirement for urgent action. This action often has to materialize in the face of unavailability of concrete scientific evidence as well as a high degree of adaptability of the legal system to rapid and frequent change. As compared to earlier, traditional treaty-making experiences, most environmental issues are mired in a significant amount of scientific uncertainty as well as high political and economic stakes for states, especially the powerful ones. Cumulatively, these factors push states to design a legal instrument that can gradually evolve and unfold, while it accommodates competing interests. Therefore, in the case of most of the recent MEAs, the so-called *hard* law turns out to be not so hard in actual practice.

At the inauguration of the instrument (entry into force), in many cases it resembles an empty shell that waits for the long and drawn-out 'fleshing' process. MEAs that emerge as end products of marathon negotiations, spread over a relatively short time span, are generally in whittled-down form to facilitate consensus. The skeleton, in turn, necessitates a step-by-step process to harden the commitments, flesh out the gaps, and work on the calculated ambiguities that could be part of the finally adopted text of the instrument. The process includes defining the core elements, removing calculated ambiguities and/or spelling out details of the mechanisms in the convention, or even launching a separate process to work on issues requiring detailed treatment (e.g., Article 27 of the Cartagena Protocol on Biosafety has called for a process to address the issue of liability and redress concerning transboundary movements of living modified organisms). This process is conditioned more by the economic and political compulsions of the state parties, as compared to

[25] Remarks by Tommy T. B. Koh, President of the Third U.N. Conference on the Law of the Sea, Montego Bay (Jamaica), December 10, 1982; see United Nations, *U.N. Convention on the Law of the Sea* (New York: UN, 1983), p. xxxiii.

the technical nature of the issue in question, availability of scientific evidence, or legal requirements.

Thus, many of the MEAs provide a bare framework, to be supplemented by the fleshing out of the subsequent legal instruments (generally known as protocols). In that sense, some of the hard legal instruments comprise *soft* obligations at their core (hard shell with a soft belly). Thus, there is a need to jettison the traditional notion that all treaties are governed by a single set of rules, in view of material differences between different types of treaties. Instead, they may well be judged from their contents, which will "affect their legal character as well."[26]

The range of issues sought to be addressed within the framework of multilateral agreements in the past four decades is quite remarkable. The states, it appears, are gradually inching more toward specialized multilateral agreements as a mode of grappling with environmental problems having global character. The range as well as complexity of these MEAs resulting from marathon multilateral negotiations, often instituted by global conferences, surpass lawmaking endeavours in other spheres of international law. As a corollary to it, various institutional structures that have emerged (e.g., conference of parties or subsidiary bodies) provide platforms for continuous institutionalized cooperation on a specific environmental issue. These institutions provide not only a servicing base to the contracting states of an MEA but also play an important role in the built-in lawmaking process of a regime.

The thickening of frameworks of MEAs has engaged an overwhelming number of states in multilateral negotiations. One of the important factors influencing these negotiations is the balancing between "national sovereignty and international interdependence."[27] The unfolding scenario reveals that more and more states are gradually opting for legal

[26] Arnold D. McNair, "The Functions and Differing Legal Character of Treaties," *British Yearbook of International Law*, vol. 11, 1930, p. 100.

[27] Richard Elliot Benedick, "Perspectives of a Negotiation Practitioner," in Gunnar Sjöstedt (Ed.), *International Environmental Negotiation* (Newbury Park: Sage Publications, 1993), p. 229.

as well as institutional cooperation within multilateral frameworks for a wide variety of environmental issues. A host of factors are influencing state behavior in this context. The process gets added color and spice from the lobbying and participation (as observers) of a number of nonstate actors that are recognized under the broad umbrella of major groups, civil society, or stakeholders.

Significantly, a notable feature of these negotiations (as well as the multilateral environmental instruments resulting therefrom) is that they do not remain a one-time affair. The very nature of the issues dealt with by these processes makes it inevitable that they remain continuous law-making enterprises (probably as industrious as the honey bees!). Most of the MEAs reflect a *process*, comprising several components that critically depend on the emergence of consensus and the political will of the states to go forward on the issue. The cumulative political and legal effect of a series of instruments adopted by the states on a given environmental issue could be described by the use of the term "regime." Irrespective of the binding or nonbinding character of the obligations contained in these instruments, they have a gradual, creeping regulatory effect on state behavior. It seems that these instruments are making significant inroads into the domestic environmental policy and lawmaking process of the states. The complex regimes established by different MEAs have generated debate about the need for and efficacy of such a form of "global governance"[28] in a given area.

[28] For writings on this issue see, generally, Peter H. Sand, *Lessons Learned in Global Environmental Governance* (Washington, DC: World Resources Institute, 1990), pp. 1–60; Peter M. Haas, "Global Environmental Governance" in Commission on Global Governance, *Issues in Global Governance* (London: Kluwer International, 1995), pp. 333–69; Rahmatullah Khan, "The Thickening Web of International Law," *ibid.*, pp. 249–62; Peter M. Haas and Ernst B. Haas, "Learning to Learn: Some Thoughts on Improving International Governance of the Global *Problematique," ibid.*, pp. 295–331. Also see Hilary French, "Strengthening Global Environmental Governance," in *Vanishing Borders: Protecting the Planet in the Age of Globalization* (New York: W.W. Norton & Company, 2000), pp. 144–62; Bharat H. Desai, "Revitalizing International Environmental Institutions: The UN Task Force Report and Beyond," *Indian Journal of International Law*, vol. 40, no. 3, 2000, pp. 455–504; "Mapping the

The Vienna Convention on the Law of Treaties (1969)[29] defines a "treaty" as "an international agreement concluded between States in written form and governed by international law, whether embodied in a single instrument or in two or more related instruments and whatever its particular designation."[30] Thus, according to the Vienna Convention definition, an international agreement that seeks to address a specific sectoral environmental issue is a treaty governed by it. The term "multilateral" has to be seen as having two or more sovereign states as parties to it. Thus MEAs fall within the ambit of traditional multilateral treaties that sovereign states design to address a *problematique*. The Vienna Convention governs such treaties regarding their formation, coming into force, and subsequent operation although the tools and techniques used, institutional forms put into place, and normative rules churned out regularly could vary from case to case.

MEAs are *prima facie* like other treaties governed by international law. What is special about them is, among other things, the process of initiating such agreements, the issues sought to be addressed, the relatively short time span within which they take shape, the scientific uncertainty that surrounds the core issue at stake, participation by a large number (in some cases, e.g., UN Convention to Combat Desertification [UNCCD], almost universal) of states, and in many cases the soft content of such agreements (defying the common understanding of such treaties as hard instruments). Furthermore, as they are not "one-time affairs," they stand apart from conventional treaties. Basically, most of the MEAs could be regarded as processes that are generally initiated by

Future of International Environmental Governance," *Yearbook of International Environmental Law* (Oxford: Oxford University press), vol. 13, 2002. pp. 43–61.

[29] The Vienna Convention has emerged from the draft articles adopted in 1966 by the ILC and subsequently came to be finalized at the Vienna Conference on the Law of Treaties in two sessions during 1968 and 1969. It comprises eighty-five articles and an annex. It entered into force on January 27, 1980. For the text of the Convention, see *ILM*, vol. 8, 1969, p. 679; *UNTS*, vol. 58, 1980. Also see, http://untreaty.un.org/ilc/texts/instruments/english/conventions/1_1_1969.pdf.

[30] Article 2 (1) (a) of the Vienna Convention; see *ibid.*

international institutions (e.g., UNEP) and taken over from them by the sovereign states. In many cases, these treaties are initiated because of some "trigger event"[31] necessitating urgent negotiations by the states to reach an agreement on regulation of the sectoral issue in question. After the states seize the matter through formal negotiations, the catalyst institution (e.g., UNEP) that initiated the lawmaking process takes a back seat.

Softness of Hard Law

The content of and final form taken by the treaties are proportional to the sense of urgency involved, paucity of time, as well as reluctance of the key actors to permit specificity into the regime so as to apportion concrete obligations to meet basic objectives. Most of these treaties, on their entry into force, warrant regular scrutiny and assessment. They also necessitate formal meetings of the states parties, at regular intervals, to carry out intensive stock taking, fill the gaps on the basis of available scientific evidence, and crystallize views of the parties regarding the best cost-effective course open to them. Such a step-by-step normative approach can not be possible without built-in softness[32] in the treaty itself.

[31] "Trigger events" could include the evidence released by the British Antarctic expedition on stratospheric ozone layer depletion, increasing cases of unregulated dumping of hazardous wastes posing a threat to humans and the environment, scientific reports on the accumulation of greenhouse gases (GHG) in the atmosphere contributing to global climatic changes, and so forth. In each of such cases, the trigger provided by these reports/incidents led UNEP on its own or in collaboration with agencies such as World Metereological Organization (WMO) to initiate negotiating processes that culminated in respective global treaties: 1985 Vienna Convention on Depletion of the Ozone Layer; 1989 Basel Convention on Transboundary Movements of Hazardous Wastes and their Disposal, and 1992 UNFCCC.

[32] On the relationship between treaties and the so-called soft-law see, for instance, Alan Boyle, "Some Reflections on the Relationship of Treaties and Soft Law," in Vera Gowlland-Debbas, *Multilateral Treaty-Making: The Current Status of Challenge to and Reforms Needed in the International Legislative Process* (The Hague: Martinus Nijhoff, 2000), pp. 25–38.

As a manifestation of such a paradoxical situation (need for a hard instrument whittled down due to the need to accommodate political convenience of the states), some of the treaties in fact boldly carry the phrase "framework convention" in their nomenclature (e.g. UNFCCC). In such cases it is expected that the parties will gradually seek to fill the gaps or calculated ambiguities left during the adoption stage of the instrument. These framework conventions could best be described as having a *hard shell with a soft belly* because of the softness of the language (content) used in the instrument as well as the intention of the states parties that these frameworks do not create conventional hard obligations (e.g., concrete timetables, quotas, ceilings, or other measures). It is that type of understanding that provides the basis for adopting the instrument in question. As a result, the negotiating states are not too much concerned about the ideal or pure form of a treaty. What they immediately look for is almost a kind of "work-in-progress" that will be refined, revised, and strengthened as and when convergence of their interests permits it. It is such political latitude and softness incorporated in flexible instruments that facilitate the participation of a large number of states.

Implied in such arrangements is a message that the parties will need to undertake a painstaking follow-up exercise to carry forward the process that could not be worked on further (due to lack of available data, scientific understanding, technical feasibility, or hard-headed economic and political interests of the negotiating states at that stage). It could lead to the adoption of concrete obligations for all or a group of the parties to the treaty or different timetables and benchmarks of performance. This practice of calculated usage of soft formulations in the text itself does not undermine the legal character of the instrument. The parties are at complete liberty to follow any form, any methodology, and any time span to realize the objectives of the treaty that they have set for themselves. In such cases, it is the decision of the parties at work to facilitate gradual crystallization of consensus on calculated ambiguity or permissive language (e.g., a lack of definition of "hazardous wastes" or use of the phrase "taking into account socio-economic conditions of the parties" or "as far as possible and as practicable").

These innovative formulations facilitate realization of the states' quest for negotiating a so-called "hard treaty," and yet keep the language used open-ended or nonbinding[33] for the time being. If such loose ends are not allowed, either the instrument will suffer premature demise or the process will have serious "holdout" problems. An absence of such flexibility could push key parties out of the treaty because they would refuse to either sign or ratify it. Therefore, in effect, such a treaty-making practice leads to a form of institutionalized cooperative instrument serving as "work-in-progress." These are the variations, flowing from competing interests of states, that are part and parcel of the giant multilateral treaty-making machine at work on diverse areas of international law. Such variations squarely fall within the ambit of the Vienna Convention on the Law of Treaties. No specific terminology or form, except the written one, is required for a treaty.[34] For instance, in the *Qatar v. Bahrain*[35] case, even an agreed "minute" of the discussions between the two parties was considered as an agreement (lack of registration or late registration under Article 102 of the UN Charter does not have any consequence for the actual validity of such treaty) to confer jurisdiction upon the ICJ. In this context, however, the intention of the negotiating states remains the material element to determine the nature of the instrument.

The follow-up measure required in the form of subsequent negotiation process could comprise amendments or adjustments to the parent treaty or preparation of a new legal instrument altogether but with more

[33] For a detailed examination of the "twilight" fate of such agreements, see Oscar Schachter, "Twilight Existence of Non-Binding International Agreements," *American Journal of International Law*, vol. 71, 1977, pp. 296–304.

[34] Article 2(1) (a) of the Vienna Convention defines a treaty as "an international agreement concluded between States in written form and governed by international law, whether embodied in a single instrument or in two or more related instruments and whatever its particular designation"; see n. 29.

[35] The Court concluded that "the Minutes of 25 December 1990, like the exchanges of letters of December 1987, constitute an international agreement creating rights and obligations for the Parties"; see Case Concerning Maritime Delimitation and Territorial Questions between Qatar and Bahrain (Jurisdiction and Admissibility), paragraphs 30 and 41 of the Judgment of July 1, 1994; see *ICJ Reports* (1994), p. 112. Also see http://www.icj-cij.org/.

concrete steps. It seems that such an arrangement provides much-needed political space for the states as they may have divergence of interests in terms of historical contribution to the problem, sharing of responsibility, domestic compulsions to not precipitate measures to carry out their obligations, and/or acceptability of the bargain by various stakeholders. The actors involved in the process could take steps ranging from ratifying the treaty through respective constitutional processes, enabling legislation to give effect to the obligations, earmarking the financial contributions for joining the treaty, and persuading the industry to take the required domestic measures (according to the prescribed threshold, such as quotas, ceilings, and timetables, and public opinion and awareness) for the treaty to take on board the civil society groups.

Apart from the instrumentality of *declaratory* statements by organs of intergovernmental organizations and multilateral conferences, normative principles and statements can also be enshrined in MEAs. This might add complexity to the hard instrument, which is *prima facie* legally binding on the parties. Such inclusion of exhortatory principles or discretionary provisions as a part of a formal multilateral instrument presents an anomalous situation. The resultant ineffectiveness of the instrument in question, in turn, "relegates them to the ranks of non-legal norms... notwithstanding their status."[36] Thus, a formal structure or form of a multilateral treaty (legal) instrument is not sufficient to ensure *hardness* or binding character of the law.

In this context, "legal hardness" means the legally binding character of a provision. Therefore, a legal norm may be regarded as "soft in all its dimensions," including its *content*, *authority*, as well as *control*

[36] It has been argued by Günter Handl that one of the theoretical challenges posed by the soft law phenomenon lies in "appreciating fully the declining reliability of formal criteria of international law as guideposts to what actually constitutes international law. Past warnings about mistaking those legal phenomena that masquerade as international law because they fit the formal categories of law as enumerated, for example, in article 38 of the Statute of the International Court of Justice, are more appropriate than ever"; see *ASIL Proceedings*, vol. 82, April 1988, p. 372.

intention.[37] It is obvious that many of the soft formulations are injected into the text of a treaty as a compromise formula or due to sheer calculated ambiguity to arrive at elusive consensus (that could be on account of lack of political will among the negotiating states, lack of concrete scientific evidence, or other factors inhibiting an agreement on the issue). The usage of such 'soft' formulations in the text of a treaty indicates that the negotiating states do not have the immediate intention of making the legal instrument effective. Such a consciously built-in contradiction – formal hard-treaty shell with a soft underbelly – primarily aims to woo recalcitrant states to enter the framework. It is apparently a "consciously premeditated technique"[38] used by negotiators to bring on board as many 'major' states as possible through accommodation of their hard-headed political and economic interests. It is the elusive *consent* of the participating states that holds the key in the matter.

It is interesting that the Vienna Convention on the Law of Treaties does not make it a prerequisite for international treaties to enunciate any specific legal rights and obligations. It merely requires an international agreement to be in "written form and governed by international law."[39] Therefore, it is entirely up to the parties to prescribe the nature and content of the agreements. Thus, it suits the negotiating states not to lay down hard commitments in the first round. The instrument will remain incomplete without subsequent steps to work out supplementary protocols or agreements to build on the normative framework prescribed in the agreement. In that case, the normative value of the framework convention remains incomplete.

There are many examples (in fact, many of the recent MEAs are frameworks) of incorporation of soft obligations in a formal multilateral treaty. Some of these agreements portray a misconception of a nonlegal norm as law. The 1985 Vienna Convention on the Depletion of the

[37] W. Michael Reisman's remarks at a panel discussion on "A Hard Look at Soft Law," *ASIL Proceedings*, vol. 82, April 1988, p. 374.

[38] *Ibid.*, p. 376.

[39] Article 2 of the Vienna Convention.

Ozone Layer was adopted following scientific warnings. When the ad hoc Working Group of Legal and Technical Experts started work (in 1981) on the issue, it was surrounded by considerable scientific uncertainty, with divided opinions as well as rejection of such concerns by some of the states. This uncertainty accounted for some of the ambiguity in the Convention and use of discretionary language for obligations of the states parties. The parties were merely required to take appropriate measures in accordance with the "means at their disposal and their capabilities."[40]

Thus the nature of obligations laid down in the initial ozone treaty was quite permissive and discretionary. The convention was tightened up with the adoption of a specific time frame for phaseout of the controlled ozone-depleting substances (ODS) in the 1987 Montreal Protocol and its subsequent adjustments and amendments (London, Copenhagen, Montreal, and Beijing), each of which also required a separate set of ratifications by the states to create a legally binding effect. In view of the availability of further scientific evidence (through satellite pictures that showed widening of the ozone hole), crystallization of political consensus, acceptance of grace periods for the developing country parties, and agreement on making available funding as well as substitutes for ODS, the parties to the Protocol very soon decided to strengthen and even move up the phaseout schedules at a series of their subsequent meetings. Thus the regulatory framework for depletion of the ozone layer has been constantly evolving, from initial loose and soft obligations to a stringent time schedule and specific obligations as well as complete phaseout of the ODS for the parties (in a stratified manner). The whole process has constantly remained under regular and institutionalized review by the parties, often as dictated by scientific projections and permitted by their own political convenience.

Similarly, the 1989 Basel Convention on Transboundary Movements of Hazardous Wastes and their Disposal came in the wake of increasing reports of unlawful hazardous waste dumping in several parts of the

[40] Article 2 on *General Obligations*, Convention for the Protection of the Ozone Layer, Vienna, March 22, 1985; *ILM*, vol. 26, 1987, p. 1529.

world, especially on the African continent. In view of the nature of the issue as well as the short time span within which the Basel Convention came to be drafted, some of the key formulations in the convention were kept vague and even left undefined. For instance, the core issue of "environmentally sound management of hazardous wastes" was merely defined as necessitating "all practicable steps,"[41] and the parties were expected to settle the issue of liability and compensation for damage resulting from transboundary movement of hazardous wastes by adopting a protocol "as soon as practicable."[42] In fact, the parties to the original convention did not define the term hazardous waste at all. It was this key component on which the regulation of export and import of wastes was to be premised. Moreover, it left discretion to the exporting state not to allow export of hazardous wastes if it has "reason to believe"[43] that they will not be managed in an environmentally sound manner (which was also left undefined). In view of sharp polarization of views and conflict of economic interests of the hazardous waste–exporting countries, consensus on these issues remained elusive.

It appears that the negotiating states expected that the economic interests of exporting and importing states would provide the basis for judging parameters of such practical steps. It is interesting that, when the parties reached an agreement in 1994, after arduous negotiations on the "Basel Ban," which sought to prohibit export of hazardous wastes from Organisation for Economic Co-operation and Development (OECD) countries to non-OECD countries, they still could not reach an

[41] Article 2(8) of the Convention on the Control of Transboundary Movements of Hazardous Wastes and Their Disposal (Basel, 1989) states: " 'Environmentally sound management of hazardous wastes or other wastes' means taking all practicable steps to ensure that hazardous wastes or other wastes are managed in a manner which will protect human health and the environment against the adverse effects which may result from such wastes"; see *ILM*, vol. 28, 1989, p. 657.

[42] Article 12 provided that: "The Parties shall co-operate with a view to adopting, as soon as practicable, a protocol setting out appropriate rules and procedures in the field of liability and compensation for damage resulting from the transboundary movement and disposal of hazardous wastes and other wastes."

[43] *Ibid.*, Article 4(2) (e).

agreement on prescribing criteria and elements for defining *hazardous wastes*,[44] which were to take shape later amid hard bargaining. This fact underscores the *softness* of obligations at the initial stage as well as the calculated ambiguity left in an MEA that was largely dictated by the economic interests of the hazardous wastes–exporting industrialized states.

We can find similar examples of the use of vague and soft obligations in other important MEAs (e.g., on climate change as well as biological diversity). They indicate exhortatory statements, such as "shall develop" or "shall adopt"[45] or fully discretionary implementation, such "as far as possible" and "as appropriate."[46] The familiar pattern of phraseology used is akin to that used in the conventions on ozone layer depletion and transboundary movements of hazardous wastes. The nature of the issues – non-availability of concrete scientific evidence to ascertain precise human contribution (e.g., in emitting greenhouse gases), circumstances of adoption, economic stakes, and reluctance of the states to go for immediate hard measures due to the cost involved – accounts for usage of such soft formulations in a hard legal instrument.

Framework Convention Approach

A sense of urgency is generally inherent in most of the multilateral environmental negotiations. Unlike traditional international lawmaking, states cannot now afford the luxury of waiting for the emergence of a hardened customary norm through the practice of states. Instead, the soft law norms are often adopted as an instant guideline for regulating states' behavior. It is interesting that even this soft law in many cases

[44] For details, see Bharat H. Desai, "Regulating Transboundary Movements of Hazardous Wastes," *Indian Journal of International Law*, vol. 37, no. 1, 1997, pp. 43–61 at 55.

[45] For example, Article 4 on "commitments" in the UNFCCC; see *ILM*, vol. 31, 1992, p. 849 at 855–9.

[46] For example, Articles 6–11 and 14, Convention on Biological Diversity; see *ILM*, vol. 31, 1992, p. 818 at 825–7.

becomes just a prelude to the formulation of hard law in the form of an MEA.

As mentioned earlier in this chapter, the rapidity (especially due to the urgency of addressing a specific environmental issue even amid scientific uncertainty) of the norm-setting process does not leave much room for the states to allow soft norms to harden, and one can often appreciate these soft norms couched even in the hard shell of a multilateral agreement. This peculiar characteristic, however, does not pose much of a problem normatively because it suits most of the states. Often, adoption of an MEA with a "soft belly" (of obligations) is a stopgap stage that allows breathing space for the normativity to harden alongside emergence of consensus in the evolution of a particular regime.

In recent years states have preferred to go for such *legal soft law* – an MEA that cannot be enforced on its own. Such multilateral legal instruments, known as *lawmaking treaties*, warrant further action on the part of the states parties to realize their basic objectives, which has been described as the *framework convention-protocol* approach in lawmaking. The factors that contribute to a state's inclination to go for this approach are complex. Multilateral treaty making is a painstaking process, especially when an overwhelming number of states (sometimes even having universal participation of the UN member states) participate in it.

In the past, efforts of the negotiating states to choose a comprehensive approach, which encompasses threadbare discussions and giving finality to all the issues on the agenda of negotiations, including concrete obligations and the dispute settlement mechanism, have proven to be exhaustive and time consuming. In such a case, the negotiating states do not envisage the use of calculated ambiguity and built-in lawmaking exercises. However, due to the nature of environmental issues, states prefer to go for exhortatory and/or discretionary language in such agreements. At the same time, they require some scientific certainty before accepting concrete obligations, especially because the legally binding obligations would entail some painful measures by states at the domestic level, which have the potential to unleash bitter political and economic implications.

In accepting a skeletal form of MEAs, states seek to grapple with scientific uncertainty on the issue in question, avoid making a hard decision in the short term, try to take as many states as possible on board, minimize holdout problems, and yet have a legal regime that brings accolades for the signatory states (keeping an eye on domestic public opinion). Often the psychological pressure is so high that few of the negotiating states prefer to be seen on the wrong side of the regulatory effort and emerging consensus. As the rationale for this approach goes, the contracting states just lay down broad policy outlines through the device of the framework convention and leave nettlesome details to be worked out in the protocols that may be negotiated at a later date.

CITES[47] has been one of the earliest examples of this approach. In fact, CITES contained endangered species listed in three appendices,[48] which the parties could review from time to time. A species name can be put in a particular annex depending on its endangered status. This approach has provided flexible built-in lawmaking for the parties, although each amendment to the lists needs to be accepted by the states for its entry into force. The UN Economic Commission for Europe's Long Range Transboundary Air Pollution Convention (LRTAP)[49] is another example of this approach. The LRTAP regime in fact comprises five[50] separate protocols designed on different long-range

[47] Convention on International Trade in Endangered Species of Wild Flora and Fauna, Washington, DC, March 3, 1973. It entered into force on July 1, 1975; see *ILM*, vol. 12, 1973, p. 1055.

[48] See, *ibid.*, Articles III, IV, and V.

[49] Convention on Long-range Transboundary Air Pollution, Geneva, November 13, 1979. Its participation is open to all member states of the UN Economic Commission for Europe. It also includes the United States, Canada, and the former Soviet Union. It entered into force on March 16, 1983; see *ILM*, vol. 18, 1979, p. 1442.

[50] The five protocols to the 1979 LRTAP Convention are: (i) Protocol on Long-term Financing of a Cooperative Programme for Monitoring and Evaluation of the Long-Range Transmission of Air Pollutants in Europe, Geneva, September 28, 1984; see

transboundary pollutants. Thus, in terms of the substance as well as precise timetables, the LRTAP has shown remarkable flexibility and built-in lawmaking. The Convention on Migratory Species of Wild Animals (CMS) also follows this new genre of treaties containing flexibility and adjustment of the regime through a list of species (in the concerned appendix)[51] as well as providing an umbrella for the development of "agreements"[52] on specific species.

ILM, vol. 27, 1988, p. 701; (ii) Protocol on the Reduction of Sulphur Emissions or their Transboundary Fluxes, Helsinki, July 8, 1987; see *ILM*, vol. 27, p. 707; (iii) Protocol Concerning the Control of Emissions of Nitrogen Oxides or their Transboundary Fluxes, Sofia, October 31, 1988; see *ILM*, vol. 28, 1989, p. 212; (iv) Protocol Concerning the Control of Emissions of Volatile Organic Compounds or their Transboundary Fluxes, Geneva, November 18, 1991; *ILM*, vol. 31, 1992, p. 573; and (v) Protocol on Further Reduction of Sulphur Emissions, Oslo, June 14, 1994; see *ILM*, vol. 33, 1994, p. 1542.

[51] See Appendix I (Endangered Migratory Species) and Appendix II (Migratory Species to be Subject to Agreements), Articles III and IV of the CMS, Bonn, June 23, 1979; *ILM*, vol. 19, 1980, p. 15.

[52] Article V of the CMS provides detailed guidelines for "agreements" that cover individual species or, more often, for a group of species listed in Appendix II. The legal character of these instruments covers legally binding agreements as well as "less formal memoranda of understanding." Their objective is to restore the migratory species to a favorable conservation status or to maintain it at that status. A series of such seven agreements and seventeen memoranda of understanding worked out under the tutelage of CMS are: Agreement on the Conservation of Seals in the Wadden Sea (1990); Agreement on the Conservation of Small Cetaceans of the Baltic and North Seas (1991); Agreement on the Conservation of Bats in Europe (1991); Agreement on the Conservation of African Eurasian Migratory Waterbirds (1995); Agreement on the Conservation of Cetaceans of the Black Sea, Mediterranean Sea and Contiguous Atlantic Area (1996); Agreement on the Conservation of Albatrosses and Petrels (2001); Agreement on the Conservation of Gorillas and their Habitats (2008); Memorandum of Understanding concerning Conservation Measures for the Siberian Crane (1993); Memorandum of Understanding concerning Conservation Measures for the Slender-billed Curlew (1994); Memorandum of Understanding concerning Conservation Measures for Marine Turtles of the Atlantic Coast of Africa (1999); Memorandum of Understanding on the Conservation and Management of the Middle-European Population of the Great Bustard (2000); Memorandum of Understanding concerning Conservation Measures for Marine Turtles of the Indian Ocean and South-East Asia (2001); Memorandum of Understanding concerning Conservation and Restoration of the Bukhara Deer (2002); Memorandum of Understanding concerning Conservation

Such framework conventions play an important role in setting in motion a normative process, through an exhortatory agreement, which is expected to evolve in due course. The process of enshrining precise legal obligations as well as a time frame for carrying them out is conditioned by the political will (coupled with economic considerations) on the part of the states. Curiously, various international actors, including civil society, play influential roles in goading states toward further regulatory measures. MEAs have generally followed the devices of protocols or agreements to strengthen the main framework conventions. Often the appendices to the convention also literally serve (as in the cases of CITES and CMS) the purpose of a protocol. Such protocols or agreements stand on their own as they are independent multilateral instruments that require a separate set of signatures and ratifications. It seems that, states having powerful economic stakes can often hold out and block the process of a protocol's entry into force whenever it impinges upon their vital interests (e.g., the 1994 Basel Ban).

Despite the flexibility and adaptability of this approach, doubts persist regarding its utility, especially because it also takes a long time for the

Measures for the Aquatic Warbler (2003); Memorandum of Understanding concerning Conservation Measures for the Western African Populations of the African Elephant (2005); Memorandum of Understanding concerning Conservation, Restoration and Sustainable Use of the Saiga Antelope (2006); Memorandum of Understanding for the Conservation of Cetaceans and their Habitats in the Pacific Islands Region (2006); Memorandum of Understanding between the Argentine Republic and the Republic of Chile on the Conservation of the Ruddy-headed Goose (2006); Memorandum of Understanding on the Conservation of Southern South American Migratory Grassland Bird Species and their Habitats (2007); Memorandum of Understanding concerning Conservation Measures for the Eastern Atlantic Populations of the Mediterranean Monk Seal (2007); Memorandum of Understanding on the Conservation and Management of Dugongs and their Habitats throughout their Range (2007); Memorandum of Understanding concerning the Conservation of the Manatee and Small Cetaceans of Western Africa and Macaronesia (2008); Memorandum of Understanding on the Conservation of Migratory Birds of Prey in Africa and Eurasia (2008); Memorandum of Understanding on the Conservation of High Andean Flamingos and their Habitats (2008). For further details on these agreements and memoranda of understanding, see http://www.cms.int (as of August 8, 2009).

framework convention as well as the protocols to enter into force. Several powerful states, the economic interests of which are to be affected, have tried to reduce the lowest common denominator to the barest minimum. Even the negotiation and acceptance of the protocols are often marred by foot-dragging and long delays. Such holding out by powerful states can often effectively cripple the protocol[53] as well as increase the abatement costs.

Regional Seas

It seems that the bulk of MEAs have a regional character. Of more than 300 MEAs negotiated since the 1972 Stockholm Conference, almost 70 percent are understood to have regional focus. The emergence of regional economic integration organizations, especially in Europe and Central America, has contributed to such legal frameworks for environment protection. A large number of regional MEAs, however, have emerged from the "Regional Seas Programme" (RSP),[54] regarded as the "jewel in the crown" of UNEP. It shows a systematic regional approach

[53] For instance, the Kyoto Climate Protocol adopted by the third meeting of the Conference of Parties to the Framework Convention on Climate Change (FCCC), at Kyoto (Japan) on December 11, 1997. It has provided commitments exclusively for the developed country parties to reduce their combined GHG emissions by at least 5.2% compared to 1990 levels by the period 2008–2012. This delicately-arrived-at compromise for reduction of GHG emissions, within a time-bound program, has been held hostage by the holdout problem due to the refusal to ratify the Kyoto Protocol (and even designing of it) by the United States, which accounts for the highest amount (almost 25%) of total global GHG emissions. Armed with the U.S. Senate vote (making it contingent on participation of key developing countries), the U.S. administration's withdrawal from the Kyoto bargain has put a question mark on meeting the targets within the initial commitment period. It could even turn out to be a bargaining tactic to put maximum pressure to delay meeting the targets and/or to permit subterfuges which will, in effect, significantly weaken developed country parties' commitments. For text of the Kyoto Protocol see, FCCC Secretariat, *The Kyoto Protocol to the Convention on Climate Change* (Bonn: FCCC, 1998).

[54] The Regional Seas Programme (RSP), launched in 1974, has been regarded as one of the biggest achievements of UNEP. The first RSP was developed in the Mediterranean with an Action Plan (1975), followed by a Convention (1976). Following success of the

to environmental problems. It seems that geographical contiguity as well as common environmental problems of the coastal states of specific regional seas provide a basic framework to embark on a regional seas instrument.

The fact that the networks of RSPs have grown around the world and so far cover 18 regions and 150 coastal states shows the workability of the concept. The underlying logic behind RSPs is that "specific environmental problems of geographically-limited areas usually are better regulated by the affected states."[55] Most of the RSPs are similar in structure but different in specifics. In a way they may be considered to be part of "comprehensive action plans oriented toward overall regional development, including coastal zone planning, monitoring and research, and technical assistance and training."[56] The web of eighteen RSPs has a staggering number of fifty instruments comprising twelve regional conventions, two special regional mechanisms, four action plans,[57] and

RSP for the Mediterranean region, RSPs for other regions were developed. The Governing Council of UNEP has, in fact, consistently endorsed a regional approach for the control of marine pollution, management of marine and coastal resources, and development of regional Action Plans for the purpose. From the first Action Plan adopted in the Mediterranean (1975), to the most recent one for the Caspian Sea (2003), the RSPs have multiplied to cover the marine environment of more than 150 of the world's coastal countries.

[55] See Kiss and Shelton, n. 3, p. 33.

[56] Peter H. Sand has described five components of the RSPs as: "(a) environmental assessment (the MEDPOL monitoring network); (b) environmental management (the 'Blue Plan' for co-ordinated development of the coastal region; and the 'Priority Actions Programme' for co-operation in coastal settlements, aquaculture, water resources, soils, renewable energy, and tourism); (c) institutional arrangements (permanent secretariat services and periodic conferences); (d) financial arrangements (trust fund shared by coastal states); and (e) regional legal instruments, following a highly uniform pattern and at least partly formulated in near identical language." See Peter H. Sand, *Transnational Environmental Law: Lessons in Global Change* (The Hague: Kluwer Law International, 1999), pp. 175–87 at 181.

[57] The eighteen RSPs are: 1. *Antarctic*: Convention on the Conservation of Antarctic Marine Living Resources (1980); entered into force: April 7, 1982 2. *Arctic*: Protection of the Arctic Marine Environment (PAME) established by the Arctic Council Ministers in Nuuk, Greenland, September 1993 3. *Baltic Sea*: The Convention on the Protection of the Marine Environment of the Baltic Sea Area, 1992, entered into force

on January 17, 2000. 4. *Black Sea*: The Convention on the Protection of the Black Sea Against Pollution was signed in Bucharest in April 1992, and ratified by all six legislative assemblies of the Black Sea countries in the beginning of 1994. 5. *Caspian Sea*: Framework Convention for the Protection of the Marine Environment of the Caspian Sea (Tehran, November 4, 2003). 6. *East Africa*: Convention for the Protection, Management and Development of the Marine and Coastal Environment of the Eastern African Region (1985). 7. *East Asian Seas*: Action Plan for the Protection and Development of the Marine Environment and Coastal Areas of the East Asian Seas Region (1981). 8. *Mediterranean*: The Barcelona Convention for the Protection of the Mediterranean Sea against Pollution (1976, as amended in 1995; entered into force July 9, 2004. 9. *North-East Atlantic*: Convention for the Protection of the Marine Environment of the North-East Atlantic (OSPAR Convention, 1992); entered into force: March 25, 1998. 10. *North-East Pacific*: Convention for Cooperation in the Protection and Sustainable Development of the Marine and Coastal Environment of the Northeast Pacific (Antigua Convention, 2002). 11. *North-West Pacific*: Action Plan for the Protection, Management and Development of the Marine and Coastal Environment of the North-West Pacific Region (1994). 12. *South Pacific*: Noumea Convention for the Protection of Natural Resources and Environment of the South Pacific Region (1986). SPREP is the secretariat for the Apia Convention 1976, the SPREP (or Noumea) Convention 1986, and the Waigani Convention 1995. 13. *Red Sea and Gulf of Aden*: Regional Convention for the Conservation of the Red Sea and Gulf of Aden (1982); entry into force: August 20, 1985. 14. *ROPME Sea Area*: Action Plan for the Protection and Development of the Marine Environment and the Coastal Areas, the Kuwait Regional Convention for Co-operation on the Protection of the Marine Environment from Pollution, and the Protocol concerning Regional Co-operation in Combating Pollution by Oil and Other Harmful Substances in Cases of Emergency adopted in 1978. 15. *South Asian Seas*: SASP is a co-operative partnership, formally adopted in 1995 for the protection and management of the shared marine waters and associated coastal ecosystems of five maritime SACEP countries (Bangladesh, India, Maldives, Pakistan, and Sri Lanka). 16. *South-East Pacific*: Permanent Commission for the South Pacific (CPPS) is the appropriate Regional Maritime Organization responsible for the coordination of the maritime policies of its Member States: Colombia, Chile, Ecuador, and Peru. The organization was established on August 18, 1952, as a result of the "Declaration on the Maritime Zone" subscribed at Santiago by the Governments of Chile, Ecuador, and Peru. Colombia joined the CPPS on August 9, 1979. 17. *West & Central Africa*: Abidjan Convention for Co-operation in the Protection and Development of the Marine and Coastal Environment of the West and Central African Region (Abidjan Convention, 1981); entered into force August 5, 1984; Action Plan for the protection and Development of the Marine Environment and Coastal Areas of the West and Central African Region (1981); entered into force: August 5, 1984. 18. *Wider Caribbean Region*: Cartagena Convention for the Protection and Development of the Marine Environment of the Wider Caribbean Region (1983); see http://www.unep.org/regionalseas/programmes/default.asp (as of August 8, 2009).

thirty-two protocols.[58] Of these, UNEP provides secretariat services for

[58] *Mediterranean*: (1) Protocol for the Prevention of Pollution in the Mediterranean Sea by Dumping from Ships and Aircraft (Dumping Protocol); adopted February 16, 1976, in force February 12, 1978. (2) Protocol for the Prevention and Elimination of Pollution in the Mediterranean Sea by Dumping from Ships and Aircraft or Incineration at Sea; adopted June 10, 1995, not yet in force. (3) Protocol on the Protection of the Mediterranean Sea against Pollution from Land-Based Sources (LBS Protocol); adopted May 17, 1980, in force June 17, 1983. (4) Protocol for the Protection of the Mediterranean Sea against Pollution from Land-Based Sources and Activities; adopted March 7, 1996, not yet in force. (5) Protocol Concerning Specially Protected Areas and Biological Diversity in the Mediterranean (SPA and Biodiversity Protocol); adopted June 10, 1995, in force December 12, 1999. (6) Protocol Concerning Cooperation in Preventing Pollution from Ships and, in Cases of Emergency, Combating Pollution of the Mediterranean Sea (Prevention and Emergency Protocol); adopted January 25, 2002, in force March 17, 2004. (7) Protocol for the Protection of the Mediterranean Sea against Pollution Resulting from Exploration and Exploitation of the Continental Shelf and the Seabed and its Subsoil (Offshore Protocol); adopted October 14, 1994, not yet in force. (8) Protocol on the Prevention of Pollution of the Mediterranean Sea by Transboundary Movements of Hazardous Wastes and their Disposal (Hazardous Wastes Protocol); adopted October 1, 1996, not yet in force. *ROPME Sea Area*: (9) Protocol concerning Regional Co-operation in Combating Pollution by Oil and other Harmful Substances in Cases of Emergency; adopted April 24, 1978, in force July 1, 1979. (10) Protocol concerning Marine Pollution Resulting from Exploration and Exploitation of the Continental Shelf; adopted 1989, in force February 17, 1990. (11) Protocol for the Protection of the Marine Environment against Pollution from Land-Based Sources; adopted 1990, in force January 2, 1993. (12) Protocol on the Control of Marine Transboundary Movements and Disposal of Hazardous Wastes and other Wastes; adopted March 17, 1998, not yet in force. *West and Central Africa*: (13) Protocol Concerning Co-operation in Combating Pollution in Cases of Emergency; adopted 1981, in force August 5, 1984. *South-East Pacific*: (14) Agreement on Regional Cooperation in Combating Pollution in the South East Pacific by Hydrocarbons and other Harmful Substances in Cases of Emergency; signed: November 12, 1981, participating countries: Chile, Colombia, Ecuador, Peru, and Panama. (15) Complementary Protocol on the Agreement for Regional Cooperation in Combating Pollution in the South East Pacific by Hydrocarbons and other Harmful Substances in Cases of Emergency; adopted July 22, 1983, in force 1987. (16) Protocol for the Protection of the South East Pacific Against Pollution from Land-Based Sources; adopted 1983, in force 1986. (17) Protocol for the Conservation and Management of Protected Marine and Coastal Areas of the South East Pacific; adopted: 1989, in force 1984. (18) Protocol for the Protection of the South East Pacific from Radioactive Pollution; adopted September 21, 1989, in force 1995. (19) Protocol on the Regional Program for the Study of the El Nino Phenomenon in the South East Pacific (ERFEN); adopted November 6, 1992, participating countries: Chile, Colombia, Ecuador, and Peru. *Red Sea and Gulf*

six[59] RSPs, and six regional organizations[60] have also come into being to implement and administer their respective RSPs.

An MEA that emerges as an end product from marathon negotiations spread over a relatively short time span generally enshrines a

of Aden: (20) Protocol Concerning Regional Co-Operation in Combating Pollution by Oil and Other Harmful Substances in Cases of Emergency; adopted February 14, 1982, in force 1985. *Wider Caribbean*: (21) The Protocol Concerning Co-operation in Combating Oil Spills; adopted 1983, in force October 11, 1986. (22) The Protocol Concerning Specially Protected Area and Wildlife (SPAW); adopted 1990, in force June 18, 2000. (23) The Protocol Concerning Pollution from Land-Based Sources and Activities (LBS); adopted October 6, 1999, not yet in force. *Eastern Africa*: (24) Protocol Concerning Protected Areas and Wild Fauna and Flora in the Eastern African Region; adopted June 21, 1985, in force May 30, 1996. (25) The Protocol Concerning Co-operation in Combating Marine Pollution in Cases of Emergency in the Eastern African Region; adopted 1985, in force May 30, 1996. *South Pacific*: (26) Protocol for the Prevention of Pollution of the South Pacific Region by Dumping; adopted 1986, in force 1990. (27) Protocol Concerning Co-operation in Combating Pollution Emergencies in the South Pacific Region; adopted 1986, in force 1990. *Antarctic*: (28) Protocol on Environmental Protection to the Antarctic Treaty; adopted 1991, in force January 14, 1998. *Black Sea*: (29) Protocol on Protection of the Black Sea Marine Environment Against Pollution from Land Based Sources; adopted 1992, in force January 15, 1994. (30) Protocol on Cooperation in Combating Pollution of the Black Sea Marine Environment by Oil and Other Harmful Substances in Emergency Situations; adopted 1992, in force January 15, 1994. (31) Protocol on The Protection of The Black Sea Marine Environment Against Pollution by Dumping; adopted 1992, in force January 15, 1994. (32) Black Sea Biodiversity and Landscape Conservation Protocol; adopted 2003, not yet in force; see www.unep.org/regionalseas (as of August 8, 2009).

[59] The six RSPs for which UNEP currently provides permanent/interim secretariat services are: Caribbean Region, East Asian Seas, Eastern Africa Region, Mediterranean Region, North-West Pacific Region, and West and Central Africa Region; see www.unep.org/regionalseas (as of August 8, 2009).

[60] These regional organizations for RSP are 1. Regional Organization for the Protection of the Marine Environment (ROMPE). It comprises Bahrain, Iran, Iraq, Kuwait, Oman, Qatar, Saudi Arabia, and the United Arab Emirates. 2. Programme of Environment for the Red Sea and the Gulf of Eden (PERSGA). It comprises Egypt, Jordan, Palestine, Saudi Arabia, Somalia, Sudan, and Yemen. 3. Permanent Commission of the South Pacific (CPPS). It comprises Chile, Colombia, Ecuador, Panama, and Peru. 4. South Pacific Regional Environment Programme (SPREP). Its members are Australia, Cook Islands, Federated States of Micronesia, Fiji, France, Kiribati, Marshall Islands, Nauru, New Zealand, Niue, Palau, Papua New Guinea, Solomon Islands, Tonga, Tuvalu, United Kingdom, United States of America, Vanuatu, and Western Samoa. 5. South Asian Cooperative Environment Programme (SACEP). It comprises

framework or a skeleton. This framework, in turn, necessitates a step-by-step process in hardening the commitments and fleshing out the skeleton (which includes defining the core elements, removing calculated ambiguities, and spelling out details of the mechanisms in the convention). There appears to be a need to jettison the traditional notion that all treaties are governed by a single set of rules in view of material differences in different types of treaties. Treaties generally need to be judged by the contents that can "affect their legal character as well."[61] This process is conditioned by the economic and political exigencies of the states parties. Thus, many of the MEAs provide a bare framework, to be supplemented by the fleshing out of the subsequent legal instruments (generally known as protocols).

Institutional Structures

It is now common knowledge that almost all multilateral agreements in the environmental field give birth to some institutional forms. These institutional forms provide a backbone for the agreement. The primary mandate of these so-called regime[62]-specific institutional mechanisms

Bangladesh, India, Maldives, Pakistan, and Sri Lanka. 6. Protection of the Arctic Marine Environment (PAME) established by the Arctic Council Ministers. It comprises Norway, Denmark, Canada, Greenland, Iceland, Faroe Islands, Finland, Russia, Sweden, and the United States; see www.unep.org/regionalseas (as of August 8, 2009).

[61] Arnold D. McNair, "The Functions and Differing Legal Character of Treaties," *British Yearbook of International Law*, vol. 11, 1930, p. 100.

[62] According to Oran R. Young, "all regimes are properly understood as social institutions. By contrast, *organizations* are physical entities possessing offices, personnel, equipment, budgets, and individual legal personalities. They play important roles in implementing and administering the provisions of many, though by no means all, international regimes" (emphasis in original); see Oran R. Young, "Perspectives on International Organizations," in Gunnar Sjostedt (Ed.), *International Environmental Negotiation* (Newbury Park: Sage Publications, 1995, p. 245. For the purposes of the present work, however, the author has considered regimes in the legal sense of constituting several intergovernmental measures/instruments on a specific *sectoral* environmental issue. Thus, for instance, the legal regime on the depletion of the ozone layer covers the 1985 Vienna Convention, 1987 Montreal Protocol, as well as series of subsequent "amendments" and "adjustments" concerning the controlled substances

is to give effectiveness to the provisions of the MEA concerned. They reflect a symbiotic relationship between the lawmaking process and the institution-building process. It is almost natural to put into place institutions that are considered so essential for international cooperation. In the context of MEAs, it seems almost inconceivable that any such treaty would not provide for institutions. They have emerged as functional necessities.

The negotiating states invariably incorporate structures that could suit the requirements of a specific sectoral issue. Included are institutions ranging from a decision-making mechanism (called Conference of Parties or Meeting of the Parties), to executive organs (e.g., bureau, standing committee, or executive committee), to other subsidiary bodies that perform advisory functions for scientific, technical, or implementation purposes (subsidiary body on science and technological advice, review panel, subsidiary body on implementation, scientific council, review committee, or other special purpose bodies), to funding mechanisms (called fund, trust fund, mechanism, facility, etc.). Generally, the practice has been to learn from institutional experiences from other treaties and to emulate them or even build on them. It is interesting to note that there are many variations among the "trust funds" that are specific to MEAs (see Table 2) and where specialized agencies are involved (e.g., the Global Environment Facility, World Heritage Fund, Prototype Carbon Fund, Rain Forest Trust Fund, and Montreal Protocol Multilateral Fund).

Most MEAs are sectoral in nature. The objectives and priorities of these agreements vary significantly from one to another, even if they fall within the ambit of a thematic area or cluster (like biodiversity related or chemicals and wastes). Still, there are some common patterns in terms of institutional structures as many focus on "sustainable development"

under the Protocol. Cumulatively, all these measures can be said to provide the legal regime on the issue of ozone depletion. Similarly, the author has considered institutional mechanisms under the regime as providing "regime-based institutions" having their *sui generis* character.

Table 2. *Comparative Status of Select MEA Trust Funds*

Name of Trust Fund	Legal Framework	Entry into Force	Objectives	Number of Parties	Fundable Activity	Contributor to the Fund	Scale of Contribution
CITES trust fund, 1979	Convention on International Trade in Endangered Species 1973	1987	Species of wild fauna or flora becomes or remains subject to unsustainable exploitation because of international trade	175	1. Costs of staff, office, and maintenance. 2. Program of work 3. Program support costs	Individual parties to the MEA	UN scale of assessment
Trust Fund for Basel Convention, 1993	The Basel Convention on the Control of Transboundary Movements of Hazardous Wastes and their Disposal, 1989	1992	Control all transboundary movement of hazardous wastes; provide assistance regarding implementation of the Basel Convention	172	Provide technical assistance to the developing countries to implement the fund	80% of the annual budget is covered by the parties; the rest may come from any party	UN scale of assessment with 25% ceiling
Mediterranean trust fund, 1979	The Barcelona Convention for the Protection of Mediterranean Sea Against Pollution, 1976; four protocols; 1995 Convention replaced 1976 Convention	1978 2004	To ensure sustainable management of natural marine and land resources and to integrate the environment in social and economic development and land use policies	22	1. Assist Mediterranean governments in assessing and controlling marine pollution 2. Personnel/ office costs of the secretariat	1. Contracting Parties to the Convention 2. Global Environment Facility 3. Mediterranean Economic Assistance	UN scale of assessment

Caribbean Trust Fund (CTF), 1993	Cartagena Convention for the Protection and Development of the Marine Environment of the Wide Caribbean Region 1983	1986	To prevent, reduce, and control pollution of the convention area to ensure sound environmental management	28	1. Assess and manage environmental pollution (AMEP) 2. Special protected areas and wildlife (SPAW)	1. Contracting parties 2. Other parties can cofinance	Amount to be paid by each party is determined by Intergovernmental Meeting (IGM), it is loosely based on UN scale of assessment
Ramsar small grants fund, 1990	1. Ramsar Convention 1971 2. Fourth conference of parties meeting (Resolution 4.3)	1975	To achieve wise use of wetlands by implementing and further developing the Ramsar wise use guidelines	159	Wise use of wetlands	1. Contracting parties 2. Other countries	Contribution from the parties: voluntary
Trust Fund to implement the Kuwait Regional Sea, 1979	Kuwait Regional Convention for Co-operation on the Protection of the Marine Environment from Pollution, 1978	1979	To prevent, abate, and combat pollution of the marine environment in the region	8	1. Environmental assessment 2. Management Legislation Institutional arrangements	Contracting parties	It seems to be loosely based on the structure of the UN

(*continued*)

Table 2 *(continued)*

Name of Trust Fund	Legal Framework	Entry into Force	Objectives	Number of Parties	Fundable Activity	Contributor to the Fund	Scale of Contribution
The World Heritage Fund	Convention for the Protection of World Cultural and Natural Heritage, 1972	1975	Protection and conservation of cultural and natural heritage	186	Conservation and protection of World Heritage sites – priority for most threatened sites	Compulsory and voluntary contributions from the states parties and private donations	
Trust Fund for Implementation of the Convention on Conservation of Migratory Species, 1993	CMS, 1979	1983	To conserve migratory species (avian, terrestrial, and aquatic) over the whole of their range	112	To promote the aims of the Convention, professional staff, scientific staff and consultants are funded.	Contracting parties	UN scale of assessment

This table is a revised and updated version (as of August 17, 2009) of the table drawn from an unpublished doctoral thesis (2005) of Anwar Sadat at Jawaharlal Nehru University, New Delhi.

(e.g., CBD, UNFCCC, and UNCCD) or seek to address the issue of sustainable use of natural resources and the environment. The variations in institutional structures among MEAs could be dictated by specific requirements of the sectoral environmental issue. The common institutional patterns include the following structures.

Conference of the Parties

The Conference of the Parties (COP) is the supreme decision-making organ of the convention. It provides an overarching umbrella for the institutions of the convention. As a plenary forum for the states parties to the convention, it has the final authority in legal and institutional matters. COP does not remain in session and, in a way, remains invisible. It generally meets every year or even at an interval of every 2 or 3 years. There are some other subsidiary bodies that cater to the specific requirement of each convention. They include technical bodies such as the Subsidiary Body on Implementation (SBI), Subsidiary Body on Science and Technology Advice (SBSTA), and the Committee on Science & Technology, Scientific Council, Heritage Fund, Multilateral Fund, and Financial Mechanism. Among all these institutions, the most visible is the secretariat,[63] the primary function of which is to provide services to the convention.

[63] For example, see Article 8, Convention on Wetlands of International Importance (1971), 11 *ILM* 963 (1972); Article 14, Convention for the Protection of the World Cultural and Natural Heritage (1972), 12 *ILM* 1385 (1972); Article XII, Convention on International Trade in Endangered Species (1972), 12 *ILM* 1055 (1973); Article 11, Convention on Long Range Transboundary Air Pollution (1979), 18 *ILM* 1442 (1979); Article IX, Convention on the Conservation of Migratory Species of Wild Animals (1979), 19 *ILM* 15 (1980); Article 7, Convention for the Protection of the Ozone Layer (1985), 26 *ILM* 1529 (1987); Article 16, Convention on the Control of Transboundary Movements of Hazardous Wastes and their Disposal (1989), 30 *ILM* 775 (1991); Article 8, UN Framework Convention on Climate Change (1992), 31 *ILM* 849 (1992); Article 24, Convention on Biological Diversity (1992), 31 *ILM* 818 (1992); and Article 23, Convention to Combat Desertification in Those Countries Experiencing Drought and/or Desertification, particularly in Africa (1994), 33 *ILM* 1332 (1994).

In the process of finding an acceptable institutional base in a host country, a two-stage exercise is triggered. As soon as the particular convention comes into force, after fulfilling the necessary ratifications requirement, the first stage is to establish an "interim secretariat" to organize the convening of the first meeting of the COP. In the second stage, the first meeting of the COP takes a a decision on the establishment of the permanent secretariat of the convention, location of the secretariat within an existing institution, and various ground rules for the functioning of the servicing arm. Along with the decision about which international institution will house the secretariat, a crucial decision is also made regarding which country will host the seat of the convention.

The multilateral environmental regulatory process is *sui generis* for various reasons. To oversee built-in lawmaking enshrined in the agreement itself, as well as for the overall supervision of the regulatory framework, the contracting parties prescribe the mechanism of the "conference of the parties." The meeting of the COP may depend on the need for normative improvement, stock taking, and decision making to provide guidance for realizing the objectives of the agreement. The COP represents a political decision-making process. It not only can interpret the provisions of the convention, but it also can give effect to the built-in lawmaking process. The entire institutional mechanism of the convention works under the supervision of the COP. Even the subsidiary bodies of the convention, which have the same membership as the COP, report to and work under the authority of the COP. The deliberations at the subsidiary body meetings and decisions made therein remain as drafts until endorsed by the COP at its regular session. Thus, the COP, representing the political process, seeks to keep the convention in tune with the changing requirements to realize the objectives of the convention.

The nature of the particular sectoral environmental issue being dealt with by the COP also involves different approaches. In some cases, the primary task of the COP may be just to lay down the threshold for certain activities beyond which states would incur responsibility (e.g., UNFCCC) or protection of certain species and natural resources (e.g., CITES). The strategy followed by the COP in such cases centers around constantly evaluating the performance and adjusting the particular regime as per scientific requirements. In some other cases, the COP may focus on the prohibition of certain activities by the states (e.g., Basel Convention) or phase out certain substances (e.g., Ozone Protocol). In the cases requiring prohibition, the COP does not try to find any "safe" levels for the regulatory process.

Thus, the COPs employ different tools and techniques to translate the goals of the convention into action. The process can be said to be "living" in the sense that, as per the political consensus, the COP uses ideas and innovations through legal concepts and formulations, which may be convenient to the states. In some cases, even "calculated ambiguity" may be the best preferred option for the COP. For instance, the compulsion of the scientific evidence appears to have forced the states to be in favor of the principle of "common but differentiated" obligations for subsequent MEAs. Sometimes, the consensus may comprise accommodation of "subterfuges" in matters ranging from apportionment of funding contributions to affixing responsibility (e.g., Kyoto Protocol).

Secretariats

It is now an established practice to have an institutional structure as a servicing arm for each convention. There is a familiar pattern among all the secretariats of the MEAs, with variations to cater to the specific requirement of each convention. The use of the term "secretariat" is common practice for such a servicing arm. In some cases, however, it has been designated as the Bureau (The Convention on Wetlands on International Importance [Ramsar Convention]),[64] the World Heritage

[64] See Article 8, Ramsar Convention, n. 62.

Centre (World Heritage Convention),[65] or the Executive Body (Long Range Transboundary Air Pollution Convention).[66]

It is common practice to have the secretariat of the protocols/agreements, which flow from the main convention, along with the secretariat for the convention itself. As per the current practice, secretariats of the MEAs are located within the already existing international institution. It is interesting, however, that it is not necessary to locate the secretariat at the headquarters of the international institution itself. Secretariats are located as per the offers made by the states and are accepted by the COP, which may be located away from the main seat of the international institution that has agreed to house the secretariat.

The secretariat of each convention performs a vital role in the process of servicing the COP and other subsidiary bodies of that convention. Servicing includes providing vital administrative, technical, and scientific support to the COP as well as to subsidiary bodies. The secretariat can also be expected to provide advice in the implementation of the convention when the contracting parties so request. The executive secretary of the convention, as chief executive officer, takes the lead not only in translating the political will of the parties, as reflected in the decisions of the COP, but also in ensuring efficient performance of the institutional mechanism. The work of various institutional mechanisms under MEAs reveals that they evolve along with the evolution and development of the regime itself. In a way, they provide a testimony to the working, in actual practice, of the institutionalized international environmental cooperation.

As a servicing arm, the secretariat acts as a pivot for the smooth running of the activities of the convention. It functions under the authority and supervision of the COP. Generally speaking, a secretariat does not possess discretionary powers. It has often been dubbed a "postal service" that acts as a conduit between contracting states and the COP. In actual

[65] See Article 14, World Heritage Convention, n. 62.
[66] See Article 11, LRTAP Convention, n. 62.

practice, some subtle differences may be observed in terms of the functions assigned to the secretariats of various conventions and, in turn, the powers exercised by them to attain the objectives of the convention. The implied powers, if any, that may be exercised by these convention bodies remain to be seen.

Conclusion

MEAs reflect the quest of the sovereign states to put in place instruments and structures to regulate specific sectoral environmental activities. Although MEAs fall within the broad rubric of treaties (as governed by the 1969 Vienna Convention on the Law of Treaties), they represent a special type of treaty that is a work-in-progress. This type of treaty comprises instruments that have, among other things, unique trigger devices that bring states to the negotiation table (e.g., scientific findings by a British Antarctic expedition on ozone-layer depletion, reports of dumping of hazardous wastes especially in the African continent, or scientific warnings about the potential effects of global warming effect); special nomenclatures (e.g., framework convention); novel tools and techniques (e.g., quotas, ceilings, and timetables); criteria of "differentiation" (e.g., grace periods for the developing countries to phase out ODS or primary responsibility for reduction of greenhouse gas emissions by the industrialized countries); built-in lawmaking mechanisms (e.g., the listing of species or special sites or amendments/adjustments to the obligations of the parties); institutional mechanisms (plenary bodies, subsidiary bodies, secretariat, funding entity); and continuous stock taking of the realization of basic objectives of the treaty.

When considering the sheer nature and evolving character of the MEA enterprise, it seems to have been developed into almost a "fine art," especially in recent years. As a corollary, it requires a special "craft" on the part of not only the sovereign states that are engaged in the process, but also of other actors. It manifests a panorama of and finesse in institutionalized international environmental cooperation that has contributed to considerable proliferation of treaties on both a regional as well as a global scale. It is apparent that MEAs have a *sui generis* character and that they trigger a series of legal implications for the parties, the institutions responsible for hosting them, and the host states. In this context, the provision for the convention secretariat, the host institution arrangement, and headquarters agreements, as well as the issue of legal capacity of the secretariats flowing from these arrangements, become crucial to unravel the entire institutionalized multilateral legal process.

4 Host Institution Arrangements

Introduction

As discussed in Chapter 3, multilateral environmental agreements (MEAs) have emerged as a unique regulatory technique. They appear to be need-based responses to address specific sectoral environmental problems. The regulatory exercise results in a legal instrument that provides fulcrum around which the entire institutionalized international environmental cooperation revolves. As a corollary to both the initial legal instrument designed by the contracting parties as well as subsequent work on a built-in lawmaking mechanism, it is usually felt necessary to have an institutional hub that services the needs of the legal regime. In this context, the issue of "location"[1] of the institutional hub (generally called the secretariat) becomes crucial.

[1] The multilateral treaty framework is an intergovernmental venture. By its very nature, the secretariat hub has to be established in the territory of one of the contracting parties. The issue of location is decided on the basis of an offer or request made and its acceptance by the respective parties. In essence, it is worked out in the pattern of a domestic contractual arrangement. If the secretariat is not an "independent" entity, the issue will need to be sorted out as to the selection of (i) a host institution and (ii) a host country. Thus, the actual location of the secretariat in such a scenario will be a product of a two-part process to narrow down the institution that will house or provide secretariat services as well as the country (and city) that will provide the venue for the location of the secretariat.

Treaty Mandate

The process of engaging a large number of sovereign states in mega-treaties – in some cases they have universal participation[2] – has spun its own web. The Charter of the United Nations (UN) is the best example of such a treaty. In the course of the past 60 years, the gigantic process of "institutionalization" within the UN has contributed to the development of what may be called the "UN system" and even the "United Nations Law." The treaties dealing with various subjects take shape as per their specific circumstances and are guided by their own internal and external dynamics.[3]

As discussed earlier in this book, the treaties that seek to govern environmental matters are *sui generis*. MEAs are treaties governed by international law, with sovereign states as their parties. They have an

[2] A perusal of the pattern of participation by the sovereign states in the marathon treaty-making enterprise indicates a steady rise in the numbers. It has been 100 plus (as of August 8, 2009) for some of the major MEAs (e.g., Ramsar, the Convention on International Trade in Endangered Species [CITES], the World Heritage Convention [WHC], the Convention on Migratory Species of Wild Animals [CMS], Ozone, Basel, the UN Framework Convention on Climate Change [UNFCCC], the UN Convention to Combat Desertification [UNCCD], the Convention on Biological Diversity [CBD], Rotterdam, and Stockholm) entered into in recent years. In a sense, this shows that the sovereign states have gradually shed their reservations regarding such treaty frameworks impinging on their cherished sovereignty. Moreover, it also underscores their willingness, among other things, to join multilateral institutionalized cooperation.

[3] For instance, this could comprise factors such as the pressure from the multinationals (e.g., Du Pont and Imperial Chemical Industries [ICI]) to phase out ozone-depleting substances in favor of the new substances that they already had in their arsenal; the role of the oil-producing countries, the alliance of small island nations (AOSIS), G77, China, as well as major industrialized countries that sought to shape the climate change negotiations to serve their own respective interests; interests of the hazardous wastes–exporting countries to get implanted calculated ambiguity and loopholes in the text of the convention so as not to adversely affect their vital trade interests; growing cacophony, lobbying, and pressure from a diverse range of civil society and business interest groups (e.g., the World Council for Sustainable Development) to influence the state-centric negotiations in multilateral environmental negotiations. Apart from this, many of the MEAs (e.g., ozone depletion and climate change) have witnessed decisive shifts in their course by scientific evidence, trade negotiations, or the global economic situation.

independent status, with at least one organ having separate existence from the member states.

The question of location of an institution in a host country[4] follows the primary determination regarding the setting up of the secretariat as an independent entity or locating it in an existing institution. In both the cases, however, it involves the location of the "seat"[5] of the secretariat in a host country. Instances of secretariats having independent existence seem to be exceptions rather than the rule. This can be seen from the growing practice of existing international institutions providing services for the new MEAs. MEAs churn out a number of institutional mechanisms, but it is the location of the secretariat that holds the key. The secretariat is also the most visible organ. The secretariat, the primary function of which is to provide services to the convention, is commonly used as a "servicing base" for the intergovernmental regulatory process as a whole on specific sectoral environmental issues. Most of the

[4] An interesting pattern seems to have emerged in this matter. Many of the MEAs are widely known by the venue of the final negotiations and adoption of the text of the instrument. For instance, the cities of Ramsar (Wetlands); Washington, DC (CITES); Bonn (CMS); Basel (hazardous wastes); Rotterdam (certain chemicals in international trade); and Stockholm (persistent organic pollutants) have become synonymous with the respective conventions that were adopted in those cities. It is interesting that three of the conventions (UNFCCC, UNCCD, and CBD) do not form part of this pattern. It seems to be the case especially because these three conventions came to be located in different cities (Bonn and Montreal) than the ones in which they were originally adopted (UNFCCC and CBD in 1992 in Rio de Janeiro as well as UNCCD in 1994 in Paris).

[5] The question of such a "seat" pertains to locating the permanent secretariat of an international institution. For a legal entity, such a seat is a prerequisite. A different question is where the seat is housed. It could be at the building of a nodal ministry dealing with a specific issue in the country where the final text of the convention was adopted, in an existing international institution already located in a particular country, or even as an independent entity. Sometimes the offer to house a secretariat is made by a state party. The choice of a specific city could be suggested by the host country, or the plenary body of the convention could express its preference. In any case, the seat ought to be located in the territory of a state that is a party to the convention. For further details on the issue see, for instance, Henry G. Schermers and Niles M. Blokker, *International Institutional Law*, 3rd ed. (The Hague: Martinus Nijhoff, 1995), pp. 319–30.

other institutional offshoots of the process generally meet at specified intervals.

An instance of an exception in this context can be seen in the separate existence (in Montreal) of the ozone "Multilateral Fund"[6] from the Ozone secretariat based at the UN Environment Programme (UNEP) offices in the Kenyan capital of Nairobi (for the 1985 Vienna Convention for the Protection of the Ozone Layer and for the 1987 Montreal Protocol on Substances that Deplete the Ozone Layer). The duration of some of the MEA subsidiary organs could vary as warranted by the function and purpose for which they are established. Unless it is desired by the contracting parties, such institutional mechanisms may not exist on a regular basis and as such do not need a formal seat. It is the secretariat[7] as

[6] The Multilateral Fund is the facilitating arm of the 1987 Montreal Protocol on the Substances that Deplete the Ozone Layer (Montreal, 1987) that entered into force on January 1, 1989; see *ILM*, vol. 26, 1987, p. 1550. For Amendments and Adjustments to the Montreal Protocol, see *ILM*, vol. 30, 1991, pp. 539 and 541; *ILM*, vol. 32, 1993, p. 874. The Fund came to be established on the basis of the London Amendments to the Montreal Protocol in 1990. The Fund is managed by an Executive Committee with an equal representation of seven industrialized and seven Article 5 countries, which are elected annually by a Meeting of the Parties. The financial and technical assistance under the Fund is provided in the form of grants or concessional loans. It is delivered primarily through four "implementing agencies": UNEP, the UN Development Programme (UNDP), the UN Industrial Development Organization (UNIDO), and the World Bank. For details, see http://www.multilateralfund.org (as of August 8, 2009).

[7] Each of the multilateral environmental agreements has a secretariat that serves as a servicing base. In general, the nature of functions and powers that are assigned to the secretariats could be more or less similar. There could, however, be some sector-specific requirement assigned to the secretariat. Furthermore, apart from the powers laid down in the convention, the secretariats are not known to possess any "implied powers." For example, see Article 8, Convention on Wetlands of International Importance (1971), 11 *ILM* 963 (1972); Article 14, Convention for the Protection of the World Cultural and Natural Heritage (1972), 12 *ILM* 1385 (1972); Article XII, CITES (1972), 12 *ILM* 1055 (1973); Article 11, Convention on Long-range Transboundary Air Pollution (LRTAP) (1979), 18 *ILM* 1442 (1979); Article IX, CMS (1979), 19 *ILM* 15 (1980); Article 7, Convention for the Protection of the Ozone Layer (1985), 26 *ILM* 1529 (1987); Article 16, Convention on the Control of Transboundary Movements of Hazardous Wastes and their Disposal (1989), 30 *ILM* 775 (1991); Article 8, UNFCCC (1992), 31 *ILM* 849 (1992); Article 24, CBD (1992), 31 *ILM* 818 (1992); and Article 23, UNCCD (1994), 33 *ILM* 1332 (1994).

a treaty body that is provided with a 'seat' and entrusted with the task of servicing the formal intergovernmental institutions (e.g., COP, MOP and other subsidiary organs) set up under the treaty. Although it flows from the treaty provisions, the secretariat is not expected to make any decisions or perform any operational functions except as mandated by the COP (plenary or supreme decision-making body). The questions of a secretariat's competence and its juridical powers are circumscribed by the original treaty instrument as well as subsequent 'host institution' and 'host country' arrangements.[8]

Establishing a Secretariat

The setting up of a secretariat is an integral part of the treaty-making process. It becomes crucial in cases of environmental treaties, as they are 'living' (or work-in-progress) instruments that continuously need institutional nurturing and service. There are familiar patterns regarding basic characteristics among MEA secretariats. To cater to the specific requirements of a convention, some variations become necessary. This can be seen in the common practice of using the term "secretariat" for the servicing arm. In some cases, however, it has been designated the "Bureau" (The Convention on Wetlands of International Importance [the Ramsar Convention]),[9] the "Heritage Centre" (World Heritage Convention [WHC]),[10] or the "Executive Body" (Longrange Transboundary Air Pollution Convention [LRTAP]).[11]

[8] These instruments, cumulatively, provide the legal framework for the secretariat to operate both within the domestic jurisdiction of the host country as well as on the international level. In exceptional cases, the original text of the convention provides for the legal capacity of the secretariat. This is generally left for the host country agreement. It, in turn, prescribes the broad contours of such juridical capacity.

[9] See Article 8, Convention on Wetlands of International Importance (Ramsar), February 2, 1971; see *ILM*, vol. 22, 1982.

[10] See Article 14, Convention Concerning the Protection of the World Cultural and Natural Heritage (Paris), November 23, 1972; see *ILM*, vol. 11, 1972, p. 1358.

[11] See Article 10, LRTAP, 1979; ratified by fifty-one states as of December 17, 2008; see http://www.unece.org/env/lrtap/lrtap_h1.htm.

The current practice of locating secretariats of MEAs within an already existing international institution has its own fallout. It is interesting, however, that it is not necessary for the secretariat to be located only at the headquarters of the international institution that has been requested to provide such a service. In fact, the question of location (seat) of the secretariat is dictated by the offers made by states that wish to host it. The best offer acceptable to the Conference of the Parties (COP) paves the way for establishment of the secretariat. Moreover, in principle, they could be in the country where the host institution is located or in a different country (even in a different continent)[12] than the headquarters of the international institution that has agreed to house the secretariat. In such cases, the secretariat in question acts as an out-posted office (i.e., an office at a different location).

Secretariats' practices in the environmental field show that they perform a vital servicing role for the COP and other subsidiary bodies of the convention. This role includes the task of providing vital administrative, technical, and scientific support to the COP as well as to the subsidiary bodies. The secretariat can also be expected to provide advice on implementation of and compliance with the convention when the contracting parties so request.

[12] It is now no longer considered necessary that the host institution that agrees to provide secretariat support to an MEA is located at its headquarters. The practice has been sustained by the advances in communication facilities as well as, in some cases, the existence of regional offices of the host institution that serve as support bases for the location of the secretariat in a different country (e.g., the UNEP regional office in Geneva). Two host institutions have experienced such secretariat services provided to MEAs that are located away from their headquarters. The UN has agreed to provide "institutional linkage" to the 1992 UNFCCC and the 1994 UNCCD and their secretariats located in Bonn (Germany). It explains the rationale for usage of prefix "United Nations" for both these conventions. UNEP has been providing secretariat support to seven MEAs: Basel, CBD, CITES, CMS, Ozone, Rotterdam, and Stockholm (with the Food and Agriculture Organization [FAO]). The secretariats of these MEAs are located in Bonn (CMS), Geneva (Basel, CITES, Rotterdam, and Stockholm), Nairobi (Ozone), and Montreal (CBD). UNEP also administers secretariats of some regional seas conventions. The Ozone Secretariat remains the only one that is located alongside the UNEP headquarters in Nairobi.

The executive secretary of the convention (as chief executive officer),[13] takes the lead not only in translating the political will of the parties into action (as reflected in the decisions of the COP), but also in ensuring effective performance of the institutional mechanism. The work of various institutional mechanisms under the MEAs reveals that they change along with the evolution and development of the treaty regime itself. They also provide a testimony to the working of the institutionalized international environmental cooperation in actual practice.

It is the text of the treaty that provides the relevant mandate regarding the nature and character of necessary host arrangements. Thus the issue gets due attention at the time of negotiating the text of the instrument itself. Almost all the MEAs that took shape in the post–Stockholm (1972) period have contained provisions for host institution arrangements. It seems that, in recent years, none of the major treaties have opted for establishment of an independent secretariat.

To begin with, in general, the text of the treaty provides that a specific institution will provide an "interim secretariat."[14] Basic considerations in this context comprise initiatives taken by an institution regarding the

[13] The executive secretary is the head of the secretariat of the convention. He or she is the chief executive officer whose selection proves crucial for the working of the secretariat. In all cases where the secretariat is being provided by a host institution, the respective head of that institution plays a decisive role in the selection process for the executive secretary of the convention secretariat. Depending on the assertiveness of the COP of the convention, however, the selection of the executive secretary, generally, conforms to its wishes. Because the task of providing a secretariat amounts to a contractual exercise (in lieu of 13 percent overhead charges) by the host institution, the head of the secretariat needs to have primary loyalty to the COP. Still, in many cases of selection or removal of the executive secretaries, the heads of the host institutions (e.g., UNEP) have asserted their authority. In most of the cases it went without a challenge, but in others it invited a strong reaction from the standing committee and/or the COP (e.g., CITES) that led to questions regarding "quality" and the nature of the services provided by the concerned host institution. In some cases, lack of transparency in the whole process has been questioned (e.g., the recent selection of the Executive Secretary of the UNFCCC).

[14] The treaty-making practice in this respect has been, generally, to provide for such an arrangement. This is especially so to put into place a mechanism to service the needs of the parties and other interim requirements until the treaty legally enters into force.

process for negotiations on a sectoral environmental issue. For instance, UNEP has initiated such negotiations on the basis of a mandate from the Governing Council and its 10-year action plan under the Montevideo Programme.[15] Moreover, organic linkage[16] of the concerned institution with the central theme of the treaty plays an important role in this respect [e.g., the World Conservation Union's (IUCN) work on species survival and other conservation issues]. Similarly, other considerations contribute

Pending this, the treaty requirements could be taken care of by either the nodal ministry of the country where the treaty came to be finalized and adopted or any existing institution that is temporarily assigned the task. An appropriate decision in the matter is sought to be made at the time of the first meeting of the COP. The COP could decide either to continue the existing interim secretariat arrangement or to entrust the task to another entity.

[15] The program is named after the first Ad-Hoc Meeting of Senior Government Officials Expert in Environmental Law took place in Montevideo from October 28 through November 6, 1981 to establish a framework, methods, and program for the development and periodic review of environmental law and to contribute to the preparation and implementation of the environmental law component of the system-wide medium-term environment program. See *Report of the Ad Hoc Meeting of Senior Government Officials Experts in Environmental Law*, UNEP/GC 10/5/Add.2, Annex, Ch. 11 (1981); *Yearbook of the United Nations*, vol. 35, 1981, pp. 839–40 and *Yearbook of the United Nations*, vol. 36, 1982, p. 1030. The UNEP Governing Council resolution 10/21 of May 31, 1982, adopted the experts' program and endorsed their conclusions and recommendations. Subsequently, the UNEP Governing Council successively adopted three more such ten-yearly programs: (i) Montevideo Programme II: "Programme for the Development and Periodic Review of Environmental Law for the First Decade of the Twenty-first Century" (UNEP Governing Council decision 17/25 of May 21, 1993); see *Yearbook of the United Nations*, vol. 47, 1993, pp. 820–1; (ii) Montevideo Programme III: "Programme for the Development and Periodic Review of Environmental Law beyond the Year 2000"(UNEP Governing Council Decision 21/23 of February 9, 2001); (iii) Montevideo Program IV: "Program for the Development and Periodic Review of Environmental Law" (UNEP Governing Council/Global Ministerial Environment Forum Decision 25/11, February 16–20, 2009).

[16] To ensure special sectoral needs of an MEA, an appropriate international institution having a close link to its objectives is preferred as a host institution. Such an entity also becomes a natural choice because it has contributed in raising awareness about the sectoral issue and provides relevant scientific and logistic assistance in convening the preliminary meeting of the government experts as well as in the drafting process for the legal instrument. The final decision in the matter is of course made by the state parties. In view of this, the entity concerned becomes a natural choice. For instance, UNEP has been such an entity at the initial stage that makes it an automatic candidate for the secretariat services for the convention.

to ensuring affinity with an organ of an international organization that has been requested to provide secretariat support.

Since 1988, the UN General Assembly has consistently followed the issue of climate change under the agenda item of "protection of global climate for present and future generations of mankind."[17] It has provided crucial political guidance to the states on the issue, brought into existence the Intergovernmental Panel of Climate Change (IPCC) [jointly sponsored by UNEP and the World Meteorological Organization (WMO)], established the Intergovernmental Negotiating Committee (INC) to negotiate the text of the legal instrument, and regularly supervised the global climate change debate. In most cases, it is the "catalyst" institution (e.g., UNEP) that acts as a natural host.

Generally, pending establishment of formal institutional mechanisms under the treaty, designating an ad hoc or interim secretariat becomes important. Moreover, it seems that, in cases of the protocols negotiated under an MEA, the respective convention secretariats are automatically expected to have interim secretariat responsibility. The interim arrangement is expected to be vetted at the first meeting of the COP (after the treaty formally comes into being). In fact, in some cases, an ad hoc secretariat could become necessary even to facilitate ongoing negotiations on the drafting of the treaty (e.g., this was felt necessary by the UN General Assembly even before formal launch of negotiations on climate change under the auspices of an INC).[18] The need, it seems, was felt to be so

[17] The General Assembly had considered the agenda item proposed by the Government of Malta on "Conservation of climate as part of the common heritage of mankind" and adopted the resolution *Protection of Global Climate for Present and Future Generations of Mankind* on December 6, 1988. The General Assembly resolution 43/53 (1988) was adopted without vote. Similar resolutions have been adopted by the General Assembly as: 54/222 of December 22, 1999; 61/201 of December 20, 2006; 62/86 of December 10, 2007; and 63/32 of November 26, 2008; see http://www.un.org/Depts/dhl/res (as of August 8, 2009).

[18] It is interesting that, as per the treaty-making practice that came to be institutionalized before the 1992 Rio Earth Summit, this pertains to the task of drafting of a legal instrument on a specific sectoral issue by an intergovernmental forum known as an Intergovernmental Negotiating Committee (INC). This body is generally provided a mandate to prepare the draft text of a legal instrument within a deadline. For instance,

pressing that, pending establishment of an ad hoc secretariat, the General Assembly authorized the UN Secretary-General to "exceptionally" convene the first session of the INC in Washington, DC, in February 1991.

Thus, the extent to which the concerned treaty is clear regarding the secretariat arrangement can greatly help in legal, administrative, and financial matters. In this context, relevant provisions of the treaty will need to be read together with subsequent decisions of the COP. It is the COP, as a supreme decision-making organ, that practically holds veto[19] power regarding the determination of the nature, shape, location, and legal character of the secretariat that will provide service. Few of the treaties contain explicit provisions regarding a possible "review" of the secretariat arrangement. Absence of such a review provision, however, does not necessarily mean that the COP, if not satisfied with

in the cases of both climate change and biological diversity, the INC was required to prepare such a text prior to the commencement of the Earth Summit on June 5, 1992. The INCs did deliver the texts around May 1992. The flip side of this process is that several issues requiring agreement have to be either deferred until the subsequent detailed convention process or inserted in the text of the instrument through usage of calculated ambiguity.

[19] As the supreme decision-making organ of the convention, the COP has the final say regarding the secretariat. Usually the decision is deferred – even when an interim secretariat is in place – until the first meeting of the COP holds its meeting. In fact, the first session of the COP is convened by the interim secretariat. For instance, Article 7 (2) of the The Vienna Convention for the Protection of the Ozone Layer provided: "The secretariat functions will be carried out on an interim basis by the United Nations Environment Programme until the completion of the first ordinary meeting of the Conference of the Parties held pursuant to article 6. At its first ordinary meeting, the Conference of the Parties shall designate the secretariat from amongst those existing competent international organizations which have signified their willingness to carry out the secretariat functions under this Convention"; see Convention for the Protection of the Ozone Layer (Vienna, 1985) and Protocol on Substances that Deplete the Ozone Layer (Montreal, 1987), both entered into force on September 22, 1988, and January 1, 1989; see *ILM*, vol. 26, 1987, p. 1529 and *ILM*, vol. 26, 1987, p. 1550.

Therefore, it is the COP that makes a decision in the matter to make a formal request to provide secretariat services to a host institution as well as subsequently supervising the services. If the COP is not satisfied with the services rendered by the concerned host institution, it can always decide to revoke the arrangement and replace the host institution.

the secretariat services provided by the host institution, can not question it and even replace it. It is an inherent power of the COP to supervise, review, and make a final decision on the relationship with the host institution as far as it performs secretariat functions.

Providing a Secretariat

The multilateral regulatory instrument designed by the states has an organic link to institutional mechanisms that germinate from it. Among them, it is the creation of a secretariat that necessitates a delicate exercise as the parties have to decide on how to go about it. They could choose an independent secretariat that can have its procedural and operative standards. There is, however, a common trend seen at the final stage of negotiation to consider formally making a request to an existing international institution to perform and/or provide such secretariat services. Generally, it is the institution that has played a role in initiating the negotiating process and/or has been working closely on the issue in question that is considered for this purpose. The crucial formulation regarding making a "call" – in terms of providing the secretariat (language could vary from "shall" to "will" to "is")[20] in the text of the treaty itself – holds the key to unraveling the complex web of the relationship between the existing international institution and the requesting decision-making body of the treaty. It is the language used that can provide the basic clue in this respect.

[20] The treaty-making practice shows an interesting pattern at work as well as an emphatic call issued in this respect to a host institution that is designated to provide secretariat services to the convention. The word "shall" is most often used in this connection. It indicates that the COP has the final say in the matter of deciding who shall provide such services. For example, the formulations used are as follows: "shall be provided" (CITES); "Secretariat is provided" (CMS); " (ECE) shall carry out . . . secretariat functions" (LRTAP); "secretariat functions will be carried out" (Basel); "secretariat functions will be carried out" (Ozone); "(UNEP) shall designate a permanent secretariat" (UNFCCC); "shall designate the secretariat" (CBD); "shall designate a Permanent Secretariat" (UNCCD); "shall be performed jointly (by UNEP ED and the FAO D-G)" (Rotterdam); and "shall be performed (by the UNEP ED)" (Stockholm).

It is the "plenary" body of the treaty (generally called the Conference or Meeting of the Parties) that has the legal capacity to make such a request and invite an entity to perform secretariat functions. The plenary body in question controls the levers of "supervising"[21] the relationship. The requested entity is described as a "host institution." It is the text of the instrument in question that has to be primarily relied on to examine the nature of the request made to an existing institution to provide secretariat support. The language used in the specific formulation holds the key in this respect.[22] As noted earlier, either ad hoc or interim secretariat responsibilities need to be assigned pending entry into force of the convention. It is the COP that has the final say in deciding on "instituting" a secretariat, its terminology, host institution, and, finally, location. There is no standard formulation used for bringing such a secretariat to fruition. The language used could vary from instrument to instrument (see Table 3).

The language formulation used to ignite the relationship with a host institution is often bland and explicit; for example, it states the secretariat functions shall be "performed" (Stockholm Convention on Persistent Organic Pollutants [POPs], Rotterdam Convention on the Prior Informed Consent Procedure for Certain Hazardous Chemicals and Pesticides in International Trade [PIC], and Ramsar Convention),[23]

[21] This is especially so since the relationship between the Conference of the Parties and the host institution is triggered on the basis of an explicit call given in the text of the convention itself. The formulation used as well as the purpose for which the relationship is brought into being shows that the MEA plenary body will duly supervise the specific contractual arrangement. For this the COP remains seized of the matter and considers it periodically by adopting decisions, where necessary.

[22] As per the treaty-making practice, the initial call given in the text of the treaty is to provide an "interim secretariat," to be followed by a permanent secretariat arrangement when the first meeting of the COP is held. The role of the interim secretariat ceases after this. However, one needs to understand, the specific language used as well as the original intention of the parties to make out the exact arrangement in this respect.

[23] See Convention on Wetlands of International Importance (Ramsar), February 2, 1971; see *ILM*, vol. 22, 1982; Rotterdam Convention on the Prior Informed Consent Procedure for Certain Hazardous Chemicals and Pesticides in International Trade (PIC), adopted on September 10, 1998, see www.pic.int; Stockholm Convention on Persistent Organic Pollutants, adopted on May 22, 2001, see www.pops.int.

Table 3. *Comparative Picture of Select MEA Provisions Concerning Host Institutions*

Convention	Interim Secretariat	Provision	Language Used	Possible Review	Functions Assigned	Special Features
1. POPs (Stockholm) 2001	UNEP (Geneva)	Article 20	Secretariat functions shall be performed by the ED of UNEP:	Three-fourths majority of the parties present and voting	Cater to meetings, assistance to parties, coordination, periodic reports, administrative, contractual arrangements, etc.	1. "Persistence" of organic pollutants that have toxic properties, resist degradation, bio-accumulates, and transported far away across international boundaries from place of origin 2. List of Annexes for regulation
2. Hazardous Wastes Protocol on Liability and Compensation, 2000	Basel Convention Secretariat (Geneva)	Article 25	Secretariat functions shall be carried out by the Secretariat of the Basel Convention.	No provision	Arrange and service meetings, prepare reports, coordination, compile information, cooperation with other entities, etc.	1. Comprehensive regime for liability and for adequate and prompt compensation for damage 2. Liability for damage due to an "incident" during a "transboundary movement" of hazardous wastes 3. Financial limits for the liability

(*continued*)

Table 3 (*continued*)

Convention	Interim Secretariat	Provision	Language Used	Possible Review	Functions Assigned	Special Features
3. Cartagena Protocol on Biosafety, 2000	CBD Secretariat (Montreal)	Article 31	Secretariat established by Article 24 of the Convention (CBD) shall serve as the secretariat to this Protocol.	No provision	Functions of the convention secretariat shall apply *mutatis mutandis*	1. Transboundary movement, handling, and use of living modified organisms 2. Advance informed agreement procedure 3. Risk assessment
4. Rotterdam PIC Procedure, 1998	UNEP (Geneva) and FAO (Rome)	Article 19	Secretariat functions shall be jointly performed by the ED of UNEP and Director-General of FAO	Three-fourths majority of the parties present and voting	Cater to meetings, assistance to parties, coordination, administrative, contractual arrangements, etc.	1. Voluntary PIC Procedure 2. Listing of chemicals subject to PIC procedure
5. Protocol to the London Dumping Convention, 1996 (to replace the 1972 Convention)	IMO (London)	Article 19	IMO shall be responsible for secretariat duties.	No provision	Convene meetings, provide advice and recommendations, develop and implement procedures, budget, and financial account, etc.	1. Protect and preserve the marine environment from all sources of pollution 2. Prevent, reduce, and where practicable, eliminate pollution caused by dumping or incineration at sea of wastes

6. UNCCD, 1994	UN Secretary-General to establish in Geneva (GA Reso. 47/188)	Article 23	COP shall designate a permanent secretariat and make arrangements for its functioning.	No provision	Arrangements for sessions of convention bodies, compile and transmit reports, facilitate assistance, coordinate activities with others, administrative and contractual arrangements, prepare reports, etc.	1. Human beings in affected or threatened areas are at the "centre of concerns" to combat desertification and mitigate the effects of drought 2. Four lists of regional implementation annexes
7. UNFCCC, 1992	UN Secretary-General to establish in consultation with UNEP ED and WMO Secretary-General	Article 8	COP shall designate at first meeting a permanent secretariat and make arrangements for its functioning.	No provision	Arrangements for sessions of convention bodies, compile and transmit reports, facilitate assistance to parties, coordinate activities with others, administrative and contractual arrangements, prepare reports, etc.	1. Climate change as a "common concern of humankind" 2. Common but differentiated responsibility for historical and current GHG emissions 3. Stabilization of greenhouse gas concentrations in the atmosphere to prevent dangerous anthropogenic interference with the climate system

(continued)

Table 3 *(continued)*

Convention	Interim Secretariat	Provision	Language Used	Possible Review	Functions Assigned	Special Features
8. CBD, 1992	UNEP ED (Montreal)	Article 24	COP shall designate at first meeting a permanent secretariat and make arrangements for its functioning.	No provision	Arrangements for sessions of convention bodies, compile and transmit reports, facilitate assistance to parties, coordinate activities with others, administrative and contractual arrangements, prepare reports, etc.	1. Conservation of biological diversity as a "common concern of humankind" 2. Conservation and sustainable use of biological diversity 3. Fair and equitable sharing of benefits from utilization of genetic resources
9. Basel Convention on Hazardous Wastes, 1989	UNEP ED (Geneva)	Article 16	COP shall designate the secretariat from existing competent intergovernmental organizations.	No provision	Arrange and service meetings, prepare and transmit reports, report on its activities, coordinate with others, communicate with parties, compile information, etc.	1. List of hazardous characteristics 2. Hazardous wastes disposal operations 3. Lists of hazardous wastes
10. Vienna Convention on Depletion of the Ozone Layer, 1985	UNEP (Nairobi)	Article 7	COP shall designate the secretariat from existing competent international organizations	No provision	Arrange and service meetings, prepare reports, functions assigned under any Protocol, coordination with other bodies, etc.	Annexes to form an integral part of the convention; effect of "amendment" to the convention

11. Montreal Protocol on the Depletion of the Ozone Layer, 1987	Ozone Secretariat (UNEP, Nairobi)	Article 12	(Ozone Secretariat) To perform the functions assigned to it by any protocol	No provision	Arrange and service meetings, report to parties, notify request for technical assistance	1. Establishment of "Multilateral Fund" for financial and technical cooperation 2. Innovative provision for "amendments" and "adjustments" to ozone-depleting substances phaseout schedules
12. CMS, 1979	UNEP ED (Bonn)	Article IX	Secretariat is provided by the ED of UNEP.	COP to make alternative arrangements if UNEP can not provide	Arrange and service meetings, liaison with parties, prepare reports, maintain list of range states, conclusion of agreements, provide general public information, etc.	1. Lists of migratory species that are endangered and have unfavorable conservation status 2. Conclusion of agreements covering the conservation and management of migratory species

(*continued*)

Table 3 *(continued)*

Convention	Interim Secretariat	Provision	Language Used	Possible Review	Functions Assigned	Special Features
13. LRTAP, 1979	ECE (Geneva)	Article 11	The Executive Secretary of the ECE shall carry out, for the Executive Body, the secretariat functions.	No provision	Convene and prepare the meetings of the Executive Body, transmit reports to the Contracting Parties, discharge the functions assigned by the Executive Body	Implementation of the existing "Cooperative programme for the monitoring and evaluation of the long-range transmission of air pollutants in Europe" and the further development of this program
14. CITES, 1973	UNEP ED (Geneva)	Article XII	Secretariat shall be provided by the ED of UNEP.	No provision	Arrange and service meetings, functions under Articles XV and XVI, scientific and technical studies, prepare reports, publish updated appendices, annual reports, etc.	Periodic publication and distribution to the Parties current editions of Appendices I, II, and III to facilitate identification of specimens of species included in those Appendices

15. World Heritage Convention, 1972	UNESCO (Paris)	Article 14	Secretariat appointed by the Director-General of UNESCO	No provision	Providing assistance to the WHC	1. Intergovernmental Committee for the Protection of the Cultural and Natural Heritage of Outstanding Universal Value (to be called the WHC) established within UNESCO 2. Director-General of UNESCO to use services of ICSPRCP, ICOMOS, and IUCN to prepare World Heritage Committee's documentation and in implementation of its decisions
16. Ramsar Convention, 1971	IUCN (Gland)	Article 8	IUCN shall perform the continuing bureau duties	Majority or two-thirds of all Contracting Parties	Assist in organizing contracting parties meetings, maintain list of wetlands, and notify on alterations to the list, etc.	1. Initiated by UNESCO 2. Maintain the list of wetlands of international importance

ICOMOS: International Council on Monuments and Sites; ICSPRCP: International Center for the Study of Preservation and Restoration of Cultural Property.

"provided" (Convention on International Trade in Endangered Species [CITES], and Convention on Migratory Species of Wild Animals [CMS]),[24] "appointed" (WHC),[25] or "carried out" (LRTAP)[26] by an existing international institution (UNEP; Food and Agriculture Organization [FAO]; International Maritime Organisation [IMO]; UN Educational, Scientific and Cultural Organization [UNESCO]; the Economic Commission for Europe [ECE]; or the International Union for Conservation of Nature and Natural Resources [IUCN], as the case may be). In some other cases, the text of the convention leaves the decision to the plenary body of the convention (COP) at its first session for a formal designation of the "secretariat from amongst those existing competent international organizations which have signified their willingness to carry out the secretariat functions" as well as ensuring arrangements for its smooth working (Basel, Convention on Biological Diversity [CBD], UN Framework Convention on Climate Change [UNFCCC], UN Convention to Combat Desertification [UNCCD], etc.).[27] This practice seems to have been well institutionalized.

It is interesting that, in almost all cases where there is an explicit reference in the formulation of secretariat services that "shall be performed" or "shall be provided" by an institution, the reference is made to the respective heads of the concerned institution (POPs, PIC, CMS,

[24] CITES of Wild Fauna and Flora (Washington), March 3, 1973; see 993 *UNTreaty Series* (UNTS), p. 243; CMS (Bonn), June 23, 1979; see *ILM*, vol. 19, 1979, p. 15.

[25] Convention Concerning the Protection of the World Cultural and Natural Heritage (Paris), November 23, 1972; see *ILM*, vol. 11, 1972, p. 1358.

[26] LRTAP (Geneva, 1979); see http://www.unece.org/env/lrtap/lrtap_h1.htm (as of August 20, 2009).

[27] See Convention on the Control of Transboundary Movements of Hazardous Wastes and Their Disposal (Basel, 1989), entered into force on May 24, 1992; see *ILM*, vol. 28, 1989, p. 657; CBD (Rio de Janeiro, 1992), entered into force on December 29, 1993; see *ILM*, vol. 31, 1992, p. 822; UNFCCC (Rio de Janeiro, 1992), entered into force on March 21, 1994; see *ILM*, vol. 31, 1992, p. 849; UNCCD (1994); see *ILM*, vol. 33, 1994, p. 1328.

CITES, WHC, etc.).[28] The reference to "host institution" (IUCN)[29] can be found only in the case of the Ramsar Convention, and not to the IUCN Director-General. In fact, commonality in formulations can be seen especially in the case of a specific reference made to the executive director (ED) of UNEP, as often it has played the role of a "catalyst" in initiating negotiations on many of the sectoral environmental issues. Thus, irrespective of the formulation used in the text of the MEA, the net effect is that the secretariat has come into effect and the task is assigned to the host institution to carry out the "function of the Secretariat."[30] It is the head of host institution (e.g., UNEP ED) who is, in turn, expected to take the steps that fully realize the role that institution is expected to play. The role of the head of the host institution could also be clearly specified by the standing committee or the COP. This is exactly what the

[28] Article 20 of the POPs states: "the Secretariat functions for this Convention shall be performed by the Executive Director of the United Nations Environment Programme, unless the Conference of the Parties decides, by a three-fourths majority of the parties present and voting, to entrust the Secretariat functions to one or more other international organizations"; Article 19 of the PIC (1998) states: "the Secretariat functions for this Convention shall be performed jointly by the Executive Director of UNEP and the Director-General of FAO, subject to such arrangements as shall be agreed between them and approved by the Conference of the Parties"; Article IX of the CMS (1979) states: "upon entry into force of this Convention, the Secretariat is provided by the Executive Director of the United Nations Environment Programme"; Article XII of the Convention on International Trade in Endangered Species of Wild Fauna and Flora (1973) states: "upon entry into force of the present Convention, a Secretariat shall be provided by the Executive Director of the United Nations Environment Programme"; Article 14 of the WHC (1972) states: "the World Heritage Committee shall be appointed by the Director-General of the United Nations Educational, Scientific and Cultural Organization."

[29] Article 8 of the Convention on Wetlands of International Importance especially as Waterfowl Habitat provides: "The International Union for Conservation of Nature and Natural Resources shall perform the continuing bureau duties under this Convention until such time as another organization or government is appointed by a majority of two-thirds of all Contracting Parties"; see *ILM*, vol. 22, 1982.

[30] UNEP, "The Relationship between the Executive Director of UNEP and the Conventions Regarding the Administration of their Secretariats," Fourth Meeting on Coordination of Secretariats of Environmental Conventions, Geneva, January 10–11, 1996; UNEP/DEP/Coord.4/3, January 4, 1996, p. 2.

CITES Standing Committee sought to do as regards UNEP ED through a special treaty provision:

> The ED will act in conformity with the provisions of Articles XI and XII of the Convention on these and other functions as may be entrusted to the Secretariat by the Parties. The ED shall ensure that the Secretary General implements the policy guidance of the CoP and between the meetings of the CoP the policy guidance of the Standing Committee in exercising the functions of the Secretariat in accordance with Articles XI and XII of the Convention and other functions as may be entrusted to the Secretariat by the Parties.[31]

It is probably to perform such a continuing role that UNEP has constituted a full-fledged Division of Environmental Conventions (DEC). It is the DEC that gives full effect to the role of UNEP headquarters to perform the secretariat role for a series of conventions. It is interesting that this relationship need not necessarily be fully effective at the main "seat" (headquarters in Nairobi)[32] of UNEP.

Except for the Ozone Secretariat (which is located at the headquarters), all other convention secretariats "administered" by UNEP are based not only away from the main seat but, in fact, on different continents. For instance, of the seven MEAs to whom UNEP provides secretariat support – Ozone, CBD, CITES, Basel, CMS, PIC (with FAO), and POPs (with FAO) – the secretariats are located in Africa, North America, and Europe. Similarly, in cases of several regional seas programs (RSPs) where UNEP directly provides secretariat support, the

[31] See Basic Principle 1 of the Agreement Signed between the Chairman of the CITES Standing Committee and ED of UNEP on June 20, 1997 (on file with the author).

[32] None of the MEAs that mandate the UNEP ED to provide secretariat services for it seek to specify the place (i.e., either at UNEP headquarters in Nairobi or elsewhere). It seems that this issue is left to the judgment of the host institution to decide. If the host institution (e.g., UNEP, UNESCO, IUCN) decides to locate the secretariat at its own headquarters, the secretariat's legal capacity will be governed by the already-existing headquarters agreement of the host institution with the host country. Only when the secretariat is sought to be located away from the seat of the host institution does the need arise for the secretariat to work out a new headquarters agreement in the host country.

task is carried out by the respective regional coordinating units (RCUs) that are located away from the headquarters.[33] This, in turn, unleashes a chain of legal implications and requires the use of multiple legal steps engaging the standing committee of the COP, the host institution, and the host country where the seat of the secretariat will be physically located.

Review Provision

Thus the power to designate an institution to perform secretariat functions rests in the convention instrument (and in the plenary body created by the convention). The MEAs themselves are brought into being only to address specific sectoral environmental problems. It seems that there is no permanence attached to these treaty-based arrangements. Theoretically speaking, the arrangements are expected to be wound up or dissolved upon realization of the basic objective or resolution of the specific environmental problem or even disappearance of the *raison d'être* of the convention. Therefore, the treaty itself is a need-based response to specific environmental challenges. If this is the case, it seems logical that secretariat arrangements could also be reviewed.[34] Such power of

[33] The RSPs work in the regions through secretariats or regional coordinating units (RCUs) and regional activity centers (RACs). The RCU is the nerve center and command post of the action plan's activities and has the overall and practical responsibility for the implementation of the decisions of member countries (or contracting parties) regarding the operation of the action plan. The RCU is responsible for the follow-up and implementation of legal documents, the program of work and of strategies and policies adopted by the member countries. For details, see http://www.unep.org/regionalseas/.

[34] In general, most of the provisions concerning secretariats in MEAs remain silent regarding the possibility of a review of the arrangements made. It seems, however, that just four of the MEAs contain an explicit provision on possible review of the secretariat arrangement (sometimes linked to three-fourths voting). These MEA provisions are: Article 20 of the Stockholm Convention (2001), which states: ". . . unless the Conference of the Parties decides, by a three-fourths majority of the Parties present and voting, to entrust the secretariat functions to one or more other international organizations"; Article 19 (4) of the Rotterdam Convention (1998), which states: "The Conference of the Parties may decide, by a three-fourths majority of the Parties present and

review can be deciphered from or even implied in the legal instrument. The competence to review secretariat arrangements is inherent in the plenary organ that made the initial request to an institution to provide or host the secretariat.

A review of the text of the sixteen selected conventions (see Table 3) shows that, in many of the cases, such a review-making power is explicitly laid down in the treaty itself. This has been linked, however, to a certain majority of the votes of the contracting parties in the plenary body of the convention. The criterion of specific majority voting (three-fourths or two-thirds) can be seen in the cases of a few conventions (POPs, PIC, and the Ramsar Convention). It is interesting that, in the case of the CMS, the COP is expected to make "alternative arrangements" only if the "United Nations Environment Programme is no longer able to provide the Secretariat."[35] In the case of other MEAs reviewed, there is no reference to a specific review mechanism. That, however, does not mean that the COP, reflecting the sovereign will of the contracting parties, can not review the secretariat arrangements already made. For instance, this inherent power was emphasized and invoked by the Standing Committee of CITES, to ask for an explanation from UNEP's DEC regarding secretariat services provided to CITES in lieu of a 13 percent overhead paid

voting, to entrust the secretariat functions to one or more other competent international organizations, should it find that the Secretariat is not functioning as intended"; Article IX of the CMS (1979), which states: "If the United Nations Environment Programme is no longer able to provide the Secretariat, the Conference of the Parties shall make alternative arrangements for the Secretariat"; and Article 8 of the Ramsar Convention (1971), which states: ". . . until such time as another organization or government is appointed by a majority of two-thirds of all Contracting Parties."

[35] The possibility of review could be triggered in this case when UNEP is deemed to be unable to continue providing secretariat services to CMS. For this, the CMS Standing Committee and the COP will need to arrive at a consensus in the matter. In essence, it will amount to an end of the original contractual arrangement put into place by the COP. Thus, what amounts to inability of UNEP could be a matter of judgment of the CMS Standing Committee and the COP. It could be helpful if, in the future, the CMS is able to extract a relationship agreement from UNEP that prescribes the criteria for arriving at such a judgment.

to the UNEP, and they even hinted that – if not satisfied – they would be free to explore alternative secretariat arrangements.[36]

Host Institution as a Secretariat

In cases where an existing international institution is requested to provide secretariat services for the convention, the purpose is to take advantage of the already-established structure. It is not only a cost-saving measure; it seeks to benefit from the expertise of the concerned institution. The underlying assumption is to put the experience, established administrative practice, and stature of the existing institution to work for the newly born convention. The parties apparently do not wish to start *de novo* the ritual of institution building for the convention when established actors have already been playing a role in the field.

The new arrangement to be created involves carving out[37] a part of the existing institution that works exclusively as and performs the role

[36] It is understood that, after the controversy surrounding one of the former secretaries-general of CITES, its Standing Committee decided to put its foot down regarding the competence of the host institution (UNEP) on arbitrary selection or removal of the head of the secretariat. The Standing Committee specially called the then-head of the UNEP DEC, Jeorge Illueca, to explain the quality and nature of services that were provided by UNEP to CITES in lieu of 13 percent overhead. In fact, a message was sought to be conveyed that, if the standing committee was not satisfied with UNEP's services, it could choose another host institution. This message probably made UNEP agree on a special relationship agreement with CITES. It was explicitly agreed that "The Executive Director will inform the Standing Committee in advance of any significant action with respect to the Secretariat which may affect the interests of the Parties or the efficient administration of the Convention, and will consider carefully the views the Standing Committee presents to him/her on such actions." Moreover, in the matter of the selection of the secretary-general, onus was placed on the UNEP ED to have an effective consultation in a manner such that "every effort will be made to appoint a Secretary General acceptable to the Standing Committee . . . "; see Basic Principles 2 and 5 of the Agreement Signed between the Chairman of the CITES Standing Committee and the ED of UNEP on June 20, 1997 (on file with the author; see Appendice II, p. 191).

[37] The formulations used in MEAs could sometimes create confusion regarding the method of providing the secretariat. In general, it seems, the issue is left to the discretion of the concerned host institution that has agreed to provide the secretariat

of a "secretariat" for the convention. It triggers the delicate relationship with an existing institution that will play the role of "host" for the functions described in an international legal instrument. To bring this entity into fruition – to work as a special convention secretariat – the head of that institution is vested with relevant authority. By doing so the COP assigns a slice of its own legal competence to the head of the host institution to carry out the task of constitution of a secretariat. This fact underscores that final say in the 'arrangement' remains with the COP. The common language, for instance, that "Secretariat functions shall be performed (provided) by the Executive Director of UNEP"[38] does not mean that the concerned person shall carry out the task personally. In fact, the case of an interesting pattern of the signing of the CBD headquarters agreement with Canada reflects this mistaken usurpation of legal capacity of the convention secretariat. It seems that the then UNEP ED, instead of the CBD executive secretary, insisted on personally signing this agreement.[39] The same ED did agree, however, to sign the "administrative arrangements"[40] agreement with the CBD's Executive Secretary.

The phrase [secretariat functions shall be performed (provided)] could be construed to mean that UNEP's ED shall put into place

services. The trend shows that whenever the secretariat is located at the headquarters of the host institution, an appropriate place is earmarked for the purpose. There are three such noticeable arrangements, namely, the Ozone Secretariat located at UNEP premises in Nairobi; the Ramsar Bureau located within IUCN premises in Gland, and the WHC located at UNESCO premises in Paris. It needs to be seen in this context as to how much this arrangement reflects the autonomous standing of the treaty body. Of these three, strangely, the WHC seems to be the only one that is treated as an integral part of UNESCO.

[38] The meaning of the phrase "secretariat services shall be performed by the Executive Director of UNEP" cannot be taken in a literal sense. If so, it could obliterate the legal capacity of the secretariat of the convention.

[39] See the Headquarters Agreement between the Executive Director of UNEP (Elizabeth Dowdeswell) on behalf of the Secretariat of the CBD, and the representative of the Government of Canada (Robert Fowler) for the Government of Canada on October 25, 1996, in New York; see Appendice VI, p. 257.

[40] This Agreement was signed between the then ED of UNEP, Elizabeth Dowdeswell and the Executive Secretary of CBD, Calestous Juma, on June 30, 1997; see Appendice III, p. 199.

a suitable institutional arrangement that will perform the role of "secretariat" for the concerned convention. Ironically, no precise pattern or contours of such an arrangement has so far been institutionalized. Each of the patterns has its own limitation as it was revealed in an assessment done by the Ramsar Bureau.[41] That role triggers a series of institutional and legal implications to ensure that an entity caters to the specific mandate laid down in the text of the instrument.

Without necessitating the laborious task of setting up a secretariat independently, the arrangement aims at earmarking (parceling out) a piece of the "requested institution" that will host the secretariat arrangement required by the convention. The practical effect will be literally to rent out part of the host institution (in lieu of 13 percent overheads) that will work as a dedicated secretariat. It is the head of the host institution who is initially expected to play a crucial role in assigning some of the staff to work as per the mandate for the secretariat. In accepting the request made by the COP to the convention, the head of UNEP agrees to carry out the relevant tasks and obligations. Thus, he is answerable to the COP as far as his role and that of the secretariat as indicated by the UNEP is concerned.[42] The convention text is generally devoid of clear guidelines[43] regarding the discharge of the UNEP ED's responsibilities. Those guidelines could be spelled out through a special relationship or administrative arrangements.

[41] See Ramsar Bureau, "Legal Status of the Ramsar Convention Secretariat," Doc. SC 36–15, Thirty-sixth Meeting of the Standing Committee of the Ramsar Convention,, Gland, February 27–29, 2008; Convention on Wetlands of International Importance (Ramsar), February 2, 1971; see *ILM*, vol. 22, 1982.

[42] In this context, the host institution is accountable to the COP and the standing committee of the convention, especially as the relationship is borne out of contractual arrangement.

[43] Almost all the texts relating to secretariats do not explicitly spell out how the head of the host institutions (UNEP ED) is to carry out the responsibility for the secretariat functions entrusted to him. The evolving trend is for the relationship agreements to spell out the details of this responsibility. For instance, see the respective relationship agreements concerning Ramsar, CITES, and CBD in Appendices I, II, and III at pp. 181, 191, and 199.

Functions of the Host Institution

The secretariat arrangements made for a sectoral environmental issue include specific functions to be performed to help the entire treaty regime run smoothly. Treaty-making practices especially during the last three decades show that a range of functions is listed in the text of the instrument itself.[44] In general, all of the secretariats are expected to make arrangements for and provide services to the meetings of the COP and the subsidiary bodies. Similarly, other important roles that the secretariat (or the host institution acting as secretariat for the convention) is required to play include providing assistance to the parties in the implementation of the convention, preparing necessary reports as required by the parties, ensuring necessary coordination with other international bodies, and putting into place the necessary administrative and contractual arrangements for the effective discharge of its functions.

Some of the functions that the secretariat is expected to perform necessitate a certain measure of international legal personality.[45] It has been made clear that the rights and duties of an entity must depend on its "purposes and functions as specified or implied in its constituent documents and developed in practice."[46] It appears that the possession of

[44] For instance, see Article 8, Convention on Wetlands of International Importance (1971), 11 *ILM* 963 (1972); Article 14, Convention for the Protection of the World Cultural and Natural Heritage (1972), 12 *ILM* 1385 (1972); Article XII, CITES (1972), 12 *ILM* 1055 (1973); Article 11, LRTAP (1979), 18 *ILM* 1442 (1979); Article IX, CMS (1979), 19 *ILM* 15 (1980); Article 7, Convention for the Protection of the Ozone Layer (1985), 26 *ILM* 1529 (1987); Article 16, Convention on the Control of Transboundary Movements of Hazardous Wastes and their Disposal (1989), 30 *ILM* 775 (1991); Article 8, UNFCCC (1992), 31 *ILM* 849 (1992); Article 24, CBD (1992), 31 *ILM* 818 (1992); and Article 23, UNCCD (1994), 33 *ILM* 1332 (1994).

[45] There appears to be consensus on the issue that the international legal personality of each of the MEA secretariats is warranted to enable them to carry out their responsibilities assigned under respective conventions. Some of the distinct tasks that a secretariat is required to perform include entering into a headquarters agreement in the host country as well as, where required, entering into relationship agreement with the host institution.

[46] See Reparations for Injuries Suffered in the Service of the UN, *ICJ Reports*, 1949, p. 180.

"treaty-making powers"[47] is an important attribute of the international legal personality of an entity such as the convention secretariat. The secretariat is a body that is created because of the concerned treaty and is expected to play a vital role in carrying out day-to-day functions as well as carrying out the decisions and the will of the contracting parties. These functions include performing a wide range of roles that bring the secretariat into a relationship with the host country agencies, the host institution itself, respective authorities of the contracting parties, other international organizations, and so forth. Such roles would necessitate a reasonable measure of international legal personality for entering into administrative and contractual relationships. Many such roles are in fact warranted because of the mandate given under the concerned treaty as well as specific decisions of the COP when it expects the secretariat to carry out operational requirements. The secretariat is expected to possess and in fact exercise a juridical personality to operate on the international level. In essence, this also means that the legal personality of the secretariat is reflected through the "signature" appended on the headquarters agreement and/or the relationship agreement. The formal procedures, including the signing of relevant papers, are in fact carried out by the head of the secretariat (or any other designated official).

Similarly, certain secretariat functions also need to be carried out under the subsequent instruments that emerge from the parent treaty. In such cases, the existing secretariat of the convention generally performs the same functions for the new instrument. Most of the protocols carry the standard clause that the secretariat functions shall be carried out by the secretariat of the convention. Such specific references are found in the 2000 (Basel Convention) Hazardous Wastes Protocol on Liability and Compensation, the 2000 Cartagena Protocol on Biosafety, and the 1997 Kyoto Protocol on Climate Change.[48] It is interesting that the 1985 Vienna Convention already contained a provision that expected its

[47] Quincy Wright, "The Jural Personality of the UN", *AJIL*, 1949, pp. 509–516.

[48] The Basel Protocol on Liability and Compensation for Damage resulting from Transboundary Movements of Hazardous Wastes and Their Disposal was adopted by the Fifth COP meeting of the Basel Convention. For text of the Protocol, see Report of

secretariat to "perform the functions assigned to it by any protocol."[49] As a corollary, the 1987 Montreal Protocol contained no reference at all as to who would perform such secretariat[50] functions. In view of the organic (original) link of the convention to subsequent protocols, no provision was made for an "interim" secretariat. Thus it is generally provided that functions of the convention secretariat "shall apply *mutatis mutandis* to this Protocol."

Cost Effectiveness

The cost factor, in general, weighs heavily in favor of the decision to locate the secretariat of a convention in an existing institution. It is the contracting parties who balance different factors in reaching such a determination. If the parties are willing to shoulder the burden of an independent secretariat, they could do so. In some cases, the secretariat is initially located in the host country that convenes the final conference of plenipotentiaries. In such cases, the host country (through the nodal ministry) performs secretariat functions, including the task of receiving instruments of ratification/accession as well as the task of registering the convention after its entry into force.[51] It is the COP that could decide to

the Conference of the Parties to the Basel Convention, Fifth Meeting, December 6–10, 1999; UNEP/CHW.5/29, December 10, 1999, Annex III, pp. 88–111; The Protocol on Biosafety to the CBD was adopted by the First Extraordinary Meeting of the COP to the CBD, Cartagena, February 22–24, 1999, and Montreal, January 24–29, 2000. See Decision EM-I/3, as well as Annex in UNEP/CBD/ExCOP/1/3, February 20, 2000 at pp. 38 and 42–65; see www.biodiv.org/biosafety; and The Kyoto Protocol to the UNFCCC, 1997; see www.unfccc.int.

[49] See Article 7, Convention for the Protection of the Ozone Layer (1985), *ILM*, vol. 26 (1987), p. 1529.

[50] See Article 12, Protocol on Substances that Deplete the Ozone Layer (Montreal, 1987), *ILM*, vol. 26, 1987, p. 1550.

[51] The task of registration of the convention is an important indicator of its entry into force. Article 102 (1) of the UN Charter requires that "Every treaty and every international agreement entered into by any Member of the United Nations after the present Charter comes into force shall as soon as possible be registered with the Secretariat and published by it." The task is to be carried out with the Treaty Section of the

shift secretariat functions to an independent place or to locate it within an existing institution. Such a decision is made on the basis of an indication from the concerned institution to host the secretariat. The exact place of the secretariat location could be decided on the basis of offers made by different contracting parties regarding building facilities, provision for administrative expenses for the secretariat, and rental and other expenses. The choice is made on the basis of the most generous offer that is available. Thus, it appears, that the host institution does not have control over the 'seat' (location) of the secretariat since it is the parties to the convention that zero in on the basis of the best offer.

In the cases of some of the smaller conventions, the parties decided to choose independent secretariats. This could be seen especially in the cases of some of the agreements[52] that took shape under the umbrella of the CMS. Moreover, some of the programs from the conventions framed under the RSP are being administered directly by UNEP. In that case, UNEP is also accountable for administering the trust funds and providing financial and budgetary services, as well as providing technical expertise and advice. Thus UNEP has much closer links, and hence is directly involved in all RSP convention projects and activities. In some other cases, RSPs are being administered by other regional organizations,[53] and still other RSPs have established independent

UN. Upon completion of the registration procedure, every treaty is provided a specific number.

[52] So far, seven agreements have been made under the CMS umbrella. These are: Agreement on the Conservation of African-Eurasian Migratory Waterbirds (1999); Agreement on the Conservation of Populations of European Bats (1994); Agreement on the Conservation of Small Cetaceans in the Baltic and North Seas (1994); Agreement on the Conservation of Cetaceans of the Black Seas, Mediterranean and Contiguous Atlantic Area (2001); Agreement on the Conservation of Seals in the Wadden Sea (1991); Agreement on the Conservation of Albatrosses and Petrels (2004); and Agreement on the Conservation of Gorillas and their Habitats (2008). The secretariat for these are: ACAP (Hobart); ACCOBAMS (Monaco); ASCOBANS (merged with CMS Jan. 2007); Eurobats (Bonn); AEWA (Bonn); and Wadden Sea (Wilhelmshaven); see www.cms.int.

[53] These programs are: (i) Commission on the Protection of the Black Sea Against Pollution Permanent Secretariat (Istanbul, Turkey); (ii) North-East Pacific Programme,

secretariats.[54] In this context, it seems, no standard formulas could be derived. Cost effectiveness of the decision, however, remains the most important factor in the issue.

Locating the Secretariat Away from the Host Institution

The primary decision by a COP to make a request to an existing institution triggers the process of a secretariat arrangement. Generally, it is the host institution that works out how to go about providing secretariat services to the COP. Still it is not always possible for the host to locate a convention secretariat at its own seat (headquarters). In fact, as discussed above, the decision in this regard is facilitated by offers made by the contracting parties to house the secretariat. It is the best offer that determines the location of the secretariat. Therefore, it does not necessarily need to coincide with the seat of the host institution. An offshoot of the growing practice of a secretariat being located away from the main seat has contributed to the fragmentation of MEA secretariats. One contributing factor could be an inadequate capacity to house the facility at

Central American Commission for Maritime Transport (Managua, Nicaragua); (iii) Regional Organization for the Conservation of the Environment of the Red Sea and Gulf of Aden (Jeddah, Saudi Arabia); (iv) Regional Organization for the Protection of the Marine Environment (Safat, State of Kuwait); (v) Comisión Permanente del Pacífico Sur (Guayaquil, Ecuador); and (vi) South Pacific Regional Environment Programme (Apia, Western Samoa); see www.unep.org.regionalseas.

[54] The independent secretariats are Protection Arctic Marine Environment (PAME), International Secretariat (Akureyri, Iceland); Commission for the Conservation of Antarctic Marine Living Resources (Tasmania, Australia); Baltic Marine Environment Protection Commission; Helsinki Commission (Helsinki, Finland); Caspian Environment Programme, Programme Coordination Unit (Baku, Azerbaijan); and Commission of the Convention for the Protection of the Marine Environment of the North-East Atlantic; OSPAR Commission (London, United Kingdom). Moreover, UNEP has been entrusted with secretariat responsibility for the following six RSPs: (i) RCU for the Caribbean Environment Programme (Kingston, Jamaica); (ii) RCU for East Asian Seas (Bangkok, Thailand); (iii) RCU of the Eastern African Region (Mahe, Seychelles); (iv) Mediterranean Action Plan (Athens, Greece); (v) RCU (Toyoma, Japan and Busan, South Korea); and (vi) RCU for the West and Central Africa Action Plan (Abidjan 20, Cote d'Ivoire). See www.unep.org.regionalseas.

the headquarters of the host such as UNEP. Therefore, if possible, co-location of secretariats having common synergies as well as use of the host's own regional offices could be explored. It is an intriguing matter as to how far the distance and dispersal from the host institution's seat contribute to the difficulty of supervision.

The issues of the effectiveness of such linkage and the possibility of interference[55] in day-to-day administration of the secretariat by the host institutions have been matters of opinion. For instance, the case of links of the convention secretariats of climate change (UNFCCC) and desertification (UNCCD) to the UN has been seen as a blessing in disguise. Such distance, however, has not necessarily been much help to the convention secretariats, such as CITES (Geneva) and CMS (Bonn) in their autonomous functioning. Thus, it seems that distance does not impinge upon the quality of the secretariat support being provided to the convention.

Chain of Legal Implications

In the process of finding an acceptable institutional base in a host country, a chain of legal implications is triggered, and it leads to a two-stage exercise. As soon as the respective convention comes into force, after fulfilling the necessary ratifications requirement, the first step is

[55] In this context, the role of the head of the host institution is crucial. The extent to which he could exercise control of the day-to-day work of the convention secretariat will decide the level of such interference. For instance, it was thought that the UN Secretary-General with his responsibilities may not meddle in the work of the secretariats (UNFCCC and UNCCD) that are provided secretariat services by the UN. However, in the case of other heads of host institutions, there have been complaints of different levels of interference. In the case of secretariats provided by UNEP, MEAs such as CITES, CMS, CBD, and even Basel have at different times complained about such interference by the UNEP ED on various issues including refusal to accord due legal status to the convention secretariats. In the case of the CBD Headquarters Agreement, the UNEP ED herself chose to affix her signature. Similarly, in the case of CMS, UNEP relented and allowed the CMS Executive Secretary to append his signature on the CMS Headquarters Agreement after a principled stand was taken by the UN Office of Legal Affairs on the issue of legal capacity of the treaty bodies.

to establish an interim secretariat to organize the convening of the first meeting of the COP. The standard formulation, for instance, could be as follows:

> The secretariat functions will be carried out on an interim basis by the United Nations Environment Programme until the completion of the first ordinary meeting of the Conference of the Parties held pursuant to article 6. At its first ordinary meeting, the Conference of the Parties shall designate the secretariat from amongst those existing competent international organizations which have signified their willingness to carry out the secretariat functions under this Convention.[56]

It is this first meeting of the COP during which the decision is made regarding the establishment of the permanent secretariat of the convention, location of the secretariat within an existing institution or independent secretariat, as well as various ground rules for the functioning of the servicing arm. In addition to the decision on which international institution will house the secretariat, a crucial decision is also made regarding the host country for the secretariat. These successive steps require a series of legal instruments among the host institution, host country, and convention secretariat. A headquarters agreement will be needed if the location of the secretariat is in a country different than the one where the host institution is situated.[57] If the convention secretariat is housed within the seat of the host institution, it does not generally require a separate headquarters agreement[58] since the host's own agreement serves that purpose.

[56] Article 7 of the Convention for the Protection of the Ozone Layer (Vienna, 1985). It entered into force September 22, 1988; see *ILM*, vol. 26, 1987, p. 1529.

[57] For instance, in the cases of CMS, UNFCCC, UNCCD, and CBD, separate headquarters agreements were entered into with the host country.

[58] For instance, the secretariats of Ozone, CITES, Basel, and Ramsar were allowed to be governed by the respective headquarters agreements of UNEP (Nairobi), International Environment House (Geneva), and IUCN (Gland).

The host institution is primarily responsible to the COP to provide secretariat services. How the secretariat services will be provided could be spelled out by the COP. It can also be placed on a sound footing by a special relationship agreement[59] between the host institution and the convention secretariat. In some cases in which the secretariat has a closer link to the host institution – when it is considered almost an integral part– specific powers are delegated. For instance, relevant authority has been delegated[60] to the Ramsar Bureau by the Director-General of IUCN.

Conclusion

The growing pattern of MEAs and state practice reveal an organic link between lawmaking and institution-building processes. As a part of the necessity for institutionalized international environmental cooperation, several convention bodies are established. There are variations regarding these bodies as they cater to specific sectoral environmental issues. It is the practice of setting up a convention secretariat, however, that has come to be commonly accepted as it acts as a fulcrum around which the entire treaty regime revolves. Because the practice of locating a secretariat in an existing institution has been consistently resorted to and institutionalized, it brings into being a relationship between the host institution and the COP. The convention secretariat is the product of that legal process of a formal request from the COP to the relevant host institution.

[59] The emerging practice in this respect so far shows three such relationship agreements between the host institution and the convention: (i) IUCN Director-General and the Ramsar Standing Committee; (ii) UNEP and CITES Standing Committee; and (iii) UNEP and CBD Secretariat. For details, see Appendices I, II, and III at pp. 181, 191 and 199.

[60] See the Delegation of Authority (by the IUCN Director-General) to the Secretary-General, Convention on Wetlands of International Importance Especially as Waterfowl Habitat (Ramsar), January 29, 1993 (on file with the author).

The choice of the host institution could be propelled by considerations of organic linkage of the institution to the sectoral issue, purely administrative convenience, or autonomy of the secretariat. The nature and quality of service provided by the secretariat are duly supervised by the COP. The arrangement triggers several crucial legal issues, which cumulatively determine the legal status of the servicing arm of the convention – the secretariat.

5 Legal Status

Introduction

The practice of multilateral environmental regulation is quite diffused, highly fragmented, and "poorly coordinated."[1] It has effectively ushered the states into an era of institutionalized international cooperation. Because the marathon practice has assumed the form of a process – rather than a one-time affair – it poses a challenge for the sovereign states to remain constantly engaged. A series of factors seems to be responsible for nurturing this vibrant process. It comprises not only an institutionalized regulatory approach to address sectoral environmental issues but also a set of institutions that are thought to be necessary to ensure that contracting state parties realize the objectives of the specific sectoral regulatory process at work.

In fact, the institutional actors have been regarded as "critical forces in shaping 'real world' environmental governance systems."[2] Such

[1] Paul C. Szasz, "International Norm-making," in Edith Brown Weiss (Ed.), *Environmental Change and International Law: New Challenges and Dimensions* (Tokyo: UNU, 1992), p. 47.

[2] Oran R. Young et Al., *Institutions and Environmental Change* (Cambridge, MA: MIT Press, 2008), p. xiii. This work, the culmination of a decade-long project on the Institutional Dimensions Programme on Global Environmental Change (IDGEC), adopted the research definition that institutions are a "system of rights, rules, and decision-making procedures." Moreover, it indicated that "institutions play a role in both causing and addressing problems that arise from human-environment interactions but that the nature of this role is complex." *Ibid.*

intergovernmental institutional structures are pressed into service for a variety of purposes.[3] Moreover, when a multilateral regulatory framework is put into place, it is built with its own set of institutional structures. This regulatory framework includes political bodies such as conference and meeting of the parties, scientific and technical bodies, funding mechanisms, and the secretariat. As compared to other institutional structures within a specific legal regime, the secretariat has become almost indispensable. It symbolizes a structural approach at work and is the most visible arm of the regulatory framework. The practice and procedures revolving around secretariat are largely governed by the international law of international institutions.[4] Still, in the specific context of the environmental field, the secretariats have emerged as *sui generis* entities. They, in fact, appear to be the most visible symbols of the sectoral multilateral regulatory process. As discussed in Chapter 4, such secretariats could take an independent form or could be provided by an existing institution that serves as a "host" institution for the purpose. This brings up several legal issues that involve the Conference of the Parties (COP), host institution, host country, and the convention secretariat.

Role of the COP

Multilateral environmental agreements (MEAs) represent sector-specific growth of a regulatory technique. It is essentially a treaty-making exercise that is unique in terms of the issues it seeks to address, embedding urgency, the underlying role of scientific evidence, innovations in

[3] These functions could comprise international environmental rule making, policy making, research, monitoring, training, project financing, and supervision. See Andrew Hurrell and Benedict Kingsbury (Eds.), *The International Politics of the Environment: Actors, Interests and Institutions* (Oxford: Oxford University Press, 1992), p. 30.

[4] For some of the authoritative works on this subject see, generally, Jan Klabbers, *An Introduction to International Institutional Law* (Cambridge: Cambridge University Press, 2002); C.F. Amerasinghe, *Principles of the Institutional Law of International Organizations* (Cambridge: Cambridge University Press, 1996); Henry G. Schermers and Niels M. Blokker, *International Institutional Law*, 3rd rev. ed. (The Hague: Martinus Nijhoff, 1995).

tools and techniques, as well as required institutional structures that provide a 'working' basis for the sovereign states. The institutional structures established within a regime are led by the COP.

In a way, MEAs are a system of the *sui generis* method of grappling with specific sectoral environmental problems. They in general depart from the traditional treaty-making enterprise known to have been followed by the sovereign states in international law. MEAs become virtual "processes"[5] rather than one-time events as they follow a step-by-step consensual approach to design response mechanisms over a period of time. In this vital process role of the plenary body of MEA – the COP – becomes most important.

In the field of international organizations (IO), a plenary organ plays a pivotal role because it has "all the members without exception"[6] having representation. Such an organ is conferred with the status of the supreme decision-making body. Even as the debate still rages whether the respective MEA-driven regime comes within the definition of an IO or not, the plenary body of the regime plays a role akin to the plenary organs of traditional IOs. It is a supreme decision-making body that is instrumental in providing direction to the regulatory process. Because the COP reflects the political will of the contracting states, all of its decisions have to be seen in a long-term perspective. Often, COP decisions trigger the process either to pick up threads of unfinished negotiations or clarify embedded calculated ambiguity under the Intergovernmental Negotiating Committee (INC) due to lack of adequate scientific evidence, paucity of time, or simply due to elusive consensus.

The process is couched in legal formulations. It is, however, essentially based on the bedrock of evolving scientific evidence, cost-effective measures, as well as political convenience of the state parties to the

[5] For that reason, the entire canvas of international law could also be described as a process because it evolves over time. For relevant work on this, see, generally, Rosalyn Higgins, *Problems and Process: International Law and How We Use It* (Oxford: Clarendon Press, 1994).

[6] C.F. Amerasinghe, see n. 4 , p. 134.

Convention. As a corollary to the exalted status of the COP within an MEA, it has the authority to decide on the seat or secretariat. The general practice of treaty making followed and the relevant text incorporated show a pattern at work in this respect. At the outset, the MEA provides an interim arrangement for the setting up of a secretariat. Such a task could be assigned to a country that provided the final venue for adoption of the agreement.

Legal Capacity/Personality

As seen earlier, the regime-based institutions brought into being are "unique"[7] in nature. They are a product of an intergovernmental treaty designed for a sectoral environmental issue. They possess the trappings of an international organization without actually being one. However, the material difference appears to be in terms of the ad hoc character of the treaty that caters to realization of a specific objective for a sectoral environmental issue. In this context, the treaty could be theoretically closed unlike traditional intergovernmental organizations (IGOs), as soon as the objective of the sector specific environmental regulatory framework is realized.

Still, the treaty-based entities need the legal capacity to carry out certain specific tasks on the international level. The question of conferment of such a legal personality still remains a moot point in actual practice. Under national legal systems, it is the human beings who generally possess primary legal personality. At the international level, it is the sovereign states that have this legal capacity as subjects of international law. Any derivative legal or juridical capacity could be conferred upon certain categories of entities that are brought into being for specific purposes. In the absence of such a legal capacity, the entities would not be in a position to perform the assigned tasks. In other words, they would not

[7] Churchill and Ulfstein have sought to examine this uniqueness of MEAs; see Robin R. Churchill and Geir Ulfstein, "Autonomous Institutional Arrangements in Multilateral Environmental Agreements: A Little Noticed Phenomenon in International Law," *AJIL*, vol. 94, no. 4, 2000, pp. 623–59 at 655.

just exist on the radar screen without such a legal capacity. Moreover, they would not be in a position "to participate meaningfully in international and national legal life."[8] The net result would be that they cannot carry out even mundane tasks such as owning some immovable property.

In the case of entities like IOs, their tasks could include the capacity to enter into treaties that create a series of legal relationships like contracts, acquisition and disposal of immovable property, as well as institution of legal proceedings. Most of such tasks need to be performed on the basis of the role of the IO as a legal entity that is distinct from its member states. The capacity to carry out these tasks is popularly described as "juridical personality," as compared to natural persons. It is a ubiquitous legal fiction created purely for functional necessity. In this legal capacity, the IOs carry out important tasks such as the headquarters agreement with the host country. Thus an absence of legal capacity could lead to several practical problems.

In the celebrated *Reparations* case advisory opinion, the International Court of Justice (ICJ) emphatically recognized that the United Nations (UN) is a subject of international law as well as capable of possessing international legal personality. The Court in this context observed that:

> In the opinion of the Court, the Organization was intended to exercise and enjoy, and is in fact exercising and enjoying, functions and rights which can only be explained on the basis of the possession of a large measure of international personality and the capacity to operate upon an international plane . . . and it could not carry out the intentions of its founders if it was devoid of international personality . . . its Members, by entrusting certain functions to it, with the attendant duties and responsibilities have clothed it with the competence required to enable those functions to be effectively discharged."[9]

[8] Henry G. Schermers and Niels M. Blokker, see n. 4, p. 975.

[9] See Reparation for Injuries Suffered in the Service of the United Nations, Advisory Opinion, *ICJ Reports* (1949), p. 174 at 179; available at http://www.icj-cij.org/docket/index.php?p1=3&p2=4&k=41&case=4&code=isun&p3=4.

In arriving at this opinion, the Court seems to have used the rationale of "functional necessity" that refers to the capability to possess certain international rights and duties without being equal to the states in international relations. It has been contended by some scholars that IOs generally exercise only "those powers which have been attributed to them" as a necessary implication whereas powers of the sovereign states are "fundamentally unlimited."[10] It appears that the basis of legal capacity of the IOs is derived from their constituent instruments. As it was shown in the case of the legal personality of the UN by the ICJ, the constructive interpretation either could be made on the basis of the language used in the instrument or implied from the functional powers conferred on the organization.

The question of legal capacity is generally sought to be addressed at the domestic level and at the international level. The former is essential by the very fact of the location of the seat of the IO within the territorial jurisdiction of the sovereign state. That competence comprises the capacity to enter into contracts, to own and dispose of immovable property, as well as to institute proceedings in the local courts. These specific instances of legal capacity at the domestic level are generally enshrined in the headquarters agreement. In fact, there could be variations in terms of legal capacity that an IO possesses in different headquarters agreements.

The question of international legal personality, however, remains crucial. As the ICJ advisory opinion in the *Reparations* case underscored, the capacity to operate on an international level is one of the important determinants of IOs as subjects of international law. An important attribute of such a capacity to operate on the international level includes treaty-making competence. This treaty-making competence of the IOs is almost akin to that of the sovereign states. Most of the established IOs seem to possess the treaty-making capacity to deal with other IOs, sovereign states, as well as other international entities. Such a capacity by

[10] Henry G. Schermers and Niels M. Blokker, see n. 6, p. 981.

its very nature could include both legally binding and non–legally binding agreements as well as arrangements. The fact that the head of the secretariat of an IO appends his signature on an instrument is a testimony to the international legal personality of the IO.

In the backdrop of this discussion one could examine the potential legal capacity of the MEAs. The phenomenal growth in the number and variety of these MEAs poses a challenge regarding their legal capacity to carry out activities both within the domestic jurisdiction of the state wherein their seat is located as well as within their international legal personality. To apply the model of IOs, the crucial question remains as to whether the MEAs are IOs. In this context there could be divergent viewpoints. Still, it seems that, because MEAs generally are sector specific and ad hoc in nature, they fall short of the full-fledged status of an IO. These MEAs have *sui generis* character and often have to decipher their legal capacity. This is demonstrated by the current debate that is prevalent among the convention secretariats.[11] In view of the differences in the history of each of the MEAs, the content of the text of the treaties, and the secretariat services being provided by an international institution (e.g., the UN Educational, Scientific and Cultural Organization [UNESCO], the International Union for Conservation of Nature and Natural Resources [IUCN], and the UN Environment Programme [UNEP]), the competence of the convention secretariats still remains a nagging issue because an MEA is a product of intergovernmental negotiations on a specific sectoral environmental issue and an overwhelming number of sovereign states are parties to it.

The question of legal capacity of the secretariat remains crucial. As a plenary body, the COP and/or standing committee could only express its view on the legal capacity of the MEA that is manifested through actions of the secretariat. It is interesting that many of the texts of MEAs remain silent as far as legal capacity is concerned. As a result, most of the

[11] For instance, the Standing Committees of the 1971 Ramsar Convention, as well as 1973 CITES, have been engaged in intensive deliberations on the "legal status" of their respective secretariats; see Web sites of both MEAs for relevant documents.

MEAs – as represented by their secretariats – try to decipher their legal capacity not only from their constituent instrument but also from their headquarters agreement (with the host state) and any specific relationship agreement (with the host institution). Thus there seem to be legitimate quest to deduce legal capacity from the chain of legal relationships that arise from various legal instruments surrounding the MEA.

Legal Character of Treaty Bodies

As seen earlier in text, the MEAs in general are not treated as full-fledged IOs, but they are akin to IOs in several respects. Variations in MEAs include the treaty bodies that are set up under the specific treaty. The overarching umbrella is of course provided by the COP. It is the supreme decision-making body of the convention; although it does not have a permanent character, it holds meetings at regular intervals in which all the state parties participate.

As a plenary organ, the COP is a repository of the standing, autonomy, and legal status of the MEA. It is the COP that is instrumental in laying down the framework of subsidiary bodies within the regime. The only visible arm of the MEA remains the secretariat, however. It is the COP that has the authority to decide the nature, competence, powers, location, as well as legal personality of the secretariat. The very arrangement for the constitution of the secretariat is formalized by the COP. It is the COP that has to decide the fate of the interim secretariat that comes into being upon adoption of the text of the treaty. Every MEA text generally comprises a statement regarding the establishment of a secretariat as well as the specific functions that are entrusted to it. A mere perusal of the provisions relating to the establishment of the secretariat in the text of the MEA does not provide any explicit indication about the extent of autonomy and legal capacity of the secretariat.

It appears that the secretariat is by and large expected to be a facilitating arm of the MEA. How much competence a secretariat possesses can be traced to the text of the convention, the role of the COP (and its executive organ, the standing committee), as well as the attitude and flexibility provided by the host institution. For instance, the functions of the secretariat enumerated in the text of the 1979 Convention on Migratory Species of Wild Animals (CMS) do not have any provisions regarding the capacity of the secretariat to enter into any administrative and contractual agreements or arrangements. In such a situation, the proponents of the implied powers theory could argue for relevant competence as necessitated by the functions assigned to the secretariat. That route can bring in an element of uncertainty as well as legal wrangling, which was amply demonstrated in a flurry of correspondence and sharp legal posturing witnessed prior to the final adoption of the 2002 Headquarters Agreement[12] of the CMS secretariat. It was indeed a treat to study and observe from the sidelines the crystallization of this instrument as well as valiant efforts of the CMS secretariat, then headed by the formidable German lawyer Arnulf Müller-Helmbrecht, to assert its legal personality.

The arguments for and against the legal capacity of the CMS secretariat (even to put its signature in its own capacity on the said headquarters agreement) opened the debate concerning the nature of autonomy that the MEA secretariats possess. In this episode, the Office of Legal Affairs of the UN (UN OLA) was insisting on a tripartite agreement among the government of Germany, the UN, and the CMS secretariat, whereas UNEP was insisting on a bilateral agreement only. Although finally the stand of the UN OLA prevailed, the initial stand of UNEP did not favor the international legal personality of the secretariat. The process underscored the graphic reality that in the practice of host institution-secretariat relationship, in many cases, the host institutions did not favor the legal personality of the secretariat, especially in the absence of any specific reference to that effect in the text of the convention. That probably could explain the gradual inclination of the

[12] See Appendice X at p. 315.

secretariats and the COP to prefer the inclusion of specific provisions in the relationship agreements.[13]

Four Models of Secretariats

As a visible organ of the MEA, a secretariat plays a pivotal role in the workings of the convention. It is a corollary to the treaty-making process. It has now almost become routine to establish a secretariat that caters to the needs of the convention. In this context, how and where a secretariat is set up remains an important question. If there is a clear intention on the part of the contracting parties to the convention, they can establish an independent secretariat. Such an independent secretariat could be akin to the secretariat of an international organization. Alternatively, the states could consider other options such as locating the secretariat within an existing specialized agency of the UN, within one of the programs of the UN or linked to the UN headquarters or any other international entity. These are the four patterns of secretariats that are currently in practice among the MEAs. Each of these models could have its own advantages and disadvantages. What specific form of secretariat is chosen for a convention, however, depends on the views of the contracting states, prevailing practice, nature of the sectoral environmental issue, and other factors.

a) **Specialized Agency:** Specialized agencies[14] of the UN are functional international organizations (see Table 4). These agencies are high profile and wedded to a specific functional area (e.g., health, labor, civil aviation, atomic energy).

[13] See Appendices I, II, and III at pp. 181, 191, and 199.

[14] These specialized agencies are basically functional international organizations. They are established by an intergovernmental agreement as per Article 57 of the UN Charter. They are designated as specialized agencies if brought into relationship with the UN in accordance with the provisions of Article 63 of the UN Charter. It is the Economic and Social Council (ECOSOC) of the UN that enters into specific relationship agreements with the concerned organization. For details on the role of the ECOSOC in this respect, see UN, *Basic Facts About the United Nations* (New York: UN, 2004), Chapter 3, p. 141.

Table 4. *Comparative Picture of Specialized Agencies of the UN*

No.	UN Specialized Agencies	Mandate	Institutional Structure	Functions	Constituent Instrument
1	UN Industrial Development Organization (UNIDO), Vienna, Austria	To reduce poverty in countries with developing and transitional economies through sustainable industrial growth. UNIDO has responsibility for promoting industrialization throughout the developing world.	General Conference, Industrial Development Board, Programme and Budget Committee	UNIDO's assistance is delivered through two core functions: a normative function as a Global Forum, and an operational function, providing technical cooperation. The broad programatic objectives and priorities of UNIDO are given in the Business Plan on the Future Role and Functions of UNIDO, endorsed by the seventh session of the General Conference in 1997, in its resolution GC.7/Res.1.	Constitution of UNIDO 1979; established by the UN General Assembly in 1966; became UN specialized agency in 1985.
2	UNESCO, Paris, France	To promote international cooperation among its member states and six Associate members in the fields of education, science, culture, and communication	Governing bodies: General Conference and Executive Board Director-General Secretariat	UNESCO functions as a laboratory of ideas and a standard-setter to forge universal agreements on emerging ethical issues. The Organization also serves as a clearinghouse – for the dissemination and sharing of information and knowledge – while helping member states to build their human and institutional capacities in diverse fields.	Constitution of UNESCO, 1946

(*continued*)

Table 4 *(continued)*

No.	UN Specialized Agencies	Mandate	Institutional Structure	Functions	Constituent Instrument
3	International Labor Organization (ILO), Geneva, Switzerland	Seeks the promotion of social justice and internationally recognized human and labor rights	Three main bodies, all of which encompass the unique feature of the Organization: its tripartite structure (government, employers, workers)	The ILO formulates international labor standards in the form of conventions and recommendations setting minimum standards of basic labor rights: It promotes the development of independent employers' and workers' organizations and provides training and advisory services to those organizations.	ILO Constitution established in 1919; became first UN specialized agency in 1946
4	International Atomic Energy Agency (IAEA), Vienna, Austria	Seeks to accelerate and enlarge the contribution of atomic energy to peace, health, and prosperity throughout the world	Board of Governors and the General Conference of all member states	To encourage and assist research on, and development and practical application of, atomic energy for peaceful uses throughout the world; fosters the exchange of scientific and technical information on peaceful uses of atomic energy	IAEA Statute, 1957, as an autonomous agency under the UN
5	Food and Agriculture Organization (FAO), Rome, Italy	To raise levels of nutrition, improve agricultural productivity, better the lives of rural populations, and contribute to the growth of the world economy	FAO is governed by the Conference of member nations, composed of eight departments	Leads international efforts to defeat hunger. Serving both developed and developing countries, FAO acts as a neutral forum where all nations meet as equals to negotiate agreements and debate policy. FAO is also a source of knowledge and information.	FAO Constitution, 1945

6	International Civil Aviation Organization (ICAO), Montréal, Canada	To ensure the safe, efficient, and orderly evolution of international civil aviation	The Organization is made up of an Assembly, a Council, and a Secretariat. The chief officers are the President of the Council and the Secretary-General.	Promotion of global aviation safety by determining the status of implementation of relevant ICAO SARPs, associated procedures, and safety-related practices. ICAO works to achieve its vision of safe, secure, and sustainable development of civil aviation through cooperation among its member states. It is the global forum for civil aviation.	Convention on International Civil Aviation (also known as Chicago Convention), 1944
7	International Fund for Agricultural Development (IFAD), Rome, Italy	To finance agricultural development projects primarily for food production in the developing countries; to enable the rural poor to overcome poverty	The Governing Council, The Executive Board	IFAD works with governments to develop and finance programs and projects that enable rural poor people to overcome poverty themselves. IFAD tackles poverty not only as a lender, but also as an advocate for rural poor people. Its multilateral base provides a natural global platform to discuss important policy issues that influence the lives of rural poor people.	Agreement Establishing IFAD, 1977
8	International Monetary Fund (IMF), Washington, DC, USA	To promote international monetary cooperation, exchange stability, and orderly exchange arrangements; to foster economic growth and high levels	The IMF is governed by, and is accountable to, its member countries through its Board of Governors.	The work of the IMF is of three main types. Surveillance involves the monitoring of economic and financial developments, and the provision of policy advice, aimed	Articles of Agreement of the International Monetary Fund, 1944

(continued)

Table 4 *(continued)*

No.	UN Specialized Agencies	Mandate	Institutional Structure	Functions	Constituent Instrument
		of employment; and to provide temporary financial assistance to countries to help ease balance-of-payments adjustment	The day-to-day work of the IMF is carried out by the Executive Board, Secretariat.	especially at crisis prevention. The IMF also lends to countries with balance-of-payments difficulties, to provide temporary financing and to support policies aimed at correcting the underlying problems; loans to low-income countries are also aimed especially at poverty reduction. Third, the IMF provides countries with technical assistance and training in its areas of expertise. Supporting all three of these activities is IMF work in economic research and statistics.	
9	International Maritime Organization (IMO), London, UK	To provide machinery for cooperation among governments in the field of governmental regulation and practices relating to technical matters of all kinds affecting shipping engaged in international trade; to encourage and facilitate the general adoption of the highest practicable standards in matters concerning maritime safety,	The Organization consists of an Assembly, a Council, and four main Committees: the Maritime Safety Committee; the Marine Environment Protection Committee; the Legal Committee; and the Technical	The worldwide implementation of the standards and regulations adopted by the Organization. IMO is primarily concerned with the safety of shipping and the prevention of marine pollution, but the Organization has also introduced regulations covering liability and compensation for damage, such as pollution, caused by ships.	The Convention establishing the International Maritime Organization, 1959

		efficiency of navigation, and prevention and control of marine pollution from ships.	Co-operation Committee. There is also a Facilitation Committee and a number of subcommittees.		
10	International Telecommunication Union (ITU), Geneva, Switzerland	To maintain and extend international cooperation between all its member states for the improvement and rational use of telecommunications of all kinds to coordinate the operation of telecommunication networks and services and advance the development of communications technology	The main legal bodies of the Union are the Plenipotentiary Conference, Council, and General Secretariat.	The three sectors of the Union – Radio communication (ITU-R), Telecommunication Standardization (ITU-T), and Telecommunication Development (ITU-D) – work to build and shape tomorrow's networks and services. Their activities cover all aspects of telecommunication, from setting standards that facilitate seamless interworking of equipment and systems on a global basis to adopting operational procedures for the vast and growing array of wireless services and designing programs to improve telecommunication infrastructure in the developing world.	International Telegraph Convention, originally founded in 1865, became UN specialized agency in 1947

(*continued*)

Table 4 *(continued)*

No.	UN Specialized Agencies	Mandate	Institutional Structure	Functions	Constituent Instrument
11	Universal Postal Union (UPU), Berne, Switzerland	To develop social, cultural, and commercial communication between people through the efficient operation of the postal service. As an intergovernmental institution, the UPU is called on to play an important leadership role in promoting the continued revitalization of postal services. It is the primary forum for cooperation between postal-sector players and helps to ensure a truly universal network of up-to-date products and services.	The Universal Postal Council of Administration, Postal Operations Council, Consultative Committee, International Bureau		The Constitution of the UPU established by the Bern Treaty 1874; became UN specialized agency in 1948
12	World Health Organization (WHO), Geneva, Switzerland	Attainment by all peoples of the highest possible level of health. Health is defined in WHO's Constitution as a state of complete physical, mental, and social well-being and not merely the absence of disease or infirmity.	The World Health Assembly, The Executive Board. The Secretariat of WHO, headed by the Director-General		WHO Constitution, 1948

13	World Intellectual Property Organization (WIPO), Geneva, Switzerland	Dedicated to developing a balanced and accessible international intellectual property (IP) system, which rewards creativity, stimulates innovation, and contributes to economic development while safeguarding the public interest.	General Assembly, a Conference, a Coordination Committee, the Secretariat, or International Bureau directed by the Director-General	WIPO's activities are conducted within the strategic framework set out in the biennial Program and Budget document and are driven by demand from member states. They fall broadly into the following areas: developing international IP laws and standards; delivering global IP protection services; encouraging the use of IP for economic development; and promoting better understanding of IP.	WIPO Convention, 1970; became UN specialized agency in 1974
14	World Bank Group, Washington, DC, USA	Facilitator of postwar reconstruction and development; present-day mandate of worldwide poverty alleviation in conjunction with its affiliate, the International Development Association	Board of Governors, Executive Directors, President of the World Bank, management and senior staff, and the vice presidents in charge of regions, sectors, networks, and functions	Reconstruction remains an important focus of its work, given the natural disasters and postconflict rehabilitation needs that affect developing and transition economies. It has, however, broadened its focus to include social sector lending projects, poverty alleviation, debt relief, and good governance.	Articles of Agreement of the International Bank for Reconstruction and Development, 1945

(*continued*)

Table 4 *(continued)*

No.	UN Specialized Agencies	Mandate	Institutional Structure	Functions	Constituent Instrument
15	World Meteorological Organization (WMO), Geneva, Switzerland		The Executive Council, the executive body, the Secretariat, headed by the Secretary-General	It is the UN system's authoritative voice on the state and behavior of the Earth's atmosphere, its interaction with the oceans, the climate it produces, and the resulting distribution of water resources.	WMO Constitution, 1951
16	World Tourism Organization (WTO), Madrid, Spain	Leading international organization in the field of tourism. It serves as a global forum for tourism policy issues and a practical source of tourism know-how.	The General Assembly, Executive Council, Regional Commissions, Committees, and the Secretariat led by the Secretary-General	It plays a central and decisive role in promoting the development of responsible, sustainable, and universally accessible tourism, with the aim of contributing to economic development. It plays a catalytic role in promoting technology transfers and international cooperation, in stimulating and developing public–private sector partnerships and in encouraging the implementation of the Global Code of Ethics for Tourism.	World Tourism Organization Constitution established in 1925; became UN specialized agency in 2003

It is interesting that, of the sixteen functional IOs having a relationship agreement with the UN, there is no agency exclusively devoted to the environment. In fact, very early on, one of the specialized agencies like UNESCO was playing a role in the environmental field. Through its Man and Biosphere program, UNESCO has been instrumental in establishing two global conventions, namely, the 1971 Convention on Wetlands of International Importance (the Ramsar Convention) and the 1972 World Heritage Convention (WHC). UNESCO provides a secretariat to the WHC. In fact, UNESCO claims to house the secretariat of the WHC (the World Heritage Centre) within UNESCO itself. It is regarded as an "integral part of the UNESCO secretariat."[15] As a corollary, the World Heritage Centre does not have a separate legal personality from the internal perspective of UNESCO. It is contended that Article 14 of the Convention stipulates that the World Heritage Committee would be assisted by a secretariat appointed by the Director-General of UNESCO. It seems that the said requirement has been fulfilled by carving out the secretariat from within the UNESCO secretariat. This presents an anomalous legal pattern and a model for a secretariat. Being an offspring of the WHC, in legal terms, the World Heritage Centre is a treaty body.

By virtue of the established practice of legal status of the treaty bodies, a secretariat is expected to have an autonomous character. Even if a secretariat is parcelled out of the secretariat of the host institution like UNESCO, the crucial question is "Does that obliterate the standing of the secretariat?" Is the legal personality of the UNESCO secretariat intertwined with the personality of the World Heritage Centre? From the point of view of international institutional law, this does create a piquant situation. This appears to be the only instance of a convention secretariat located within the secretariat of a UN specialized agency that has not been provided with a separate legal personality.

[15] E-mail communication from John Donaldson, UNESCO Legal Office (Paris), July 5, 2003.

For all practical purposes, the general conference of UNESCO and, under its supervision, the Director-General will have the capacity to put into place any agreements, arrangements, or other matters. Another important facet of the peculiar legal position of the World Heritage Centre is that it is governed by the Headquarters Agreement (July 2, 1954)[16] between UNESCO and France. This headquarters agreement recognizes the legal personality of the organization. In the absence of any special arrangement or delegation of authority by UNESCO's Director-General to the director of the Centre, the convention secretariat (World Heritage Centre) needs to operate under the umbrella of the legal capacity of UNESCO. As such, the WHC story remains a legal aberration.

b) **International NGO:** At the time of negotiation of the convention, there are certain international entities (governmental and non-governmental) that work in a specific area (e.g., wildlife, birds, wetlands, and conservation). The role of these entities in the implementation of the convention could be important. As a result, sometimes the convention secretariat is placed under the tutelage of that international entity. An important criterion in this respect appears to be the organic link between the international entity and the convention secretariat. A leading example of this model is provided by the 1971 Ramsar Convention. It seems that the IUCN played an important part in the evolution of the Ramsar Convention. After the entry into force of the Convention, IUCN was requested by the COP to provide services for the Ramsar Bureau (Secretariat). This Bureau was carved out of the IUCN headquarters in Gland. It occupies a portion of the building. As compared to the traditional view regarding autonomy of the treaty

[16] See the headquarters agreement between UNESCO and France, signed in Paris on July 2, 1954. It entered into force on November 23, 1955, as per Article 32 of the Agreement (on the exchange of the instrument of ratification by the Government of the French Republic and the notification of approval by UNESCO).

bodies, the Ramsar Bureau and Secretary-General work under the supervision of the IUCN Director-General. In view of this, it is contended that the Ramsar Bureau has no legal standing.

In fact, the Director-General of IUCN has the overall legal authority for the workings of the Ramsar Convention. The Ramsar Bureau arrangement departs from the WHC, however, especially with respect to the explicit "delegation of authority" provided by the IUCN Director-General. As a result, the Ramsar Bureau appears to possess only limited legal capacity as circumscribed by the terms of the delegation of authority. Even this limited exercise of legal capacity will be conditional upon the extent of scrupulous adherence to the terms of the delegation of authority by the IUCN Director-General. In view of the limitations imposed by the delegation of authority and various problems perceived by the Ramsar Bureau, the Ramsar Standing Committee is currently assessing the issue of the legal status of the Ramsar Bureau. This process involves comparing and considering potential advantages from other patterns of MEA secretariat arrangements. It seems that the triggering of the process has unravelled the suppressed yearning for a full legal personality for the secretariat of the Ramsar Convention.

c) **UN Headquarters:** The UN General Assembly has been playing an active role through the global conferencing in the environmental field. The Assembly, as a plenary organ of the UN, provides political guidance to the sovereign states in the identification of global sectoral environmental issues. In fact, the Assembly, just before the Rio Earth Summit, had identified some environmental issues (e.g., climate change, desertification, and biodiversity) as "common concerns of humankind." As a sequel to this emphatic pronouncement by the Assembly, the negotiating process was set in motion under an INC. These processes led to crystallization of the UN Framework Convention on Climate Change (UNFCCC), the Convention on Biological Diversity (CBD) in 1992, as well as the UN Convention to Combat Desertification (UNCCD) in

> 1994. Of these three, only two carry the prefix "United Nations." This prefix itself connotes the linkage of the UNFCCC[17] and the UNCCD[18] to the UN headquarters. This linkage has come about primarily because the UN General Assembly played a pivotal role in the drafting of these conventions. Moreover, the arrangement was put into place explicitly by virtue of the request made by the COP of the respective conventions to the General Assembly. Upon acceptance of the said request, the requirement for secretariat support has been given effect to by the UN. In this context, the process through which the secretariat arrangement has been worked out and the association with the UN headquarters give an edge to the convention.

The use of the prefix UN appears to add prestige to the concerned secretariat. The discussions that this author has had with the concerned heads of the secretariats showed that the heads have preference for the arrangement (linkage with the UN), especially because of the different chain of command involved. In fact, the executive secretary reports to the secretary-general through the under-secretary-general heading the Department of Management (on administrative and financial matters) and through the under-secretary-general heading the Department of Economic and Social Affairs (on other matters). In practical terms, it means the least interference in the day-to-day functioning of the secretariat by the Secretary-General of the UN. This model has caught the

[17] For UNFCCC, it was the COP decision 14/CP.1 that decided that "the Convention secretariat shall be institutionally linked to the United Nations, while not being fully integrated in the work programme and management structure of any particular department or programme"; see www.unfccc.int. Also see DOC. UNFCCC/CP/1995/5/Add. 4, 6 April 1995, pp. 1–7 (on file with the author).

[18] For UNCCD's linkage with the UN, it was the General Assembly Resolution 51/180 that approved the arrangements (interim) for the secretariat. It was the COP decision 3/COP.1 that accepted the offer of the UN Secretary General (DOCS. A/AC.241/44 and 55) to provide the secretariat support; see Report of the COP on its First Session, Rome, Sept. 29–Oct. 10, 1997; ICCD/COP(1)/11/Add. 1, Dec. 22, 1997 (on file with the author).

attention of the other MEA secretariats. Some of them are toying with the idea of adopting this model not only for prestige but also for sheer convenience.

The secretariats of UNFCCC and UNCCD are located in the German city of Bonn, so this model of secretariat accommodates the entities at a distance from the UN headquarters in New York. It seems that the respective COPs and the General Assembly have put in place a reasonable working relationship. As a result, it is the Secretary-General of the UN who is responsible for the selection process of the executive secretaries of both UNFCCC and UNCCD. It is contended that this model imparts transparency to the selection of the head of the convention secretariat. Still, after the process of nominations and short listing is over, how the final decision is made remains mysterious. Except for the apparent role of the UN Secretary-General in the selection of the Executive Secretary, there does not appear to be much interference in the workings of the convention bodies. This relative lack of interference from the host institution (UN) probably ensures that the secretariat exercises latitude in its work and exercises legal capacity both within the country of its seat (host country) as well as on the international level. For both UNFCCC and UNCCD, the bulk of the provisions of the headquarters agreement for UN Volunteers (UNV) applies. It is interesting that, after accepting the requests of the COPs of UNFCC and UNCCD, the General Assembly has not so far obliged any other convention secretariat to have the status of the UN-administered secretariat.

d) **UNEP-Administered Secretariat:** UNEP is a premier UN entity for environmental protection. It is a program and a subsidiary organ of the UN General Assembly (established by resolution 2997 of December 15, 1972). Although the constituent instrument of UNEP is not explicit regarding its role in lawmaking, it has been playing a catalytic role in the matter. In fact, UNEP has a mandate under its Montevideo Programme to catalyze sectoral environmental agreements. As a result, UNEP performs the role

> of a 'mother' and helps in nurturing many of the MEAs. As a corollary, UNEP is assigned the responsibility of carrying out the function of the secretariat, which generally takes place even prior to the entry into force of the convention. The rationale for assigning secretariat responsibility to UNEP seems also to be the availability of an established administrative structure.

This arrangement could vary from convention to convention. For instance, the text of the Convention on International Trade in Endangered Species (CITES) itself designated UNEP as a secretariat. In other cases like the 1989 Basel Convention and the 1992 CBD, the decision to designate UNEP for the secretariat support was decided at the first meeting of the COP. In this respect, various formulations have been used, including designating the UNEP's Executive Director to carry out functions of the secretariat, requesting UNEP to provide a secretariat, or even designating UNEP as the secretariat.

As a result of UNEP's engagement in the lawmaking process, a good number of convention secretariats are being administered by it. Now there are at least seven conventions that are being serviced by UNEP. These secretariats are located in Nairobi (Ozone), Geneva (Basel and CITES), Montreal (CBD), and Bonn (CMS). Two more secretariats also located in Geneva are the Stockholm and Rotterdam secretariats, which are being administered jointly with the Food and Agriculture Organization (FAO). These convention secretariats are being serviced by the Division of Environmental Conventions within UNEP. In fact, because UNEP provides secretariat services to the concerned conventions, it is paid 13 percent overhead. This arrangement is put into place and works entirely at the discretion of the COP (meaning that, if the COP is not satisfied with the services provided by UNEP, in principle the secretariat could be shifted elsewhere). It also means that, if the COP considers it appropriate, the secretariat could have independent status or could be hosted by another international institution. The issue of quality of service provided and the treatment meted out to the secretariat (including appointment of the head of the secretariat) have often become bones of contention.

The fact that UNEP has been asked to provide secretariat services for a specific convention is construed as authorizing the executive director to work out the structure and composition of the servicing arm of the convention. In this respect, the executive director is, of course, accountable to the COP of the convention. It is the executive director who has a decisive say in the selection of the Executive Secretary of the convention despite the fact that a selection process is put into place for that purpose. In a way, there are pro forma contentions that UNEP "exercises limited control over secretariats, mainly ensuring that UN Rules and Regulations are followed in personnel and administrative matters."[19] It is also argued that "the secretariats have their own legal capacity according to the headquarters Agreements... In matters of finance and personnel, UNEP still has a consultative function (e.g. the trust funds for each convention are administered from UNEP headquarters)."[20]

Apart from selecting the head of the secretariat, UNEP also has a significant say in the employment of officials of the secretariats. The nature and depth of these effective controls on the composition and work of the secretariat could be deciphered from this emphatic assertion by the executive director:

> It can appoint, promote, and terminate staff. As a consequence of the staff as its employees, the host organisation must also be able to direct officials in personnel and administrative matters. UNEP provides support services to the conventions in the area of Human Resources management and budget and financial management. Each convention is different and the nature of the elements of the support UNEP provides is tailored to the needs of that convention, hence the fact that some relationships are guided by written agreements while others are not. Any potential difficulties that arise are addressed on

[19] Alexandre Timoshenko's (Legal, Economics and Other Instruments Unit, UNEP, Nairobi) communication to the author dated July 6, 2000 (on file with the author).

[20] Alinka Konrad's (Intern) e-mail communication to the author dated July 17, 2000 (on file with the author).

> as – needed or case-by-case basis. UN Rules and Regulations govern the functioning of UNEP in administrative matters.[21]

Still, it seems, while rendering secretariat services to the convention, UNEP is expected to take into account the perception of the COP and the Standing Committee.

Possibilities of Conflict

The setting up of a secretariat as a part of an existing international entity is almost institutionalized. This process shows that the pattern of convention secretariats – as provided by a host institution – is generally acceptable as compared to independent secretariats to the state parties to the respective conventions. *Prima facie*, the advantage of the practice could be obvious in terms of taking advantage of an established institutional setup, as well as the synergy and organic link to an institution that has a direct interest in the area of the convention. As indicated earlier in text, the arrangement could work without any potential trouble provided the respective parties comply with their part of the deal. It seems, however, that the relationship between the host institutions and the COP (or standing committee) could in some cases result in acrimony.

Because the secretariat acts as a link between the COP and the host institution such as UNEP, it has dual lines of accountability. This delicate position of the secretariat needs to be duly respected, especially by the host institution. It is the secretariat that is required to carry out the decisions of the COP. Ironically, in some cases the host institutions have tried to put pressure on the secretariats not only in staffing and finance but also in other routine matters. Thus, the potential areas of conflict could cover a wide canvas, ranging from appointment of the head of the secretariat to the range and ambit of the secretariat's legal capacity. This could even include mundane issues such as domain name of the Web site!

[21] Communication (Ref: OED/AH/1765) to the author from Dr. Klaus Toepfer, Executive Director of UNEP, October 6, 2003 (on file with the author).

Appointment of a Secretary-General

It has been seen that heads of the host institutions have been asserting their unfettered right to choose the head of the secretariat. This choice often goes unchallenged. For instance, when Iwona Rummel-Bulska was shifted as Executive Secretary of the Basel Convention and Per Bakken was sent from UNEP headquarters, it caused considerable disquiet. The action itself was not questioned by the COP or the standing committee, however. In contrast, when the UNEP's Executive Director removed the Secretary-General of CITES, it caused almost a storm. The COP and the standing committee took serious note of it. It led to a debate on working out a proper relationship arrangement with UNEP to define contours of the relationship and to preempt any potential interference. In fact, the then-head of the UNEP Division of Environmental Conventions, Jorge Illueca, was called to Geneva to provide an explanation to the standing committee regarding the "quality" of services provided by UNEP to CITES in lieu of 13 percent overhead being paid by the convention. It finally led to negotiations and adoption of a special relationship agreement between the CITES Standing Committee and the Executive Director of UNEP.[22]

It is interesting that, in a move apparently aiming at clipping the wings of UNEP's Executive Director, one of the (three) "basic principles" clearly requires that "The Executive Director will inform the Standing Committee in advance of any significant action with respect to the secretariat which may affect the interests of the Parties or the efficient administration of the convention, and will consider carefully the views the standing committee presents to him/her on such actions."[23] Even with respect to the appointment of the secretary-general, there is an explicit requirement that the UNEP Executive

[22] Agreement Between the CITES Standing Committee and the Executive Director of UNEP, June 20, 1997; sent with a communication from Jim Armstrong, Deputy Secretary-General, CITES (on file with the author).

[23] *Ibid.*, Principle 2, p. 1 of the Agreement.

Director will have *effective* "consultation" with the CITES Standing Committee. The consultation prescribed in the relationship agreement is not to be superficial or an eyewash but of such a nature that "every effort will be made to appoint a Secretary General acceptable to the Standing Committee."[24] The case of the Secretary-General of CITES underscores the potential problematic nature that the appointment of a head of a secretariat could be. In such cases wherein the UNEP Executive Director asserts his power to appoint the head, its acceptability could depend on the attitude and stand that the COP and/or the standing committee take in the matter.

In this context, the IUCN–Ramsar Bureau (secretariat) relationship[25] provides a model of a working arrangement even when the Bureau does not seem to have a legal personality. Still, in a refreshing stance, the Director-General of IUCN agreed to put into place an arrangement called *delegation of authority*. The said *delegation* covers earmarking of the authority of the IUCN Director-General to the Ramsar Secretary-General, especially concerning staff matters. It is interesting that each of the items listed in the delegation (financial and budgetary, personnel management, and facility management) is also followed by limitations on it. In essence, this arrangement shows that the primary (and original) legal capacity of the Ramsar Convention is vested in the IUCN Director-General.[26] The IUCN Director-General, in turn, has parceled out this authority to the Ramsar Secretary-General. The smooth working of this arrangement could be conditional on the scrupulousness with which the IUCN Director-General respects the terms of the *delegation of authority*.

[24] *Ibid.*, para. 5, p. 2.

[25] Delegation of Authority to the Secretary-General Convention on Wetlands of International Importance Especially as Waterfowl Habitat (Ramsar), January 29, 1993 (on file with the author).

[26] *Ibid.* The Supplementary Note states that: "IUCN, as the legal persona to which the Ramsar Bureau is attached, must inevitably retain ultimate liability for the actions of the Secretary General, in exercising the authority delegated to him" (on file with the author).

It appears that the Ramsar Bureau is uncomfortable with the present IUCN-linked secretariat arrangement. It has triggered a process mandated by the COP *prima facie* to revisit the matter and consider possible options for the secretariat (see Table 5).[27] The ninth meeting of the Ramsar COP resolved to instruct the secretary-general:

> (T)o engage in a consultative process with appropriate bodies such as the IUCN and UNESCO, as well as the government of the host country and other interested organisations and governments, regarding the options, as well as legal and practical implications for the transformation of the status of the Ramsar Secretariat towards an international Organisation or other status whilst still recognising and maintaining its links with IUCN and the host country.[28]

In a detailed assessment note on the legal status of the Ramsar Secretariat, it has listed some of the problems (e.g., budgetary disputes with IUCN, control of financial procedures by IUCN, legal standing of the secretariat subject to the delegation of authority by the IUCN Director-General) that are specifically related to the secretariat being provided by the IUCN.

In a similar quest, the CITES Secretariat is also following the matter concerning legal personality both within the host country and on the international level. Although the CITES Secretariat contends that it has operated under the assumption that it possesses such a legal personality, this is construed as implicit rather than explicit in nature. The Secretariat

[27] The Ramsar Bureau had initiated an extensive consultation process regarding its legal status with different convention secretariats as well as relevant international organization. It came out with this preliminary analysis of the possible solutions to the various problems faced by the Secretariat; see 36th Meeting of the Standing Committee, Gland (Switzerland), February 27–29, 2008, Ramsar Convention on Wetlands of International Importance, Doc. SC 36–15; available at http://www.ramsar.org/sc/36/key_sc36_doc15.htm. Also see SC37–2, Agenda Item 5.2, at http://www.ramsar.org/sc/37/key_sc37_agenda_papers.htm (as of August 5, 2009).

[28] Legal Status of the Ramsar Convention Secretariat, 36th Meeting of the Standing Committee, Convention on Wetlands (Ramsar Iran, 1971), Gland, Switzerland, February 27–29, 2008, DOC. SC36–15, para. 2 (on file with the author).

Table 5. *Ramsar Case: Possible Solutions to Problems of MEA Secretariat Personality and Host Institutions*

	Potential Result		
Issue/Problem	Option 1: IUCN to continue hosting of the secretariat with significant improvement	Option 2: Ramsar Secretariat to be registered as a legal International Governmental Organization	Option 3: Ramsar Secretariat to be administered by a UN agency such as UNEP or UNESCO
1. Difficulty in obtaining travel visas for our staff without international organization legitimization	May remain unsolved	Would be solved	Would be solved
2. Difficulty in obtaining recognition of our delegation at major international meetings	Being solved	Would be solved	Would be solved
3. Problem of not being able to obtain work permits for spouses of non-Swiss staff members	Will remain unsolved	Will remain unsolved	Will remain unsolved
4. Potential impossibility in making binding contracts as Ramsar, which has no legal power to sign contracts	Unsolved	Would be solved	May remain unsolved
5. Legal liability of IUCN for Ramsar actions (in case of staff disputes, the Regional Initiatives, misappropriation of funds, etc.)	Remains unsolved	Would be solved	Would be solved
6. Difficulty that some parties have in paying contributions to Ramsar in the absence of legal identity	Will remain unsolved	Would be solved	Would remain unsolved

7.Non-Swiss employees do not pay Swiss taxes and may be losing privileges in their communities	Will remain unsolved	Will remain unsolved	Will remain unsolved
8. IUCN controls our financial procedures in ways that may not be suitable for us.		Would be solved	May remain unsolved
9. When in the field, our staff does not have access to a network of logistical and security assistance, as UN staff would, for example.	Will remain unsolved	Will remain unsolved	Will be solved
10. New problems that may emerge when adopting an option	Current problems remain	Ramsar would need to set up its own social security and pension schemes. Ramsar could continue to engage IUCN or UNEP for specific services required. Find a new alternative for office space (including rent and running cost), administrative, financial, and accounting services that are currently provided by IUCN. Need to get a higher budget to cover new salary scale and provide social security allowances.	Need to get a higher budget to cover new salary scale and provide social security allowances. Find a new alternative for office space (including rent and running cost), administrative, financial, and accounting services that are currently provided by IUCN.

Source: 36th Meeting of the Standing Committee, Convention on Wetlands (Ramsar, Iran, 1971), Gland, Switzerland, 27–29 February 2008; Doc. SC 36–15, pp. 10–11.

appears to be concerned about its "derivative legal personality,"[29] which could lead to questions regarding its treaty-making capacity or even a mundane issue like allocation for the ".int" domain on the Internet.

Thus, it seems that seeds of potential conflicts could lie in the host institution arrangement that the convention has with an international institution (like UNEP). Each of the four models of institutional arrangements discussed has its own problems. None of them seems to provide an ideal choice for the consideration of locating a secretariat within an existing international institution.

Treaty-Making Power

As seen earlier in text, the secretariat of an MEA is a product of the legal mechanism put into place by the convention. The secretariat is brought into being as one of the subsidiary organs by the COP. Acting under the overall supervision of the COP, the secretariat works as *a servicing arm*. As a corollary, the secretariat is expected to work within the boundaries of authority provided by the COP. Still, the question of legal capacity both within the domestic jurisdiction of the host country and on the international level becomes crucial. Because most of the convention secretariats are located within an existing international institution, the extent of legal capacity that they are allowed to exercise remains a moot question.

The question of the treaty-making power of the secretariat is generally sought to be addressed in the headquarters agreement. The standard formulation inserted in most of the headquarters agreements is *legal capacity or personality*[30] (i.e., construed as capacity to (i) contract, (ii)

[29] Legal Personality of the Convention and the Secretariat, 54th Meeting of the Standing Committee, CITES, Geneva, Switzerland, October 2–6, 2006; SC54 Doc 8, p. 1. Also detailed notes of Marceil Yeater, November 8 and 14, 2007 (on file with the author).

[30] For instance, see Article 1 of the Headquarters Agreement between UNESCO and France (1954); Article 2 of the Agreement between the Secretariat of the CBD and the Government of Canada concerning the Headquarters of the Convention Secretariat (1996); Article 4 of the Agreement among the UN, the Government of the Federal Republic of Germany, and the Secretariat of the UNFCCC (1996); Article 4 of the Agreement between the UN, the Government of the Federal Republic of Germany,

acquire and dispose of movable and immovable property, and (iii) institute legal proceedings). It shows that these agreements only address the question of the legal capacity of the secretariat to contract only within the host country. This capacity is derived only at the specific concession provided by the host country in which the seat of the secretariat is located. An advantage of this concession is to enable the secretariat to carry out those essential tasks that are necessitated by its sheer existence in the host country.

The element of international legal capacity is an important attribute of the functions of the secretariat as a treaty body. This capacity is not generally exercised automatically by the secretariat. Any such capacity is to be either explicitly mandated or implied by the COP. The UN practice reveals that such legal capacity is not automatically extended, even to the secretariats that are linked to the UN. Most secretariats seek to derive international legal capacity through their COPs. It is still possible, however, for the secretariat to embark on the implied powers[31] doctrine drawing on the objectives and purposes of a specific multilateral legal framework on a sectoral environmental issue. The doctrine could have some relevance because almost all MEAs follow the tradition of constituent instruments of international organizations (IOs) in the sense that their legal capacity is not explicitly defined therein. As a result, it makes sense to reasonably follow the dictum of the ICJ in the *Reparations* opinion that, if the powers are not expressly provided, they could be deemed to have been "conferred upon it by necessary implication as being essential to the performance of its duties."[32] We could consider the

and the Secretariat of the UNCCD (1998); and Article 4 of the Agreement between the Government of the Federal Republic of Germany, the UN, and the Secretariat of the CMS (2002). Original copies of all the headquarters agreements are on file with the author.

[31] See, for details on this doctrine, C.F. Amerasinghe, *Principles of the Institutional Law of International Organizations* (Cambridge: Cambridge University Press, 1996), p. 137; Jan Klabbers, *Introduction to International Institutional Law* (Cambridge: Cambridge University Press, 2002), pp. 67–73; and Henry G. Schermers and Niels M. Blokker, *International Institutional Law* (The Hague: Martinus Nijhoff, 1995), p. 979.

[32] See the majority opinion in *Reparations for Injuries Suffered in the Service of the United Nations*, ICJ Reports 1949, p. 182.

international legal capacity of the convention secretariat as *sui generis* (international entity), as well as *sine qua non* for the discharge of their mandate and obligations under a multilateral legal instrument.

Headquarters Agreements

The question of a headquarters agreement for the location of the seat of the convention secretariat holds the key to smooth functioning of the entire convention process. The four models of secretariats examined earlier in text do not have a uniform pattern concerning the headquarters agreement. There are variations in the secretariat services provided by different international entities. Similarly, there are variations in headquarters agreements either specially designed for or made applicable to the convention secretariats provided by a host institution. From the standpoint of international institutional law, no convincing explanation is available about differences in headquarters agreements governing a specific convention secretariat. The scenario is almost akin to the differences regarding the legal personality of the convention secretariats.

One category of headquarters agreements that is discernible is the headquarters agreement of the host institution also governing the headquarters of the convention secretariats. This seems to be the case of the Ozone Convention Secretariat located within UNEP Headquarters (Nairobi), the WHC Secretariat located within UNESCO Headquarters (Paris),[33] and the Ramsar Bureau located within IUCN Headquarters (Gland). Thus, the UNEP Headquarters Agreement between the UN and the Republic of Kenya serves the need for a headquarters agreement for the Ozone Secretariat.[34] Similarly, CITES and Basel Conventions that are located in the International Environment House in Geneva are governed by the Headquarters Agreement between the

[33] Headquarters Agreement between UNESCO and France, Paris, July 2, 1954; entry into force November 23, 1955 (on file with the author).

[34] Communication from Dr. Alexandre Timoshenko, Office-in-Charge, Legal Economics and other Instruments Unit, UNEP, Nairobi, dated July 13, 2000 (on file with the author).

UN and the Government of Switzerland.[35] The CBD Secretariat is serviced by UNEP but located in Montreal, Canada. It is governed by a special Headquarters Agreement between the CBD Secretariat and the Government of Canada.[36] It is interesting that there is a separate Headquarters Agreement between the provincial Government of Quebec and the CBD Secretariat.[37]

It seems that the case concerning the headquarters agreement for the CMS Secretariat[38] has witnessed a curious set of developments regarding the legal status of the CMS Secretariat. This was especially so with respect to the competence of the secretariat to negotiate as well as sign and seal the agreement in its own capacity. There was a flurry of correspondence involving the CMS Secretariat, UNEP Headquarters, and the UN OLA. The core issue in the process was a strange treatment of the CMS Secretariat as a "joint subsidiary body of UNEP and the Convention." It led to usage of a hybrid term of "UNEP/CMS Secretariat" while making reference to the secretariat. Giving a sharp but principled reaction to the usage of this terminology, the UN OLA rejected it,[39] especially because the secretariat is a "non-UN treaty body"[40] under

[35] Agreement between the IUCN and the Swiss Federal Council, December 17, 1986 (original French version on file with the author).

[36] The Headquarters Agreement between the Government of Canada and the Secretariat of the Convention on Biological Diversity was signed in New York, NY, on October 25, 1997 (on file with the author).

[37] See the Agreement between the Secretariat of CBD and the Government of Quebec, Montreal, March 12, 2001 (original French version on file with the author). Also see Privileges and Immunities of the Secretariat of the Convention on Biological Diversity Order, November 20, 1997, *Canada Gazette* Part II, vol. 131, no. 25, December 10, 1997.

[38] Agreement between the Government of the Federal Republic of Germany, the United Nations and the Secretariat of the Convention on the Conservation of Migratory Species of Wild Animals concerning the Headquarters of the Convention Secretariat, Bonn, September 18, 2002 (copy of the original German and English versions on file with the author).

[39] Communication from Ralph Zacklin, Assistant Secretary-General for Legal Affairs, UN and Donald Kaniaru, Director, ELI/PAC, UNEP, May 19, 1998 (on file with the author).

[40] Communication from Ralph Zacklin, Assistant Secretary-General for Legal Affairs, UN and Donald Kaniaru, Director, Environmental Law and Institutions, UNEP, June 3, 1998 (on file with the author).

Article IX (1) of the CMS Convention. The secretariat has its own standing, as determined by the relevant text of the convention, in accordance with applicable rules of international law. In fact, the UN OLA took a clear position that the:

> Secretariat servicing arrangements provided by the United Nations either directly or through its subsidiary body UNEP do not affect the independent status of the conventions and agreements concerned... Agreements with host countries, which have been negotiated by the United Nation serviced secretariats of some of these conventions and agreements concluded in the name of the entity concerned on the basis of its legal personality and have not been based on the United Nations legal personality.[41]

In view of this postion, the UN OLA had taken a stand that the CMS Headquarters Agreement should be a *tripartite* one between the Government of Germany, the UN, and the CMS Secretariat. After a lot of haggling and correspondence, the UNEP Headquarters finally fell in line with the legal position of the UN OLA, resulting in the September 18, 2002, CMS Headquarters Agreement.[42] It was duly signed by the then CMS Executive Secretary, Arnulf Mueller-Helmbrecht, for the Secretariat of the Convention. The agreement was promptly put into the formal ratification process by the German side with the Federal Government approving it on May 21, 2003, and forwarding it to the *Bundestag* and *Bundesrat*.[43]

[41] Communication from Ralph Zacklin, Assistant Secretary-General for Legal Affairs, UN OLA to the author, July 26, 2000.

[42] Agreement between the Government of the Federal Republic of Germany, the United Nations and the Secretariat of the Convention on the Conservation of Migratory Species of Wild Animals concerning the Headquarters of the Convention Secretariat. It was signed in Bonn on September 18, 2002, by Julius G. Luy, Ambassador, and Jurgen Trittin, Federal Minister for the Environment, Nature Conservation and Nuclear Safety (for Germany), Shafqat Kakakhel, Deputy Executive Director of UNEP (for the UN), and Arnulf Mueller-Helmbrecht, Executive Secretary (for CMS); (copy of the original agreement on file with the author).

[43] Communication from Juergen Trittin, Federal Minister for the Environment, Nature Conservation and Nuclear Safety, Government of Federal Republic Germany, Berlin,

As far as two UN-linked conventions – UNFCCC and UNCCD – are concerned, they did not seem to have any problems working out their respective headquarters agreements.[44] Both of these instruments followed the standard UN position on according separate legal personality (from the UN) to the convention secretariats as treaty bodies. Moreover, both of these agreements adopted the format and content *mutatis mutandis* of the headquarters agreement of the UN Volunteers Programme (UNV).[45] As a corollary, UNFCCC and UNCCD adopted the UNV model of *juridical personality and legal capacity* in the host country.

Thus, it appears that various headquarters arrangements among the convention secretariats follow a specific pattern in terms of according legal personality and treaty-making capacity to the secretariats in their own right. In the cases where the host institutions deemed it fit, they made their own respective headquarters agreements with the host countries applicable to the convention secretariats. That arrangement could be purely for the sake of convenience, however. It does not in any manner reflect upon the legal capacity of the secretariats to work out such arrangements in their own right.

Conclusion

The advent of MEAs on the international scene has led to the growth of various kinds of treaty bodies. In general, at the apex level the COP has full legal capacity. That capacity is in turn passed on, under its authority,

to Klaus Toepfer, Executive Director, UNEP and Arnulf Mueller-Helmbrecht, CMS Executive Secretary, June 2, 2003 (on file with the author).

[44] See Agreement between the Government of the Federal Republic of Germany, the United Nations and the secretariat of the UNCCD, concerning the Headquarters of the Convention Permanent Secretariat, Bonn, August 18, 1998 and Agreement among the United Nations, the Government of the Federal Republic of Germany, and the Secretariat of the UNFCCC, concerning the Headquarters of the Convention Secretariat, Bonn June 20, 1996 (on file with the author).

[45] Agreement between the Federal Republic of Germany and the United Nations concerning the Headquarters of the United Nations Volunteers Programme, New York City, November 10, 1995 (copy of the original on file with the author).

to the secretariat as a treaty body. The said legal capacity of the secretariat is borne out of sheer functional necessity. As seen earlier in text, MEAs possess *sui generis* legal standing on the international level, whereas their legal capacity within the domestic jurisdiction of the host country is facilitated by their headquarters agreements. The four models of secretariats seen in the field provide different flavors of the institutional practice as well as experiments that the contracting parties perform while putting in place an MEA. It can be deciphered that, by and large, the host institutions accept – sometimes grudgingly – the legal capacity of the convention secretariats. This is notwithstanding the treatment meted out to the CMS Secretariat on the occasion of the drafting of its headquarters agreement. Such an attitude could be the product of a lack of clarity in the text of the convention, ignorance of the practice of institutional law, lack of assertiveness on the part of the COP and the standing committee, and institutional egos. Such a negative attitude toward a treaty body could not but take its own toll on the work of the secretariat. Similarly, the "closed door" attitude in UNESCO circles regarding the lack of legal capacity of the World Heritage Centre still remains problematic from a scholarly point of view. It could at best be regarded as an aberration in the field because it negates the legal status of the WHC as a treaty body.

The potential problems in the relationship between host institution and convention secretariat cannot be entirely ruled out. Efforts made by the Ramsar Bureau, the CITES Secretariat, and the CBD Secretariat to work out a specialized *relationship agreement* with the host institution provide a possible way out for other convention secretariats. These efforts could help clarify many of the sources of conflict and demarcate respective areas of jurisdiction and accountability to prevent issues of turf. In this context, the COPs and standing committees of the respective MEAs will need to launch a process to formulate a workable relationship agreement that could facilitate the carrying out of objectives of the primary legal instruments.

6 Conclusions

The practice of multilateral environmental regulation is an inescapable by-product of the age of multilateralism. It seeks to ensure that the sovereign states adopt the spirit of multilateralism and come together on a common platform to address some of the global *problematique*. It is also largely based on the premise that global problems need global solutions. In this context, there has been a transition in the attitude of the states from the era of "common heritage" to the "common concerns of humankind." It is possible that the sheer identification of some of these common concerns could be colored by the promotion of the national interest of a state or a group of states, economic factors, technology control regimes, financial jugglery, or just a quest for engaging the key countries in the midst of their developmental journey. It is also noteworthy that, in this age of multilateral regulation, the processes are also influenced by scientific reports. As a result, this admixture produces unique products that are now popularly described as multilateral environmental agreements (MEAs).

One of the salient facets of MEAs is that they provide an institutionalized platform for sovereign states to engage in addressing a commonly identified problem. This platform in practice revolves around a regulatory framework of a sectoral environmental agreement. The mushrooming growth in the number of MEAs in the past four decades is a testimony to this process at work. Both the nature and scope of the regulatory technique in the environmental field have seen significant transformation over the years. It is also buttressed by the quantum jump in the number of environmental concerns, which initially started with the conservation agenda and shifted gear to larger marathon concerns (e.g., climate change, biodiversity, and desertification) before culminating in the trend of phasing out highly toxic chemicals and wastes. At the subterranean level, the regulatory process has been fueled by the consequences of a global wild chase for economic miracles. Thus, cumulatively, the marathon multilateral environmental regulation process also provides a large sectoral chess board for application of science, economics, politics, and law.

The regulatory process comprises both built-in lawmaking and institutional building processes. Because of the very nature of the regulatory process, there is an element of uncertainty surrounding it. Moreover, scientific uncertainty, economic considerations, and political compulsions of contracting parties lead to the use of calculated ambiguity within the instrument itself. There are many loose ends left in the instrument that need to be picked up by the convention process to be elaborated through a step-by-step process. As a result, the sector-specific regulatory mechanism acts literally as work in progress. Along with the lawmaking exercise, the process includes the evolution of an institutional framework within the convention. Apart from the plenary body, each convention also has several subsidiary bodies, including the secretariat. There are innovations involving these processes, and these take into account the needs of sectoral environmental issues and vital interests of the states parties to respective MEAs.

The treaty-based institutional framework needs competence to meet the objectives of the convention. The primary legal capacity that centrally eases the workload of the convention emanates from the plenary body called the Conference of Parties/MOP). It is now generally accepted that each MEA carries a *sui generis* standing in international law that is separate from the contracting parties to it. In this parlance, MEAs, having an ad hoc character, are generally not regarded as international organizations (IOs). Notwithstanding this, the MEA is not devoid of the legal capacity to either operate on the international level or carry out specific functions within the domestic jurisdiction of the host state.

The sheer necessity of an MEA, through its secretariat, to meet its objectives leads to a chain of legal implications involving the host institution, host country, and other legal entities. As the state practice (as well as that among the MEAs) reveals, the secretariat generally possesses the standing – under the authority of the COP – to act by its own authority. There are, however, some problems in this respect, especially due to either an unclear view of the host institution or a reluctance to allow the secretariat the status of a treaty body under international institutional law.

Barring few exceptional cases, most of the convention secretariats in recent years have come to be located within an existing international institution. It is interesting that this question of "location" is unaffected by physical distance (sometimes even continents apart) of the convention secretariats from their host institutions. This phenomenon can be witnessed especially in the case of secretariat services being provided by the United Nations (UN) headquarters as well as the UN Environment Programme (UNEP; Nairobi). In these cases, the actual location of the secretariats is decided on the basis of offers made by participating countries in terms of office building, financial support, staff benefits, and other considerations. In view of this, the seat of the secretariat is not necessarily located at the headquarters of the host institution.

Thus, as a part of the chain of legal events that starts with a formal request by the COP to an existing international institution such as the UN or UNEP, the actual determination of location of the secretariat is a separate event altogether. The decision of the host institution to provide secretariat support to the convention is not at all influenced by the considerations of the actual place where the secretariat will come to be located. In this respect, the decision is made on the basis of availability of the best offers from the states parties to the convention. It is important to note that location of the secretariat has no effect on its legal capacity. There seem to be a standard practice among the UN entities is to offer secretariat support to convention secretariats, as well as the legal capacity they possess as treaty bodies. In fact, the Office of Legal Affairs of the UN (UN OLA) has taken a forthright position that the convention secretariats are not subordinate to either the UN or to UNEP when they provide secretariat services.

The issue of host institution arrangements assumes considerable importance in the life of a convention secretariat. It has been seen that there are wide variations in secretariat services provided by host institutions. Notwithstanding the clear legal position of the UN OLA, host institutions have tried to assert control over the MEA secretariats. That is precisely why the term "providing a secretariat" is subject to close legal scrutiny. It is more so in view of a sort of contractual arrangement with the convention through payment of, on average, a 13 percent overhead charge to the host institutions in lieu of the secretariat services. This arrangement often gets derailed and creates conflicting situations between the host institution and the convention secretariat. It seems, in actual practice, that whenever the COP or the standing committee does not keep track of the situation and assert itself to ensure the capability of the secretariat to realize the objectives of the convention it could lead to possible disregard for the secretariat legal capacity by an assertive host institution. Without this oversight, the relevant convention secretariats have been subjected to sometimes quite humiliating treatment on even petty issues, such as the size of the host institution's name or logo or the domain name for the Web site of the secretariat. Of course, there are other larger issues such as appointment of the head of the secretariat or legal capacity of the head of the secretariat to put his or her signature in his or her own capacity on the headquarters agreement of the secretariat. Unfortunately, headquarters agreements generally do not throw much light on some of these critical legal issues. As a result, a trend has grown among the secretariats to insist on a proper relationship agreement with the respective host institution. The three such agreements so far put into place (the Convention on Wetlands of International Importance [Ramsar Convention], the Convention on International Trade in Endangered Species [CITES], and the Convention on Biological Diversity [CBD]) indicate the preference to clearly delineate the respective roles of the host institution and the convention secretariat. This arrangement could possibly prevent conflicts; however, it could work only if the arrangement is duly respected by the host institution. Alternatively, the COP or the standing committee that generally enters into the relationship agreement could assert its authority and seek clarifications from the host institution regarding the nature of the services that they are providing to the convention. In case of their assessment to the contrary, the COP could always consider alternatives for the host institution. The recent assessment justifiably carried out by both the Ramsar Bureau and the CITES Secretariat point in this direction.

It appears that convention secretariats have a unique position in international institutional law. These ad hoc institutional arrangements present a challenge in the field of international law to cope with several issues concerning their actual working in the field as well as with intra-institutional issues. The four different models of convention secretariats seen in the field have their own strengths and weaknesses as well as present distinct sets of problems, which could be resolved through a spirit of solidarity and cooperation between the host institution and the COP. The convention secretariat is sandwiched between these two institutions and has to grapple with a sense of dual loyalty to the two masters.

If the basic purpose of institutionalized international environmental cooperation is to be realized on a specific sectoral issue, the convention secretariat will need to be adequately strengthened. The secretariats need to be provided with the necessary wherewithal and the legal capacity to work smoothly both within the domestic jurisdiction of the host country as well as on the international level. This will necessitate concerted political resolve by the COP, understanding from the host institution, as well as jettisoning institutional egos to attain the best results. In view of the fact that each sectoral convention is different and that the nature of secretariat support provided by the host institution also is different, therefore, it will be best to put into place an appropriate relationship agreement for all the MEA secretariats. (At present, only

Ramsar, CITES, and CBD have them.) Such documentation of specific turfs could help address and avert potential conflicts and difficulties in an institutionalized way rather than through an ad hoc firefighting (case-by-case) approach.

It is also incumbent on the concerned host institutions to duly respect the legal sanctity of the treaty bodies rather than treat them merely as their subordinates or appendages. Only in the situation where there is a harmonious relationship between the host institution and the convention secretariat will the contracting state parties be able to realize in letter and spirit the basic objectives of their respective MEAs. The issue could be duly addressed as a part of the larger intergovernmental debate on 'international environmental governance' in the UN system. The considerable churning and reports under the auspices of the UN Secretary-General's High-level Panel on Environment, Development and Humanitarian Assistance (9 November 2006) and UN General Assembly mandated Informal Consultative Process on the Institutional Framework for the UN's Environmental Activities (co-chaired by Switzerland and Mexico; 10 February 2009) as well as UNEP's annual Governing Council/Global Ministerial Environment Forum have not yet yielded appropriate roadmap for future of MEAs. It is high time that the UN General Assembly provides appropriate legal and political 'guidance' to the member states to address the issue squarely. Pending the debate on the lawmaking approach through MEAs as well as their efficacy as 'governance tools,' UNEP could possibly launch a formal process to address a series of legal issues afflicting various MEAs. The initiative will help in removing ambiguity as regards legal status of the secretariats as well as several other issues that provide room for potential conflicts with host institutions and undermine their effectiveness as multilateral environmental regulatory tools. It could also contribute to the current UNEP Governing Council/Global Ministerial Environment Forum-led intergovernmental deliberations on the future of MEAs as a part of the larger agenda on international environmental governance.

APPENDICES

Part I Relationship Agreements

Appendix I Delegation of Authority to the Secretary General Convention on Wetlands of International Importance Especially as Waterfowl Habitat (RAMSAR)*

Introduction

(A) Article 8.1 of the Ramsar Convention provides that IUCN shall perform the continuing bureau duties under the Convention until such time as another organization or government is appointed by a majority of two-thirds of all Contracting Parties.

This was accepted by IUCN at the Ramsar plenipotentiary Conference in 1971.

(B) In 1987, by decision of the Third Meeting of the Conference of the Contracting Parties to the Convention, the Bureau was established as an integrated unit within IUCN, headed by a Secretary General administratively responsible to the Director General of IUCN who was in turn responsible to the Conference of the Parties for financial and personnel administration. The Conference also established a Standing Committee of the Contracting Parties empowered, *inter alia*, with supervision of the Bureau's programme, policy, and budget.

This change, whereby IUCN was asked to provide an integrated Bureau rather than perform itself continuous bureau duties, was accepted by IUCN in a letter from the IUCN Director General to the Ramsar Standing Committee in June 1987.

* Agreement signed between the Director-General of IUCN and CMS Standing Committee Chairman on January 29, 1993 (on file with the author).

(C) In 1990, by decision of the Fourth Meeting of the Conference of the Contracting Parties, the Bureau was transformed into an independent unit co-located with the headquarters of IUCN. The Secretary General was given sole responsibility for administration of Convention funds and for all administrative matters other than those requiring the exercise of legal personality. For those latter matters, formal responsibility rests with the Director General of IUCN. In addition the mandate of the Standing Committee was expanded to include supervision for personnel issues.

The Director General of IUCN, who participated in the discussion of these changes indicated to the Conference that he concurred with the terms of the decisions.

(D) The development of the Convention over the years including increased membership from countries throughout the world, and an expanded conservation programme, has led the Standing Committee to seek increased authority and flexibility for the Secretary General in the implementation of the Convention's programme.

(E) In keeping with the decision of the Conference of the Parties and in the desire to assure effective and efficient management of Convention affairs, the Director General of the IUCN makes the following delegations of Authority to the Secretary General:

(I) Financial and Budgetary Matters

(A) Background

The Resolution on Financial and Budgetary Matters (annex to C.4. 13 Rev.) of the Fourth Meeting of the Conference of the Contracting Parties directs the Secretary General to administer Convention funds in accordance with certain terms of reference related to financial administration. The Resolution on Secretariat Matters (annex to C.4. 15 Rev.)

provides that the Convention budget, as approved by the Conference of the Contracting Parties, shall be administered by the Secretary General, with budgetary disbursal in accordance with the budgetary provisions and instructions given by the Conference or by the Standing Committee. The Resolution on the Standing Committee (annex to C.4. 14 Rev.) empowers the Standing Committee to supervise, as a representative of the Conference, the execution of the Bureau's budget. At the request of the Conference, and in agreement with the Standing Committee, the Director General of IUCN has established a separate Ramsar bank account.

(B) Delegation

The authority of the Director General of IUCN to receive and expend Convention funds, including payment of Bureau staff salaries and benefits; purchase and rental of supplies, materials, and equipment; authority to enter into contracts; and otherwise provide for the financial administration of the Convention's funds by means of a separate Ramsar account is hereby delegated to the Secretary General. The Secretary General, with the approval of the Standing Committee, may purchase services from IUCN to assist with financial administration.

(C) Limitations

(1) As the exercise of this authority reflects upon the fiscal and institutional integrity of IUCN, the Director General reserves the right to impose limitations upon the above delegation of authority, subject to the agreement of the Standing Committee, or to request the Standing Committee for a review of Bureau financial practices by the Standing Committee or an outside agency.
(2) Nothing in this delegation shall excuse the Secretary General from the requirement to provide for an annual audit of Convention accounts to the Contracting Parties, copies of which shall be provided to the Director General of IUCN.

(II) Personnel Management

(A) Background

The Resolution on Secretariat Matters (annex to C.4. 15 Rev.) of the Fourth Meeting of the Conference of the Contracting Parties indicates that the Bureau of the Convention shall be comprised of the Secretary General, appointed by the Director General of IUCN in consultation with and on the basis of a proposal from the Standing Committee, and other staff members appointed by the Director General of IUCN in consultation with and upon the proposal of the Secretary General. That Resolution also indicates that the IUCN salary scale along with IUCN personnel provisions shall apply to Bureau personnel, subject to the approval of the Standing Committee. The Resolution on the Standing Committee (annex to C.4. 14 Rev.) empowers the Standing Committee to supervise, as a representative of the Conference, Bureau personnel matters.

(B) Delegation

The authority of the Director General of IUCN to select, hire or dismiss Bureau staff and assign salary levels, tasks and job descriptions, set performance standards, evaluate performance, and provide for employee awards, all in line with IUCN personnel provisions is hereby delegated to the Secretary General.

All staff positions within the Bureau, except that of the Secretary General, shall be classified by the Secretary General, after consultation with the Director General, in accordance with IUCN classification standards to assure that similar positions in the two bodies are salaried at the same level and that transfers of staff between IUCN and Bureau are not impeded.

To enhance co-operation, the Secretary General will be invited to designate a staff member to sit in an ex officio capacity on the IUCN Staff Liaison Committee, the Secretary General will participate ex officio in appropriate IUCN Management Committee and all Bureau staff are invited to IUCN staff meetings. Finally the Secretary General, with the approval of the Standing Committee, may purchase services from IUCN to assist with personnel administration.

(C) Limitations

(1) This delegation does not apply to the selection or removal of the Secretary General, or to the establishment of a salary grade and scale, tasks and job description, performance evaluation and employee awards for the Secretary General, which shall require agreement with the Standing Committee. Furthermore the Standing Committee may request the IUCN Director General to suspend certain IUCN personnel provisions for Bureau staff in view of Convention finances.

(2) As the exercise of this authority reflects upon the institutional integrity of IUCN as well as upon questions of equity for staff under contract with IUCN, the Director General reserves the right to impose limitations upon the above delegation of authority, subject to the agreement of the Standing Committee.

(III) Facility Management

(A) Background

The Resolution on Secretariat Matters (annex to C.4. 15 Rev.) of the Fourth Meeting of the Conference of the Contracting Parties provides that the Convention Bureau shall be co-located with the Headquarters of IUCN, as an independent unit funded from the Convention budget. In 1988 the Swiss Federal Government, Government of the Canton of Vaud, and the Government of the Commune of Gland provided IUCN with funds and the use of a parcel of land for the construction of a new headquarters facility. It was noted by Swiss officials on numerous occasions that the facility was being provided for both IUCN and the Ramsar Bureau.

On 6 November 1991 the Director General of IUCN and the Chairman of the Ramsar Standing Committee signed a Memorandum of Understanding on Headquarters Facilities which provided for allocation of space within the new building for the Ramsar Bureau, appropriate indication on the building and its grounds to reflect the fact that the facility was also the home of the Bureau, and for reimbursement by Ramsar of its fair share of the cost of maintenance, heating, lighting, and ventilation as well as the possibility to contract for other agreed costs and services. Provision was also included for consultations between the Director General of IUCN and the Secretary General of the Ramsar Bureau in the case of any dispute or for any request by Ramsar for additional space in the building.

(B) Delegation

The authority of the Director General of IUCN for facility management for that space within the IUCN Headquarters Building assigned to the Convention Bureau is hereby delegated to the Secretary General. This authority shall include office arrangements and equipment, and siting of staff members. The Secretary General, with the approval of the Standing Committee, may purchase facility services from IUCN. The Secretary General shall agree with the Director General on matters such as the maintenance, fittings, decoration, use of common space or other issues relating to the Headquarters building where an uniform approach is necessary.

(C) Limitations

(1) The Secretary General is not authorized to waive or abridge those regulations imposed by Swiss law upon the IUCN Headquarters Building for reasons of health, safety, or access to the disabled.
(2) As the exercise of this authority reflects upon the institutional reputation of IUCN, the Director General reserves the right to advise the Standing Committee of any space usage viewed as

inappropriate or inconsistent with general space usage within the facility and may impose limitations upon the above delegation of authority, subject to the agreement of the Standing Committee. Requests for reduced Bureau space usage or for an expansion of Bureau offices, either within the facility on external to it, shall be the subject of written agreement between the Director General of IUCN and the Standing Committee.

Interpretation

In the event of differences of interpretation of administrative requirements under the Convention, or under the above-mentioned delegations of authority, such differences shall first be subject to consultation between the Director General and the Secretary General, or if requiring policy attention, in writing between the Director General and the Chairman of the Standing Committee. In the event that they cannot be resolved at these levels, referrals shall be made to the governing bodies of both IUCN and Ramsar.

Supplementary Note

This note records certain points raised in discussion of the formal paper on Delegation of Authority, which seem more appropriately dealt with in a separate memorandum.

Legal and Financial Liability

IUCN, as the legal persona to which the Ramsar Bureau is attached, must inevitably retain ultimate liability for the actions of the Secretary General, in exercising the authority delegated to him.

It is agreed that in his own interests, and in order to minimize any risk to IUCN, the Secretary General will:

(a) ensure that adequate and up-to-date accounts are kept by the Bureau, so as to disclose any excesses of expenditure over income promptly, and before they become difficult to correct. The internal accounting procedures used will be agreed between the Secretary General and the Director of Finance of IUCN, and statements of the financial position of the Bureau will be made to the Standing Committee twice yearly, at mid- and end-year, and copied to the Director General of IUCN;

(b) give early warning to IUCN of the likely termination of any contracts, including contracts of staff employment, which could lead to financial or legal liability;

(c) ensure that potential risks of financial or legal liability are, to the maximum extent practicable, covered by insurance, and that the Director General of IUCN is informed of the nature and extent of such cover. In particular, the Secretary General will ensure that all Bureau staff are insured against claims for alleged professional negligence.

In the event that the Secretary General decides to pay staff salaries other than through IUCN, the arrangements will be discussed with the Director General who will need to be satisfied that they provide adequately for deduction of taxes and other charges, and for payments to a fund that can be drawn upon to compensate staff who become entitled to unemployment benefit.

Personnel Management

The costs of all Ramsar staff salaries and associated benefits will be provided for in the budget of the Convention. The Ramsar budget will also bear the costs of severance payments, repatriation, unemployment benefit and other costs in respect of Bureau staff whose contracts are terminated on the decision of the Secretary General. Where staff have served both the Bureau and IUCN, severance costs will be divided in accordance with the cost sharing agreement between the Director General and the Chair of the Standing Committee dated 27 February 1992.

It is agreed that IUCN cannot be required to take onto its own direct payroll staff engaged by the Secretary General but no longer required by the Ramsar Bureau, unless IUCN has an appropriate vacancy.

Cooperation and Reporting

The Director General and Secretary General will report annually to the Standing Committee on the cooperation between them. Such reports will be as brief and informal as possible: the aim is to minimise the time devoted by the Standing Committee to such administrative details.

Appendix II Agreement between the CITES Standing Committee and the Executive Director of UNEP*

CONSCIOUS of the need to maintain flexibility and adaptability in the management of the CITES Secretariat and in the provision of services to the Parties to the Convention;

AWARE that the responsibilities and functions of the Standing Committee and the Executive Director of the United Nations Environment Programme (UNEP) with regard to the implementation of Articles XI and XII of the Convention need to be clarified;

RECOGNIZING that the decisions of the Conference of the Parties shall guide the Implementation of CITES and management of its Secretariat;

DESIRING to further improve the relationship between CITES and UNEP; and

RECOGNIZING that the 37th meeting of the Standing Committee recommended that the Agreement between the Standing Committee and the Executive Director of UNEP, signed in June 1992, be revised;

The CITES Standing Committee and the Executive Director of UNEP agree as follows:

* Agreement signed between the Chairman of the CITES Standing Committee and the Executive Director of UNEP on June 20, 1997 (on file with the author).

Basic Principles

1. The Executive Director will act in conformity with the provisions of Articles XI and XII of the Convention and the rules and regulations of the United Nations on these and other functions as may be entrusted to the Secretariat by the Parties. The Executive Director shall ensure that the Secretary General implements the policy guidance of the Standing Committee in exercising the functions of the Secretariat in accordance with Articles XI and XII of the Convention, and other functions as may be entrusted to the Secretariat by the Parties.
2. The Executive Director will inform the Standing Committee in advance of any significant action with respect to the Secretariat which may affect the interests of the Parties or the efficient administration of the Convention, and will consider carefully the views the Standing Committee presents to him/her on such actions.
3. Where consultations between the Executive Director and the Standing Committee are required under this agreement, they shall be conducted through the Chairperson of the Committee who shall seek the views of the members and reflect these in his or her reply. On specific issues, the Chairperson may designate another member of the Standing Committee to conduct such consultations.

Personnel Management

4. Personnel Selection

   All personnel selection shall be performed expeditiously by UNEP and the Secretary General. The aim should be to ensure that any vacancies occurring among the senior professional staff should be filled by replacements on fixed term appointments with 6 months. Any unforeseen delays in filling senior posts shall be explained in writing to the Chairperson of the Standing Committee, as representative of the Parties, upon his/her written request. All vacancy announcements shall be drafted carefully and in conformity with UN rules, and the UN shall ensure its circulation to all the Parties. All selection panels for posts at the Secretariat shall be convened in accordance with United Nations rules and regulations. Only candidates with the requisite knowledge, experience, and expertise shall be considered for posts at the CITES Secretariat. For senior posts, the Executive Director or his/her designated official (Secretary General), shall consult with and take into consideration the views of the Standing Committee in establishing selection panels, as appropriate.[1]

5. Selection of the Secretary General

   The Secretary General (the Chief Officer of the Secretariat of the Convention) shall be appointed by the Executive Director of UNEP in accordance with the United Nations personal rules, and after consultation with the Standing Committee. The consultation will be such that every effort will be made to appoint a Secretary General acceptable to the Standing Committee, while recognizing that the United Nations personnel rules will govern the appointment.

6. Selection of Other Staff

   Other staff members will also be appointed under the United Nations personnel rules, which provide for consultation with the Secretary General. The consultation will be such that every effort will be made to appoint candidates the Secretary General considers acceptable for the effective conduct of the business of the Secretariat.

7. The appointment of individuals to posts in the Secretariat financed by Governments or other Institutions over and above their normal contributions to the CITES Trust Fund (e.g. secondments) will be confirmed through the applicable appointment process of

[1] In accordance with UN staff rules and regulations, selection panels for all posts are established by the Executive Director, who has delegated this authority to the Secretary-General.

the United Nations Environment Programme, and will be subject to the terms of an agreement negotiated between the originating Government agency and UNEP.

8. Performance of the Secretary General

   In appraising the performance of the Secretary General, the Executive Director will provide the Standing Committee with the applicable performance appraised criteria. On an annual basis, the Standing Committee will submit its comments to the Executive Director on the performance of the Secretary General. The Executive Director will reflect these comments in his/her performance evaluation of the Secretary General. The Executive Director will consult with the Standing Committee on issues of concern to him/her in the performance of the Secretary General. The Executive Director will extend or discontinue the contract of the Secretary General after consultation with the Standing Committee.

9. Performance of Other Personnel

   The evaluation of the performance of the incumbents of all other posts shall be in accordance with the applicable Staff Rules of the United Nations, which provide for the full participation of the supervisors of the Secretariat.

Financial Management

10. Budget Oversight and Execution

    The Standing Committee oversees on behalf of the Parties the development and execution of the Secretariat budget as derived from the Trust Fund and other sources. The Executive Director will be guided by the specific Resolutions established at each meeting of the Conference of the Parties with respect to matters related to the financing and budgeting of the Secretariat taking into account the availability of resources. The Executive Director shall consult with the Standing Committee before taking actions or implementing decisions which cause an unforeseen change in the budget of the Secretariat.

11. To assist the Standing Committee in fulfilling its responsibilities, the Executive Director shall ensure that a report is submitted to each meeting of the Committee showing details of the expenditure for each of the years of the triennium in question which has been allocated by the Conference of the Parties which is projected or committed, and has been incurred. The reports should allow year on year comparison with the final year of the preceding triennium and show the amount of unspent balance held in the Trust Fund. In the year preceding a Conference of the Parties, the Executive Director shall additionally provide the Standing Committee with detailed expenditure proposals for the next biennium identifying priorities and the scope for savings, including those from increased efficiency. This information shall be included in the report as indicated in paragraph 16 of this Agreement.
12. Administrative Support Charge
Recognizing the current process within UNEP in collaboration with the United Nations to determine an adequate mechanism to report administrative support cost, as called for in UNEP Governing Council decision 19/24B, UNEP will provide to the Parties as detailed an accounting as possible of services provided to CITES with the understanding that the level of detail will be consistent with the needs of the Parties. This information shall be included in the report as indicated in paragraph 16 of the Agreement. Progress on the implementation of this paragraph will be assessed at the 42nd meeting of the Standing Committee.
13. Externally Financed Projects
Proposals for externally financed projects shall be submitted in the established format to the Standing Committee which has the authority to approve proposals. Upon approval by the Standing Committee, the CITES Secretariat shall then discuss the proposal with the implementing body and finalize the document with the

assistance of the UNEP Programme Support Unit in Geneva. The requisite project document shall then be signed by the Secretary General of CITES, the relevant implementing body and UNEP. UNEP will give authorization to commit resources for the project subject to the actual receipt of the externally provided finance in the CITES account. Any changes in the current practice of administering these projects will be subject to negotiations between the Executive Director and the Standing Committee.

14. Location and Custody of the Trust Fund
In accordance with Rule 8.1 of the Financial Rules and Regulations of the United Nations, the Controller, in consultation with UNEP and the CITES Secretary General, has designated a bank in Geneva in which the CITES Trust Fund shall be located. The annual reports of the United Nation auditors on the management and investment of the Trust Fund account shall be provided to the CITES Standing Committee, for transmission to all CITES Parties.

Management Review

15. UNEP, in consultation with the Standing Committee or at its request, may as appropriate commission an independent management review of services provided by the CITES Secretariat, in the interest of promoting cost efficiency, transparency, and furthering the goals of the Convention. UNEP shall keep the Committee fully informed about any such reviews which are undertaken.
16. UNEP Report
UNEP shall submit an annual report on its provision of and support to the Secretariat, including the implementation of this Agreement and the administration of the Secretariat for consideration at each meeting of the Standing Committee and meetings of the Conference of the Parties. In the event that the Standing Committee meets more than once a year, the required

information, in particular that set out in paragraph 11, will be updated accordingly. This report will be utilized by the Standing Committee and UNEP to monitor and enhance the implementation of this Agreement.

17. Revision of this Agreement

This agreement may, at the request of either party to it, be reviewed at any time. Such a request shall be made at least four months in advance, and shall then be addressed at the next meeting of the Standing Committee or the next meeting of the Conference of the Parties, whichever comes first.

Appendix III Administrative Arrangement between UNEP and the Secretariat of the CBD*

Preamble

The Executive Director of the United Nations Environment Programme (UNEP) and the Executive Secretary of the Convention on Biological Diversity (CBD);

Pursuant to Decision I/4 of the first meeting of the Conference of the Parties of the CBD which designated the UNEP to carry out the functions of the Secretariat of the Convention while ensuring its autonomy to discharge the functions referred to in Article 24;

Recalling Decision 18/36 of the Eighteenth Session of the Governing Council of the UNEP which welcomed the designation of the UNEP to carry out the functions of the Secretariat of the Convention while ensuring its autonomy to discharge the functions referred to in Article 24;

Aware that Decision II/19 of the second meeting of the Conference of the Parties accepted the offer of Canada to host the Permanent Secretariat of the CBD in Montreal;

Recalling Decision III/23 of the third meeting of the Conference of the Parties invited the Executive Director of the UNEP and the Executive

* Agreement signed between the Executive Director of UNEP (Elizabeth Dowdeswell) and the Executive Secretary of the CBD (Calestous Juma) on June 30, 1997 (on file with the author).

Secretary of the CBD to develop procedures, making an effort to conclude by 27 January, 1997, with respect to the functioning of the Permanent Secretariat of the CBD, to clarify and make more effective their respective roles and responsibilities;

Cognizant that Decision III/23 stressed further that the procedures must be in accordance with the United Nations financial and staff rules and regulations and with decision I/4 of the Conference of the Parties and should as far as possible, and where appropriate, follow the Personnel, Financial and Common Services arrangements agreed to between the United Nations and the Framework Convention on Climate Change;

Aware that some of the services required by the Secretariat of the CBD in accordance with Article 24 of the Convention and the appropriate decisions of the Conference of the Parties are provided by the United Nations Office at Nairobi;

Hereby decide to apply the following, effective immediately:

I. Personnel Arrangements

1. The Executive Secretary of the CBD will be appointed by the Executive Director of UNEP after consultation with the Conference of the Parties through its Bureau. The level and term of office of the appointment will be determined by the Conference of the Parties. The term of office may be extended by the Executive Director of UNEP after consultation with the Conference of the Parties. Consultations on these matters will be conducted through the Bureau of the Conference of the Parties. The Executive Director of UNEP will also consult the Bureau when appraising the performance of the Executive Secretary of the CBD and will provide the Bureau with the applicable performance criteria to be used in such appraisal. On an annual basis, the Bureau will submit its comments to the Executive Director of UNEP on the performance of the Executive Secretary of the CBD. The Executive

Director of UNEP will reflect these comments in her/his performance evaluation of the Executive Secretary of the CBD. The Executive Director of UNEP will consult the COP, through its Bureau, on issues of concern to her/him in the performance of the Executive Secretary of the CBD.

2. In accordance with the relevant staff rules, the Executive Director of UNEP will, in full consultation with the Executive Secretary of the CBD, appoint CBD staff whose appointment will be limited to service with the Convention, unless mutually agreed otherwise and in accordance with United Nations Rules and Regulations.
3. Posts and their levels are established by the Conference of the Parties for classification and recruitment purposes in conformity with the principles laid down by the General Assembly of the United Nations.
4. The Executive Secretary of the CBD will make recommendations to the Executive Director of UNEP on the promotion of all staff up the D1/L-6 level and on the (non) extensions of appointments of all staff of the Convention at or below the D1/L-6 level, except for terminations under article X of the Staff Regulations. The provisions of ST/SGT/213/Rev. 1, concerning the designation of staff members performing significant functions in financial management, personnel management and General Services administration, shall be applicable to CBD. All appointments and promotions to posts above the D1/L-6 level, or termination of appointment above the D1/L-6 level, requires prior approval of the Secretary General of the United Nations.
5. The Executive Director of UNEP will, in full consultation with, and on the recommendation of the Executive Secretary of the CBD, appoint, promote and terminate project personnel up to D1/L-6 level, except for terminations under article X of the Staff Regulations. In all cases, contracts will be offered by the Executive Director of UNEP for service of the Secretariat of the Convention, and their duration is subject to availability of resources

in the Trust Funds established by the Conference of the Parties to the CBD.

6. An Appointment and Promotion Board for CBD will be established at the seat of the Convention Secretariat by the Executive Director of UNEP in full consultation with the Executive Secretary of the CBD, to advise the Executive Director of UNEP on all matters related to appointments, promotions, and review of staff. The Board will consider all the appointments and promotions of staff in the General Services and related categories and in the Professional category up to D1/L-6 level.
7. The CBD Appointment and Promotion Board, which will make its recommendations to the Executive Director of UNEP for final approval, will follow the relevant UN Staff Regulations and Rules, the procedures of the Appointment and Promotion Board at UN Headquarters and the policies of the Secretary-General of the United Nations in personnel question. The Board will consist of four members and four alternates. Members and alternate members will be appointed by the Executive Director of UNEP in full consultation with the Executive Secretary of the CBD. A representative of the Human Resources Management Services of the United Nations Office in Nairobi (HRMS/UNON) will be an ex-officio member of the Board and will serve as its Secretary. The Executive Director of UNEP, in full consultation with the Executive Secretary of the CBD, will ensure that the other members and alternates are appointed after consultation with the CBD staff representative body referred to in paragraph 8 of this agreement. Such members and alternates will be appointed for fixed periods, normally of one year, subject to renewal.
8. Consistent with the Staff Regulations and Rules of the United Nations, a CBD staff representative body will be established, taking into account, as appropriate, the existing staff representative body(ies) at the seat of the Convention Secretariat and will be consulted on all matters related to staff.

9. Movements of staff between the Convention Secretariat and other parts of UNEP will be subject to the same conditions and arrangements as are applicable to staff serving with voluntarily funded programmes of the United Nations.
10. The principle of recruitment on as wide a geographical basis as possible will govern the Professional staff in accordance with the guidelines for voluntarily funded programmes.
11. Job descriptions are prepared and submitted to UNEP by the Executive Secretary for posts approved by the Conference of the Parties.
12. Once a post is classified, a recruitment process is carried out according to the following procedures:
    (a) Vacancy announcements are issued to all Parties/signatories to the CBD, "internally" to request candidates within UNEP and the UN system, and "externally" to elicit applications worldwide;
    (b) Upon completion of the time limited given for applications (which should not exceed six weeks), the HRMS/UNON submits the list of candidates and their detailed applications to the Executive Secretary;
    (c) The Secretariat will constitute a panel to prepare a short list and advise the Executive Secretary on the most suitable candidate. The panel will normally follow agreed procedures for its selection including interviewing the short listed candidates;
    (d) The Appointment and Promotion Board of the CBD, referred to in paragraphs 6 and 7 of this agreement, will review the recommendations and submit its advice to the Executive Director of UNEP for final approval;
    (e) The selected candidate(s) will be offered appointment(s) by the Executive Director of UNEP after consultation with the Executive Secretary of the CBD, in accordance with paragraphs 3, 4, and 5 of this agreement.

13. As an “external” recruitment process takes time, fixed-term appointments of short-term duration of less than one year (up to a maximum of eleven months) can be made as an interim solution, while the normal recruitment process is completed in accordance with the provisions of paragraphs 3, 4, 5, and 6 of this agreement.
14. The selection and terms of employment of consultants, within available allotments, will be decided by the Executive Secretary, in accordance with United Nations procedures.
15. Posts for General Services follow the International Civil Aviation Organization (ICAO) (the lead UN agency in Montreal) job classification standards. The procedure for selecting the most qualified candidate is also similar to that of the professional candidate. For these purposes, renewable contracts of up to but not exceeding eleven months for General Service staff may be offered by the Executive Secretary of the CBD.
16. The appropriate UN bodies, such as the Joint Appeal Board, the Joint Disciplinary Committee, the Claims Board and the Advisory Board on Compensation Claims, will have jurisdiction as regards all staff serving with the Convention.
17. Professional staff will normally be pay-rolled at UNEP Headquarters and their salaries deposited monthly in the individual bank accounts nominated by the staff unless agreed otherwise by UNEP and the CBD Secretariat.
18. For health insurance, Professional and General Services staff are enrolled in the Canadian Medicare which is a branch of Sunlife Medical Insurance. Enrollment is made once staff member starts working and the staff member’s portion of the premium is charged to his/her salary. The administration of this service is provided by ICAO.
19. Staff attendance, annual sick leave will be monitored by the Executive Secretary of the CBD or the person to whom he/she delegates this responsibility.

II. Financial Arrangements

General Provisions

20. The Financial Regulations and Rules of the United Nations will govern these financial and common services arrangements. These arrangements will also be consistent with the financial rules adopted by the Conference of the Parties.
21. Taking into account that the resources of CBD are contributions from the Parties to the CBD and are distinct from the United Nations resources, the financial transactions of the CBD Secretariat that utilize these resources will be exempted from such restrictions as the Secretary-General of the United Nations may from time-to-time impose regarding the employment of staff and consultants and the use of funds for operational requirements, including the restrictions currently in force due to the financial situation of the United Nations.
22. The financial and common support services of the CBD Secretariat will be provided by UNEP, UNON or any other United Nations entity, as appropriate, and as agreed by the Executive Director of UNEP, in full co-operation with the Executive Secretary of the Convention.

III. Contributions and Funds

23. The Executive Director of UNEP, with approval of UNEP's Governing Council, has established the following trust funds to support the Convention process:
    (a) Special account for the Core Administrative Budget of the CBD (General Trust Fund for the CBD-alpha code BY);
    (b) Special fund for additional voluntary contributions to the core budget for approved activities under the CBD (General Trust Fund for additional voluntary contributions in support of approved activities under the CBD-alpha code BE);

(c) Special fund for voluntary contributions to facilitate the participation of Parties in the CBD process (General Trust Fund for voluntary contributions to facilitate the participation of Parties in the process of the CBD-alpha code BZ).

24. The trust funds, referred to in paragraph 21 above, will be subject to arrangements related to Appendix D of the Staff Regulations and Rules. The related resources and expenditures will be accounted for under a separate account to be established by the United Nations for this purpose.

25. For the purpose of recording funds and expenditures, the trust funds, referred to in paragraph 21 above, will be administered in accordance with UN Rules and Regulations with the following exception:

No operational reserve will be maintained under the Core Administrative Budget of the Convention account on the understanding that the CBD Working Capital Reserve will be maintained and administered under that account. No operational reserves will be maintained under the other trust fund accounts.

26. The CBD secretariat will be exempt from the requirement to submit cost plans and annual substantive and programme performance reports to the UNEP. It will, however, adopt appropriate financial planning and reporting practices corresponding to its own administrative needs and to such purposes as may be determined by the Conference of the Parties.

27. Notifications (invoices) of contributions due from parties to the Convention will be processed on the basis of the Executive Secretary's communication on approval of the CBD indicative scale of contribution amount for each Party, in co-operation with the Fund Management Branch of UNEP, as appropriate. Notifications (invoices) are to be sent by the CBD Secretariat to all Parties by 1 October of the year proceeding the year for which contributions are due. Pledged contributions will be recorded under the trust funds in accordance with the rules and regulations

governing the acceptance of such pledges. Contributions of the CBD accounts shall be deposited in the following account:

UNEP Trust Funds Account No. 015-002756
UNEP Bank Account
Chase Mahattan Bank
New York, N.Y. 10017

28. UNEP will promptly advise the Executive Secretary by facsimile or any other appropriate means of communication, of the receipt of the contributions and acknowledge receipt to the donors. On a monthly basis, UNEP will provide to the Executive Secretary an up-to-date report of the status of pledges, payments of contributions and expenditures.

IV. Treasury

29. All contributions to the Convention are deposited in the Trust Funds referred to in paragraph 21 of this agreement, and in accordance with the terms of reference for such trust funds, it is the prerogative of the Secretary-General of the United Nations to invest all available cash surpluses in the account to achieve the best possible investment returns. The Treasurer of the United Nations will therefore invest CBD monies that may not be immediately required. The interest earned on the Convention trust funds will be credited to the relevant trust funds.

V. Budget

30. The budget of the Convention is approved by the Conference of the Parties. The Executive Secretary may commit resources only if such commitments are within the budget approved by the Conference of the Parties and within available resources.
31. The Executive Secretary will prepare draft allotments and staffing tables for activities under the Convention's budget, for final

approval of the Executive Director of UNEP. These allotments constitute the authority to the Executive Secretary to enter into commitments and expend resources, including the extension of staff contracts. The Executive Secretary of the CBD has the responsibility to adhere to all applicable UN Regulations and Rules when exercising this authority.

32. Certification authority for expenditures from each of the Convention trust funds will reside with the Secretariat-based Fund and Administrative Officer, who will consult fully with the Executive Secretary of the CBD on such matters. The Secretariat-based Fund and Administrative Officer, in full consultation with the Executive Secretary, can delegate this authority to the responsible Fund Programme Management Officer in UNEP when necessary.

VI. Accounting and Reporting

33. UNEP/UNON will maintain, in full consultation with the Executive Secretary, the accounts for CBD, approve payments on behalf of the CBD Secretariat, provide payroll services, record obligations, disbursements and expenditures and provide a timely, up-to-date report of all accounts to the Executive Secretary in accordance with established procedures.
34. No disbursement will be made if funds are not available within the trust funds established for the Convention.
35. A bank account will be maintained in Montreal to support the day-to-day transactions of the Secretariat. This account shall be replenished as and when required. The Montreal Bank Account is not intended for the receipt of contributions, except in extraordinary circumstances and in accordance with United Nations Rules and Regulations. In such circumstances, the Executive Secretary will record the related reasons and provide them to UNEP.
36. On a monthly basis, UNEP/UNON will provide the Executive Secretary with up-to-date information on the status of allotment,

trial balance and unliquidated obligations. The final accounts will be submitted to the Executive Secretary for certification and submissions to the Board of External Auditors and reporting to the Conference of Parties in accordance with CBD Financial Procedures.

VII. Procurement of Goods and Services

37. The Executive Secretary may approve procurement of goods and services up to a maximum of US$70,000 for each transaction provided that:
    (a) except as provided in (c) below, contracts involving commitments in excess of US$20,000 will be let only after competitive budding or calling for proposals if proposals are called, a comparative analysis of such proposals shall be kept on record;
    (b) contracts will be awarded to the lowest acceptable bidder, provided that where the interest of the Convention so required, all bids may be rejected. In such case the Executive Secretary will record the related reasons and provide them to UNEP;
    (c) the Executive Secretary may award contracts without calling for proposals or formal invitations to bid, in the circumstances set out in paragraphs (b) to (h) to financial rule 110.19; in such cases, appropriate reasons will be recorded and provided to UNEP.

    For any transaction in excess of US$70,000, procurement will be handled under the procedures set out in financial rule: 111.17(d), as applicable to UNEP.
38. Travel of the CBD Secretariat staff will be authorized by the Executive Secretary and will be at standards not higher than those which the United Nations may set from time to time. Travel of delegations under the terms of the Special Fund for Voluntary Contributions to Facilitate Participation of Parties in the

CBD process will be governed by ST/SGB/107/Rev. 6 and related legislative decisions of the Conference of the Parties, or donor requirements.

VIII. Reimbursement for Services provided to the Secretariat

39. All trust funds established for the CBD are subject to 13 per cent programme support reimbursement on actual recorded expenditures.
40. The above programme support funds will be used in part for financing the full and effective requirements of the administrative/personnel unit of the CBD Secretariat in Montreal. The remaining will be used for financing the services provided to the CBD Secretariat, including recruitment, services by UNEP/UNON to the APB referred to in paragraphs 6, 7 and 12 (d) of this agreement, and the provision of human resources development staff by UNEP/UNON when required.

IX. Conference and Other Services

41. UNEP/UNON will facilitate the co-ordination and provision of conference services to the sessions of the COP and its subsidiary bodies in full co-operation with the Executive Secretary of the CBD. The Executive Secretary of the CBD will consult with UNEP/UNON when subcontracting services to other institutions.

X. Revision of this Agreement

42. The provisions of this agreement or their application may, at the request of either party be reviewed at any time. Such a request will be made at least four months in advance, and will then be addressed at the next meeting of the Bureau of the COP or the next meeting of the COP, whichever comes first.

PART II Headquarters Agreements

Appendix IV Headquarters Agreement between UNESCO and France*

The Government of the French Republic and the United Nations Educational, Scientific and Cultural Organization,

Considering that by Resolution 28 adopted at its 6th session, the General Conference of the United Nations Educational, Scientific and Cultural Organization decided to build the permanent headquarters of the Organization at Paris,

Considering further that the Government of the French Republic has for this purpose by contract dated 25 June 1954 granted to the United Nations Educational, Scientific and Cultural Organization the use of such land as is necessary for the establishment of its permanent headquarters and the construction of its buildings, and

Desiring to regulate, by this Agreement, all questions relating to the establishment of the permanent headquarters of the United Nations Educational, Scientific and Cultural Organization in Paris and consequently to define its privileges and immunities in France,

Have appointed as their representatives for this purpose the following, that is to say: For the United Nations Educational, Scientific and Cultural

* Headquarters Agreement between the Director-General of the UNESCO (Luther H. Evans) for the UNESCO and the representative of the French Republic (Monsieur Guérin de Beaumont, State Secretary for Foreign Affairs) for the Government of the French Republic, signed in Paris on July 2, 1954 (on file with the author).

Organization (hereinafter called 'the Organization'), Mr. Luther H. Evans, Director-General; For the Government of the French Republic, Monsieur Guérin de Beaumont, State Secretary for Foreign Affairs, who have agreed as follows:

Agreement between the Government of the French Republic and the United Nations Educational, Scientific and Cultural Organization regarding the Headquarters of UNESCO and the Privileges and Immunities of the Organization on French Territory

[Signed in Paris on 2 July 1954; Came into force on 23 November 1955 in accordance with Article 32 thereof.]

Legal Personality of the Organization

Article 1

The Government of the French Republic recognizes the legal personality of the Organization and its capacity:

(a) To contract;
(b) To acquire and dispose of movable and immovable property;
(c) To be party to judicial proceedings.

The Permanent Headquarters of the Organization

Article 2

The permanent Headquarters of the Organization (hereinafter called 'Headquarters') shall comprise the land described and defined in Annex A of this Agreement, and all the buildings that are or may be in future built thereon.

Article 3

The Government of the French Republic agrees to take all necessary measures to ensure that the Organization shall have full and uninterrupted use of the land and buildings which constitute its Headquarters.

Article 4

1. The Government of the French Republic grants to the Organization the right of free radio communication on French territory in the manner defined in Annex III of the International Telecommunication Convention made at Buenos Aires in 1952, for broadcasting its programmes and for participation in the radio network to be established between the United Nations and its Specialized Agencies.
2. Special agreements to be negotiated between the Organization and the appropriate French authorities, and, if necessary, between the Organization and international institutions concerned, will set out the terms upon which the aforesaid broadcasts and radio communications are to be made.

Article 5

1. The Headquarters shall be under the control and authority of the Organization.
2. The Organization shall have the right to make internal regulations applicable throughout Headquarters in order to enable it to carry out its work.
3. Subject to the provisions of the preceding paragraph, the laws and regulations of the French Republic shall apply at Headquarters.

Article 6

1. Headquarters shall be inviolable. Agents and officials of the French Republic shall not enter Headquarters to discharge any

official duty save with the consent or at the request of the Director-General and in accordance with conditions approved by him.

2. The execution of legal process, including the seizure of private property may take place in Headquarters only with the consent of and under conditions approved by the Director-General.
3. Without prejudice to the terms of this Agreement, the Organization shall not permit its Headquarters to become a refuge from justice for persons against whom a penal judgement has been made or who are pursued *flagrante delicto*, or against whom a warrant of arrest or a deportation order has been issued by the competent French authorities.

Article 7

1. The Government of the French Republic undertakes to protect Headquarters and to maintain order in its immediate vicinity.
2. At the request of the Director-General and in accordance with his instructions, the French authorities shall make available whatever police force may be necessary to maintain order within Headquarters.

Article 8

1. The appropriate French authorities shall endeavour, within the limits of their powers, on equitable terms, and in accordance with requests made by the Director-General of the Organization, to provide public services such as postal, telephone and telegraph service, electricity, water and gas supplies, public transport, drainage, collection of refuse, fire protection and snow removal.
2. Subject to the provisions of Article 10, the Organization shall be granted, in respect of tariffs charged for public services supplied by the French Government or public bodies under its control, such reductions as are granted to French administrative services.

3. In case of *force majeure* involving a partial or total suspension of public services, the Organization shall receive, for its requirements, priority equal to that received by the French administrative services.

Access to Headquarters

Article 9

1. The competent French authorities shall not impede the transit to or from Headquarters of any persons having official duty at Headquarters or invited there by the Organization.
2. For this purpose the French Government undertakes to authorize the entry into France without delay and without charge for visas, of the following persons for the term of their duty or mission with the Organization:
   - (a) Representatives of Member States, including alternates, advisers, experts and secretaries at sessions of the various organs of the Organization or at conferences and meetings called by it;
   - (b) Members of the Executive Board of the Organization, alternates, advisers and experts;
   - (c) Permanent delegates of Member States accredited to the Organization, deputies, advisers and experts;
   - (d) Officials and experts of the Organization and of the United Nations and the Specialized Agencies;
   - (e) Members of the governing bodies and officials of nongovernmental organizations having consultative status, the offices of which are at Headquarters;
   - (f) The families – spouses and dependent children – of the above-mentioned persons;
   - (g) All those invited on official business by the General Conference, the Executive Board or the Director-General of the Organization;

(h) Representatives of non-governmental organizations having consultative status, representatives of the press, radio, cinema and of other information agencies who are accredited to the Organization, after consultation with the French Government and provided that the persons concerned have not been previously prohibited from entering French territory.

3. Without prejudice to any special immunities which they may enjoy, the persons mentioned in paragraph 2 may not, during the whole period in which they are performing their duties or missions, be compelled by the French authorities to leave French territory, save where they have abused the privileges accorded to them in respect of their visits by carrying out activities unconnected with their duties or missions with the Organization and subject to the following provisions.
4. No measures for the expulsion from French territory of the persons mentioned in paragraph 2 may be taken without the approval of the Minister of Foreign Affairs of the Government of the French Republic. Before giving his approval, the Minister of Foreign Affairs shall consult the authorities mentioned hereafter.
5. The authorities mentioned in the preceding paragraph are:
   (a) In any case concerning the representative of a Member State or his family – the Government of the Member State concerned;
   (b) In any case concerning a member of the Executive Board or his family – the Chairman of the Executive Board;
   (c) In the case of any other persons – the Director-General of the Organization.
6. Persons who enjoy diplomatic privileges and immunities by virtue of this Agreement may not be required to leave French territory save in accordance with the procedure customarily applicable to diplomats accredited to the Government of the French Republic.

7. It is understood that the persons referred to in paragraph 2 are not exempt from any reasonable application of the rules governing quarantine and public health.

Arrangements for Communication

Article 10

1. Without prejudice to the provisions of Article 4 and in so far as is compatible with any international conventions, regulations and arrangements to which it is party, the Government of the French Republic shall grant to the Organization for communication by post, telephone, telegraph, radio-telephone, radio-telegraph and radio-photo-telegraph, terms at least as favourable as those granted by it to other governments, including diplomatic missions, as regards priorities, tariffs and taxes on mail, cablegrams, telegrams, radio-telegrams, photo-telegrams, telephone calls and other communications and also as regards charges payable for press and radio communications.
2. The Government of the French Republic shall grant full facilities to the Director-General of the Organization and his principal officials for press or radio statements.

Article 11

1. The official correspondence of the Organization shall be inviolable.
2. The official statements of the Organization shall not be subject to censorship. This immunity extends to publications, films, negatives, photographs, and visual and sound recordings addressed to or dispatched by the Organization, and also material displayed at exhibitions which it may organize.
3. The Organization may make use of codes and may dispatch and receive correspondence by courier or pouch. Courier and pouch

services shall be accorded the same privileges and immunities as diplomatic couriers and pouches.

Property, Funds and Assets

Article 12

The Organization, its property and assets wherever located and by whomsoever held, shall enjoy immunity from every form of legal process, except in so far as in any particular case the Organization has expressly waived immunity or where a waiver is implied by contract. It is, however, understood that no waiver shall extend to any measure of execution.

Article 13

Should the Organization set up offices or occupy conference rooms outside Headquarters but inside France, these premises shall be inviolable, in accordance with the conditions of Article 6.

Article 14

1. The property and assets of the Organization wherever located and by whomsoever held shall be immune from search, confiscation, requisition, expropriation or any other form of constraint, either executive, administrative or legislative.
2. The archives of the Organization and, in general, all documents belonging to or held by it shall be inviolable wherever they are located.

Article 15

1. The Organization, its assets, income and other property shall be exempt from all direct taxation. The Organization shall, however, pay taxes charged for services rendered.
2. The Organization shall be exempt

(a) From all duty and taxes, other than taxes for services rendered, collected by the customs authorities, and from all prohibitions and restrictions on imports and exports in respect of articles imported by it for official use. It is understood, however, that articles imported free of duty may not be transferred to other parties on French territory, save on conditions to be agreed upon between the Organization and the competent French authorities;

(b) From all duty and taxes, except taxes payable for services rendered, collected by the customs authorities, and from all prohibitions and restrictions on imports and exports in respect of publications, cinematograph films, photographic slides and documents which the Organization may import or publish in the course of its official activities.

Article 16

The Organization shall pay, under general laws and regulations, all indirect taxes which form part of the cost of goods sold and services rendered. Nevertheless, any such taxes levied in respect of purchases made or activities undertaken officially by the Organization may be reimbursed by lump sums to be agreed between the Organization and the French Republic.

Article 17

1. The Organization may, without being subject to any financial control, regulations or moratoria:
   (a) Receive and hold funds and foreign exchange of all kinds and operate accounts in all currencies;
   (b) Freely transfer its funds and foreign exchange within French territory and from France to another country and vice versa.
2. The competent French authorities shall grant all facilities and assistance to the Organization with a view to obtaining the most favourable conditions for all transfers and exchanges. Special

arrangements to be made between the French Government and the Organization shall regulate, if necessary, the application of this Article.

3. In exercising its rights under this Article, the Organization shall take account of all representations made by the Government of the French Republic in so far as it considers that these can be complied with without prejudice to its own interests.

Diplomatic Privileges, Immunities and Facilities

Article 18

1. Representatives of Member States of the Organization at sessions of the various organs of the Organization and at conferences and meetings called by it; members of the Executive Board, alternates, permanent delegates accredited to the Organization and their deputies shall enjoy, during their stay in France on official duty, such privileges, immunities and facilities as are accorded to diplomats of equal rank belonging to foreign diplomatic missions accredited to the Government of the French Republic.
2. These privileges, immunities and facilities shall extend to the spouses and children under 21 of the above-mentioned persons.
3. Only the heads of delegations of Member States to the General Conferences of the Organization, the Chairman of the Executive Board and permanent delegates accredited to the Organization with the rank of ambassador or minister plenipotentiary shall be assimilated to heads of diplomatic missions.

Article 19

1. Without prejudice to the provisions of Articles 23 and 24, the Director-General and the Deputy Director-General of the Organization shall, during their residence in France have the status accorded to the heads of foreign diplomatic missions accredited to the Government of the French Republic.

2. Without prejudice to Articles 22 and 24, the directors of departments, the heads of services and bureaux and officials defined in Annex B of this Agreement, and the spouses and dependent children of the persons designated in paragraphs 1 and 2 of this Article shall be accorded during their residence in France the privileges, immunities and facilities and other courtesies accorded to members of foreign diplomatic missions in France.
3. The persons mentioned in paragraphs 1 and 2 of this Article may not, if they are of French nationality, claim immunity in the French courts in respect of judicial proceedings concerning matters extraneous to their official duties.

Article 20

The Organization shall, in due course, communicate to the Government of the French Republic the names of the persons mentioned in Articles 18 and 19.

Article 21

The immunities provided for in Articles 18 and 19 are accorded in the interests of the Organization and not for the personal benefit of the individuals themselves. Such immunities may be waived by the Government of the state concerned in respect of its representatives and their families; by the Executive Board in respect of its members and their families and of the Director-General and his family; and by the Director- General in respect of the other officials of the Organization mentioned in Article 19, and their families.

Officials and Experts

Article 22

Officials governed by the provisions of the Staff Regulations of the Organization:

(a) Shall be immune from legal process in respect of all activities performed by them in their official capacity (including words spoken or written);
(b) Shall be exempt from all direct taxation on salaries and emoluments paid to them by the Organization;
(c) Subject to the provisions of Article 23, shall be exempt from all military service and from all other compulsory service in France;
(d) Shall, together with their spouses and the dependent members of their families, be exempt from immigration restrictions and registration provisions relating to foreigners;
(e) Shall, with regard to foreign exchange, be granted the same facilities as are granted to members of diplomatic missions accredited to the Government of the French Republic;
(f) Shall, together with their spouses and dependent members of their families, be accorded the same facilities for repatriation as are granted to members of diplomatic missions accredited to the Government of the French Republic in time of international crisis;
(g) Shall, provided they formerly resided abroad, be granted the right to import free of duty their furniture and personal effects at the time of their installation in France;
(h) May temporarily import motor cars free of duty, under customs certificates without deposits.

Article 23

1. French officials of the Organization are not exempt from military service or any other obligatory service in France. Nevertheless, those whose names have, by reason of their duties, been placed upon a list compiled by the Director-General and approved by the French authorities, may, in case of mobilization, be assigned to special duties in accordance with French law.

2. These authorities shall, on the request of the Organization and in case of a call-up for national service applicable to other officials of French nationality, grant such temporary deferments as may be necessary to avoid the interruption of essential work.

Article 24

Privileges and immunities are granted to officials in the interests of the Organization and not for the personal benefit of the individuals themselves. The Director-General shall agree to waive the immunity granted to an official in any case in which he considers that such immunity would impede the course of justice and can be waived without prejudice to the interests of the Organization.

Article 25

1. While performing their functions or engaged on mission on behalf of the Organization, experts other than the officials mentioned in Articles 19 and 22 shall, in so far as is necessary for the effective discharge of their functions, and also during journeys made in the course of duty or for the period of their missions, be granted the under-mentioned privileges and immunities:
   (a) Immunity from personal arrest and seizure of personal baggage, except if caught in the act of committing an offence. The competent French authorities shall, in such cases, immediately inform the Director-General of the Organization of the arrest or of the seizure of baggage;
   (b) Immunity from judicial process in respect of all acts done by them in the performance of their official functions (including words spoken or written). Such immunity shall continue notwithstanding that the persons concerned are no longer performing official functions for the Organization or on mission on its behalf;

(c) The same facilities concerning the regulation of foreign exchange as those accorded to officials of foreign governments on temporary official mission.

2. The Director-General of the Organization shall agree to waive the immunity of an expert in any case in which he considers that this can be done without damage to the interests of the Organization.

Article 26

The Organization shall constantly co-operate with the competent French authorities for the proper administration of justice, the due carrying out of police regulations and in order to avoid any possible abuse arising out of the exercise of the immunities and facilities provided for in this Agreement.

Laissez-passer

Article 27

United Nations *laissez-passer* held by officials of the Organization shall be recognized and accepted by the Government of the French Republic as valid travel documents.

Settlement of Disputes

Article 28

The Organization shall make provision for appropriate modes of settlement of:

(a) Disputes arising out of contracts or other disputes in private law to which the Organization is party;

(b) Disputes involving any official of the Organization who, by reason of his official position, enjoys immunity if this immunity has not been waived by the Director-General.

Article 29

1. Any dispute between the Organization and the Government of the French Republic concerning the interpretation or application of this Agreement, or any supplementary agreement, if it is not settled by negotiation or any other appropriate method agreed to by the parties, shall be submitted for final decision to an arbitration tribunal composed of three members; one shall be appointed by the Director-General of the Organization, another by the Minister of Foreign Affairs of the Government of the French Republic and the third chosen by these two. If the two arbitrators cannot agree on the choice of the third, the appointment shall be made by the President of the International Court of Justice.
2. The Director-General or the Minister of Foreign Affairs may request the General Conference to ask an advisory opinion of the International Court of Justice on any legal question raised in the course of such proceedings. Pending an opinion of the Court, the two parties shall abide by a provisional decision of the arbitration tribunal. Thereafter, this tribunal shall give a final decision, taking into account the advisory opinion of the Court.

General Provisions

Article 30

The provisional Agreement of 10 March 1947 between the Government of the French Republic and the Organization shall terminate on the entry into force of this Agreement.

Article 31

1. This Agreement is made in accordance with the provisions of Section 39 of the Convention on the Privileges and Immunities of

the Specialized Agencies, which provides for special agreements between a state and a Specialized Agency for the carrying out of the provisions of the above-mentioned Convention, taking into account the particular needs of an Agency at its headquarters.

2. The accession of the Government of the French Republic to the Convention on the Privileges and Immunities of the Specialized Agencies shall not be deemed to modify the application of the provisions of this Agreement.
3. It is, however, understood that, should that Convention be revised, the Minister of Foreign Affairs of the Government of the French Republic and the Director-General of the Organization shall confer with a view to deciding what necessary amendments should be made to this Agreement.
4. All amendments to the provisions of this Agreement must be submitted to the competent authorities of the Organization and to the Government of the French Republic. No such revision shall come into force save in accordance with the procedure set out in Article 32.

Article 32

This Agreement and any amendment made thereto shall come into force on the exchange of the instrument of ratification by the Government of the French Republic and the notification of approval by the Organization.

Done at Paris on 2 July 1954, in two copies in the French and English languages, both texts being equally authoritative.

ANNEX A

The permanent Headquarters of the Organization is established on an area of 30,350 square metres of land, situated in Paris in the 7th *arrondissement,* between Place de Fontenoy, Avenue de Saxe, Avenue Ségur, Avenue de Suffren and Avenue de Lowendal. This area was granted to the Department of Foreign Affairs by decree dated 22 December 1952 and let to the Organization by lease dated 25 June 1954 and is designated by the area coloured pink on the plan annexed to the said lease.

ANNEX B

The officials of the Organization who shall benefit from the provisions of Article 19, paragraph 2, are, in addition to the directors of departments and heads of services and bureaux, the following:

(a) Officials in a grade equivalent or superior to grade P-5;
(b) As a transitional measure, those officials who, under the provisional Headquarters Agreement entered into by the Government of the French Republic and the Organization, enjoyed the privileges and immunities accorded to members of diplomatic missions in France;
(c) Officials in grades corresponding to the grades of officials of any other intergovernmental institution to whom the Government of the French Republic may grant diplomatic privileges and immunities by a Headquarters Agreement.

V Agreement between the United Nations and the Republic of Kenya regarding the Headquarters of the United Nations Environment Programme*

The United Nations and the Republic of Kenya

Considering that the United Nations General Assembly, by resolution 2997 (XXVII) of 15 December 1972, has established institutional and financial arrangements for the United Nations Environment Programme, and, in response to an offer by the Government of Kenya, has, by resolution 3004 (XXVII) of 15 December 1972, decided that the Environment Secretariat shall be located at Nairobi;

Considering that the Convention on the Privileges and Immunities of the United Nations adopted by the General Assembly of the United Nations on 13 February 1946, to which the Republic of Kenya is a party, is *ipso facto* applicable to the United Nations Environment Programme;

Considering that it is desirable to conclude an agreement, complementary to the convention on the Privileges and Immunities of the United Nations, to regulate questions not envisaged in that Convention arising as a result of the establishment of the headquarters of the United Nations Environment Programme at Nairobi;

* Headquarters Agreement between the Executive Director of UNEP (Maurice F. Strong) for the UNEP and the Minister for Foreign Affairs of the Republic of Kenya (Munyua Waiyaki) for the Republic of Kenya, signed in Nairobi on 26 March 1975 (on file with the author).

Have agreed as follows:

Article I

Definitions

Section – 1

In this Agreement,

(a) The expression "the UNEP" means the institutional and financial arrangements for the United Nations Environment Programme established by the General Assembly of the United Nations in resolution 2997 (XXVII) of 15 December 1972, and such other institutional and financial arrangements as may from time to time be made for the United Nations Environment Programme. The United Nations Environment Programme shall, in particular, in accordance with resolution 2997 (XXVII), include the following:
   (i) the Government Council of the United Nations Environment Programme (hereinafter referred to as "the Governing Council");
   (ii) the Executive Director of the United Nations Environment Programme;
   (iii) the Environment Secretariat;
   (iv) the Environment Fund; and
   (v) the Environment Co-ordination Board;

(b) The expression "Executive Director" means the Executive Director of the UNEP or any officer designated to act on his behalf;

(c) The expression "officials of the Environment Secretariat" means the Executive Director and all members of the staff of the UNEP, except those who are locally recruited and assigned to hourly rates;

(d) The expression "the Government" means the Government of the Republic of Kenya;

(e) The expression "appropriate Kenyan authorities" means such government, municipal or other authorities in the Republic of Kenya as may be appropriate in the context and in accordance with the laws and customs applicable in the Republic of Kenya;

(f) The expression "Laws of the Republic of Kenya" includes:
  (i) the Constitution of the Republic of Kenya; and
  (ii) legislative acts, regulations and orders issued by or under authority of the Government or appropriate Kenyan authorities;

(g) The expression "headquarters seat" means
  (i) the headquarters area with the building or buildings upon it, as may from time to time be defined in supplemental agreements referred to in section 3 of article II hereof; and
  (ii) any other land or building which may from time to time be included, temporarily or permanently, therein in accordance with this Agreement or by supplemental agreement with the Government;

(h) The expression "Member State" means a State which is a Member of the United Nations, or a member of one of the specialized agencies, or a member of the International Atomic Energy Agency, or any other State designated by the General Assembly as eligible to participate in the UNEP;

(i) The expression "General Convention" means the Convention on the Privileges and Immunities of the United Nations approved by the General Assembly of the United Nations on 13 February 1946.

Article II

The Headquarters Seat

Section – 2

(a) The permanent headquarters of the UNEP shall be in the headquarters seat, and shall not be removed therefrom unless the

United Nations should so decide. Any transfer of the headquarters temporarily to another place shall not constitute a removal of the permanent headquarters unless there is an express decision by the United Nations to that effect.

(b) Any building in or outside of Nairobi which may be used with the concurrence of the Government for meetings convened by the UNEP shall be temporarily included in the headquarters seat.

(c) The appropriate Kenyan authorities shall take whatever action may be necessary to ensure that the UNEP shall not be dispossessed of all or any part of the headquarters seat without the express consent of the United Nations.

Section – 3

The Government grants to the UNEP, and the UNEP accepts from the Government, the permanent use and occupation of a headquarters seat as may from time to time be defined in supplemental agreements to be concluded between the UNEP and the Government.

Section – 4

(a) The United Nations shall for official purposes have the authority to install and operate a radio sending and receiving station or stations to connect at appropriate points and exchange traffic with the United Nations radio network. The United Nations as a telecommunications administration will operate its telecommunications services in accordance with the International Telecommunication Convention and the Regulations annexed thereto. The frequencies used by these stations will be communicated by the United Nations to the Government and to the International Frequency Registration Board.

(b) The Government shall, upon request, grant to the UNEP for official purposes appropriate radio and other telecommunications facilities in conformity with technical arrangements to be made with the International Telecommunication Union.

Section – 5

The UNEP may establish and operate research, documentation and other technical facilities. These facilities shall be subject to appropriate safeguards which, in the case of facilities which might create hazards to health or safety or interfere with property, shall be agreed with the appropriate Kenyan authorities.

Section – 6

The facilities provided for in sections 4 and 5 may, to the extent necessary for efficient operation, be established and operated outside the headquarters area. The appropriate Kenyan authorities shall, at the request of the UNEP, make arrangements, on such terms and in such manner as may be agreed upon by supplemental agreement, for the acquisition or use by the UNEP of appropriate premises for such purposes, and for the inclusion of such premises in the headquarters seat.

Article III

Extraterritoriality of the Headquarters Seat

Section – 7

(a) The Government recognizes the extraterritoriality of the headquarters seat, which shall be under the control and authority of the UNEP as provided in this Agreement.

(b) Except as otherwise provided in this Agreement or in the General Convention, and subject to any regulation enacted under section 8, the laws of the Republic of Kenya shall apply within the headquarters seat.

(c) Except as otherwise provided in this Agreement or in the General Convention, the courts or others appropriate organs of the Republic of Kenya shall have jurisdiction, as provided in applicable laws, over acts done and transactions taking place in the headquarters seat.

Section – 8

(a) The UNEP shall have the power to make regulations, operative within the headquarters seat, for the purpose of establishing therein conditions in all respects necessary for the full execution of its functions. No law of the Republic of Kenya which is inconsistent with a regulation of the UNEP authorized by this section shall, to the extent of such inconsistency, be applicable within the headquarters seat. Any dispute between the UNEP and the Republic of Kenya as to whether a regulation of the UNEP is authorized by this section, or as to whether a law of the Republic of Kenya is inconsistent with any regulation of the UNEP authorized by this section, shall be promptly settled be the procedure set out in section 35. Pending such settlement, the regulation of the UNEP shall apply and the law of the Republic of Kenya shall be inapplicable in the headquarters seat to the extent that the UNEP claims it to be inconsistent with the regulation of the UNEP.

(b) The Executive Director shall from time to time inform the Government, as may be appropriate, of regulations made by him in accordance with sub-section (a).

(c) This section shall not prevent the reasonable application of fire protection or sanitary regulations of the appropriate Kenyan authorities.

Section – 9

(a) The headquarters seat shall be inviolable. No officer or official of the Republic of Kenya, or other person exercising any public authority within the Republic of Kenya, shall enter the headquarters seat to perform any duties therein except with the consent of, and under conditions approved by, the Executive Director. The service of legal process, including the seizure of private property, shall not take place within the headquarters seat except with the express consent of, and under conditions approved by, the Executive Director.

(b) Without prejudice to the provisions of the General Convention or article XI of this Agreement, the UNEP shall prevent the headquarters seat from being used as a refuge by persons who are avoiding arrest under any law of the Republic of Kenya, who are required by the Government for extradition to another country, or who are endeavoring to avoid service of legal process.

Article IV

Protection of the Headquarters Seat

Section – 10

(a) The appropriate Kenyan authorities shall exercise due diligence to ensure that the tranquility of the headquarters seat is not disturbed by any person or group of persons attempting unauthorized entry into or creating disturbances in the immediate vicinity of the headquarters seat, and shall provide on the boundaries of the headquarters seat such police protection as may be required for these purposes.

(b) If so requested by the Executive Director, the appropriate Kenyan authorities shall provide a sufficient number of police for the preservation of law and order in the headquarters seat.

Section – 11

The appropriate Kenyan authorities shall take all reasonable steps to ensure that the amenities of the headquarters seat are not prejudiced and that the purposes for which the headquarters seat is required are not obstructed by any use made of the land or buildings in the vicinity of the headquarters seat. The UNEP shall take all reasonable steps to ensure that the amenities of the land in the vicinity of the headquarters seat are not prejudiced by any use made of the land or buildings in the headquarters seat.

Article V

Public Services in the Headquarters Seat

Section – 12

(a) The appropriate Kenyan authorities shall exercise, to the extent requested by the Executive Director, their respective powers to ensure that the headquarters seat shall be supplied with the necessary public services, including, without limitation by reason of this enumeration, electricity, water, sewerage, gas, post, telephone, telegraph, local transportation, drainage, collection of refuse and fire protection and that such public services shall be supplied on equitable terms.

(b) In case of any interruption or threatened interruption of any such services, the appropriate Kenyan authorities shall consider the needs of the UNEP as being of equal importance with those of essential agencies of the Government, and shall take steps accordingly to ensure that the work of the UNEP is not prejudiced.

(c) The Executive Director shall, upon request, make suitable arrangements to enable duly authorized representatives of the appropriate public services bodies to inspect, repair, maintain, reconstruct and relocate utilities, conduits, mains and sewers within the headquarters seat under conditions which shall not unreasonably disturb the carrying out of the functions of the UNEP.

(d) Where gas, electricity, water or heat is supplied by appropriate Kenyan authorities, or where the prices thereof are under their control, the UNEP shall be supplied at tariffs which shall not exceed the lowest comparable rates accorded to Kenyan governmental administrations.

Article VI

Liaison Functions

Section – 13

The Government shall take all necessary measures to facilitate the establishment of offices at Nairobi by international non-governmental organizations duly accredited to the UNEP, for the sole purpose of liaison with the UNEP.

Article VII

Communications, Publications and Transportation

Section – 14

(a) All official communication directed to the UNEP or to any officials of the Environment Secretariat, at the headquarters seat, and all outward official communications of the UNEP, by whatever means or in whatever form transmitted, shall be immune from censorship and from any other form of interception or interference with their privacy. Such immunity shall extend, without limitation by reason of this enumeration, to publications, still and moving pictures, films and sound recordings.

(b) The UNEP shall have the right to use codes and to dispatch and receive correspondence and other official communications by courier or in sealed bags, which shall have the same privileges and immunities as diplomatic couriers and bags.

Section – 15

(a) The Government recognizes the right of the UNEP freely to publish and broadcast within the Republic of Kenya in the fulfillment of its purpose.

(b) It is, however, understood that the UNEP shall respect any laws of the Republic of Kenya, or any international conventions to which the Republic of Kenya is a party, relating to copyrights.

Section – 16

The UNEP shall be entitled for its official purposes to use the railroad facilities in the Republic of Kenya at tariffs which shall not exceed the lowest comparable passenger fares and freight rates accorded to Kenyan governmental administrations.

Article VIII

Freedom from Taxation

Section – 17

(a) The UNEP, its assets, income and other property shall be exempt from all forms of direct taxes, provided, however, that such tax exemption shall not extend to the owner or lessor of any property rented by the UNEP.
(b) While the UNEP will not generally claim exemption from indirect taxes which constitute part of the cost of goods purchased by or services rendered to the UNEP, including rentals, nevertheless when the UNEP is making important purchases for official use on which such taxes or duties have been charged or are chargeable, the Government shall make appropriate administrative arrangements for the remission or refund of such taxes or duties. With respect to such taxes or duties, the UNEP shall at all times enjoy at least the same exemptions and facilities as are granted to Kenyan governmental administrations or to chiefs of diplomatic missions accredited to the Republic of Kenya, whichever are the more favorable. It is further understood that the UNEP will not claim exemption from taxes which are in fact no more than charges for public utility services.

(c) In any transaction to which the UNEP is a party, the UNEP shall be exempt from all taxes, recording fees, and documentary taxes.
(d) Articles imported or exported by the UNEP for official purposes shall be exempt from customs duties and other levies, and from prohibitions and restrictions on imports and exports.
(e) The UNEP shall be exempt from customs duties and other levies, prohibitions and restrictions on the importation of service automobiles, and spare parts thereof, required for its official purposes.
(f) The Government shall, if requested, grant the UNEP such facilities for the procurement of gasoline or other fuels and lubricating oils for each such automobile operated by the UNEP in such quantities as are required for the work of the UNEP and at such special rates as may be established for diplomatic missions in the Republic of Kenya.
(g) Articles imported in accordance with sub-sections (d) and (e) or obtained from the Government in accordance with sub-section (f) of this section, may be sold by the UNEP in the Republic of Kenya at any time after their importation or acquisition, subject to the Government regulations concerning payment by the buyer of customs duties and other levies.

Article IX

Financial Facilities

Section – 18

(a) Without being subject to any financial controls, regulations or moratoria of any kind, the UNEP may freely:
  (i) purchase any currencies through authorized channels and hold and dispose or them;
  (ii) operate accounts in any currency;

(iii) purchase through authorized channels, hold and dispose of funds, securities and gold;

(iv) transfer its funds, securities, gold and currencies to or from the Republic of Kenya, to or from any other country, or within the Republic of Kenya; and

(v) raise funds through the exercise of its borrowing power or in any other manner which it deems desirable, except that with respect to the raising of funds within the Republic of Kenya, the UNEP shall obtain the concurrence of the Government.

(b) The Government shall assist the UNEP to obtain the most favorable conditions as regards exchange rates, banking commissions in exchange transactions and the like.

(c) The UNEP shall, in exercising its rights under this section, pay due regard to any representations made by the Government in so far as effect can be given to such representations without prejudicing the interests of the UNEP.

Article X

Social Security and Pension Fund

Section – 19

The United Nations Joint Staff Pension Fund shall enjoy legal capacity in the Republic of Kenya and shall enjoy the same exemptions, privileges and immunities as the UNEP itself.

Section – 20

The UNEP shall be exempt from all compulsory contributions to, and officials of the Environment Secretariat shall not be required by the Government to participate in, any social security scheme of the Republic of Kenya.

Section – 21

The Government shall make such provision as may be necessary to enable any official of the UNEP who is not afforded social security coverage by the UNEP to participate, if the UNEP so requests, in any social security scheme of the Republic of Kenya. The UNEP shall, in so far as possible, arrange, under conditions to be agreed upon, for the participation in the Kenyan social security system of those locally recruited members of its staff who do not participate in the United Nations Joint Staff Pension Fund or to whom the UNEP does not grant social security protection at least equivalent to that offered under Kenyan law.

Article XI

Transit and Residence

Section – 22

(a) The Government shall take all necessary measures to facilitate the entry into and sojourn in Kenyan territory and shall place no impediment in the way of the departure from Kenyan territory of the persons listed below; it shall ensure that no impediment is placed in the way of their transit to or from the headquarters seat and shall afford them any necessary protection in transit:

(i) Members of permanent missions and other representatives of Member States, their families and other members of their households, as well as clerical and other auxiliary personnel and the spouses and dependent children of such personnel;

(ii) Officials of the Environment Secretariat, their families and other members of their households;

(iii) Officials of the United Nations or of one of the specialized agencies or of the International Atomic Energy Agency, attached to the UNEP, and those who have official business with the UNEP, and their spouses and dependent children;

(iv) Representatives of other organizations, with which the UNEP has established official relations, who have official business with the UNEP;

(v) Persons, other than officials of the Environment Secretariat, performing missions authorized by the UNEP or serving on committees or other subsidiary organs of the UNEP, and their spouses;

(vi) Representatives of the press, radio, film, television or other information media, who have been accredited to the UNEP in its discretion after consultation with the Government;

(vii) Representatives of other organizations or other persons invited by the UNEP to the headquarters seat on official business. The Executive Director shall communicate the names of such persons to the Government before their intended entry.

(b) This section shall not apply in the case of general interruptions of transportation, which shall be dealt with as provided in section 12 (b), and shall not impair the effectiveness of generally applicable laws relating to the operations of means of transportation.

(c) Visas, where required for persons referred to in this section, shall be granted without charge and as promptly as possible.

(d) No activity performed by any person referred to in sub-section (a) in his official capacity with respect to the UNEP shall constitute a reason for preventing his entry into or his departure from the territory of the Republic of Kenya or for requiring him to leave such territory.

(e) No person referred to in sub-section (a) shall be required by the Government to leave the Republic of Kenya save in the event of an abuse of the right of residence, in which case the following procedure shall apply:

(i) No proceeding shall be instituted to require any such person to leave the Republic of Kenya except with the prior approval of the Minister for the time being responsible for foreign affairs of the Republic of Kenya;

(ii) In the case of a representative of a Member State, such approval shall be given only after consultation with the Government of the Member State concerned;

(iii) In the case of any other person mentioned in sub-section (a), such approval shall be given only after consultation with the Executive Director, and if expulsion proceedings are taken against any such person, the Executive Director shall have the right to appear or to be represented in such proceedings on behalf of the person against whom such proceedings are instituted; and

(iv) Persons who are entitled to diplomatic privileges and immunities under section 29 shall not be required to leave the Republic of Kenya otherwise than in accordance with the customary procedure applicable to members, having comparable rank, of the staffs of chiefs of diplomatic missions accredited to the Republic of Kenya.

(f) This section shall not prevent the requirement of reasonable evidence to establish that persons claiming the rights granted by this section come within the classes described in sub-section (a), or the reasonable application of quarantine and health regulations.

Section – 23

The Executive Director and the appropriate Kenyan authorities shall, at the request of either of them, consult as to methods of facilitation entrance into the Republic of Kenya, and as to the use of available means of transportation, by persons coming from abroad who wish to visit the headquarters seat and who do not enjoy the privileges provided by section 22.

Article XII

Representatives to the UNEP

Section – 24

Representatives of Member States to meetings of or convened by the UNEP, and those who have official business with the UNEP, shall, while exercising their functions and during their journey to and from Kenya, enjoy the privileges and immunities provided in article IV of the General Convention.

Section – 25

Members of permanent missions to the UNEP shall be entitled to the same privileges and immunities as the Government accords to members, having comparable rank, of diplomatic missions accredited to the Republic of Kenya.

Section – 26

Permanent missions to the UNEP of States members of the Governing Council and those of Member States shall enjoy the same privileges and immunities as are accorded to diplomatic missions in the Republic of Kenya.

Section – 27

The Executive Director shall communicate to the Government a list of persons within the scope of this article and shall revise such list from time to time as may be necessary.

Article XIII

Officials of the Environment Secretariat

Section – 28

Officials of the Environment Secretariat shall enjoy within and with respect to the Republic of Kenya the following privileges and immunities:

(a) Immunity from legal process of any kind in respect of words spoken or written, and of acts performed by them in their official capacity, such immunity to continue notwithstanding that the persons concerned may have ceased to be officials of the Environment Secretariat;
(b) Immunity from seizure of their personal and official baggage;
(c) Immunity from inspection of official baggage, and if the official comes within the scope of section 29, immunity from inspection of personal baggage;
(d) Exemption from taxation in respect of the salaries, emoluments, indemnities and pensions paid to them by the UNEP for services past or present or in connection with their service with the UNEP;
(e) Exemption from any form of taxation on income derived by them from sources outside the Republic of Kenya;
(f) Exemption from registration fees in respect of their automobiles;
(g) Exemption, with respect to themselves, their spouses, their dependent relatives and other members of their households, from immigration restrictions and alien registration;
(h) Exemption from national service obligations, provided that, with respect to Kenyan nationals, such exemption shall be confined to officials whose names have, by reason of their duties, been placed upon a list compiled by the Executive Director and approved by the Government; provided further that should officials, other

than those listed, who are Kenyan nationals, be called up for national service, the Government shall, upon request of the Executive Director, grant such temporary deferments in the call-up of such officials as may be necessary to avoid interruption of the essential work of the UNEP:

(i) The right to purchase petrol free of duty for their vehicles on similar terms as are accorded to members of diplomatic missions accredited to the Republic of Kenya;

(j) Freedom to acquire or maintain within the Republic of Kenya or elsewhere foreign securities, foreign currency accounts, and other movables and the right to take the same out of the Republic of Kenya through authorized channels without prohibition or restriction;

(k) (i) Freedom to purchase one dwelling house within the Republic of Kenya for strictly personal use, and the right to finance such purchase through local mortgage arrangements under the same conditions applicable to Kenyan citizens;

(ii) In the event of sale of such house, the right to take out of the republic of Kenya, through authorized channels, the proceeds of the sale, after repayment of any outstanding local loan or local mortgage, in transferable currency;

(l) The same protection and repatriation facilities with respect to themselves, their spouses, their dependent relatives and other members of their households as are accorded in time of international crisis to members, having comparable rank, of the staffs of chiefs of diplomatic missions accredited to the Republic of Kenya; and

(m) The right to import for personal use, free of duty and other levies, prohibitions and restrictions on imports:

(i) their furniture, household and personal effects, in one or more separate shipments, and thereafter to import necessary additions to the same;

(ii) one automobile, and in the case of officials accompanied by their dependents, two automobiles every three years, unless the UNEP and the Government agree in particular cases that replacements may take place at an earlier date, because of loss, extensive damage or otherwise;

(iii) reasonable quantities of certain articles including liquor, tobacco, cigarettes and foodstuffs, for personal use or consumption and not for gift or sale; the UNEP may establish a commissary for the sale of such articles to its officials and members of delegations. A supplemental agreement shall be concluded between the Executive Director and the Government to regulate the exercise of these rights;

(n) Automobiles imported in accordance with sub-section (m) (ii) of this section may be sold in the Republic of Kenya at any time after their importation, subject to the Government regulations concerning payment by the buyer of customs duties;

(o) Officials of the Environment Secretariat who are locally recruited shall enjoy only those privileges and immunities provided in the General Convention, it being understood, nevertheless, that such privileges and immunities include exemption from taxation on pensions paid to them by the United Nations Joint Staff Pension Fund. Such officials shall also have access to the Commissary to be established in accordance with paragraph (m) (iii) of this section.

Section – 29

In addition to the privileges and immunities specified in section 28:

(a) The Executive Director and officials of the Environment Secretariat having the rank of Assistant Secretary-General and above shall be accorded the privileges and immunities, exemptions and facilities accorded to Ambassadors who are heads of missions;

(b) A senior official of the Environment Secretariat, when acting on behalf of the Executive Director during his absence from duty, shall be accorded the same privileges and immunities, exemptions and facilities as are accorded to the Executive Director; and

(c) Other officials having the professional grade P-5 and above, and such additional categories of officials as may be designated, in agreement with the Government, by the Executive Director in consultation with the Secretary-General of the United Nations on the ground of the responsibilities of their positions in the UNEP, shall be accorded the same privileges and immunities, exemptions and facilities as the Government accords to members, having comparable rank, of the staffs of chiefs of diplomatic missions accredited to the Republic of Kenya.

Section – 30

(a) The Executive Director shall communicate to the Government a list of officials of the Environment Secretariat and shall revise such list from time to time as may be necessary.
(b) The Government shall furnish persons within the scope of this article with an identity card bearing the photograph of the holder. This card shall serve to identify the holder in relation to all Kenyan authorities.

Article XIV

Experts on Mission for the UNEP

Section – 31

Experts (other than officials of the Environment Secretariat coming within the scope of article XIII) performing missions authorized by, serving on committees or other subsidiary organs of, or consulting at its request in any way with, the UNEP shall enjoy, within and with respect to the Republic of Kenya, the following privileges and immunities so far as may be necessary for the effective exercise of their function:

(a) Immunity in respect of themselves, their spouses and their dependent children from personal arrest or detention and from seizure of their personal and official baggage;

(b) Immunity from legal process of any kind with respect to words spoken or written, and all acts done by them, in the performance of their official functions, such immunity to continue notwithstanding that the persons concerned may no longer be employed on missions for, serving on committees of, or acting as consultants for, the UNEP, or may no longer be present at the headquarters seat or attending meetings convened by the UNEP;
(c) Inviolability of all papers, documents and other official material;
(d) The right, for the purpose of all communications with the UNEP, to use codes and to dispatch or receive papers, correspondence or other official material by courier or in sealed bags;
(e) Exemption with respect to themselves and their spouses from immigration restrictions, alien registration and national service obligations;
(f) The same protection and repatriation facilities with respect to themselves, their spouses, their dependent relatives and other members of their households as are accorded in time of international crisis to members, having comparable rank, of the staffs of chiefs of diplomatic missions accredited to the Republic of Kenya;
(g) The same privileges with respect to currency and exchange restrictions as are accorded to representatives of foreign Governments on temporary officials missions; and
(h) The same immunities and facilities with respect to their personal and official baggage as the Government accords to members, having comparable rank, of the staffs of chiefs of diplomatic missions accredited to the Republic of Kenya.

Section – 32

Where the incidence of any form of taxation depends upon residence, periods during which the persons designated in Section 31 may be present in the Republic of Kenya for the discharge of their duties shall not be considered as periods of residence. In particular, such persons shall be exempt from taxation on their salaries and emoluments received from the UNEP during such periods of duty.

Section – 33

(a) The Executive Director shall communicate to the Government a list of persons within the scope of this article and shall revise such list from time to time as may be necessary.
(b) The Government shall furnish persons within the scope of this article with an identity card bearing the photograph of the holder. This card shall serve to identify the holder in relation to all Kenyan authorities.

Article XV

Settlement of Disputes

Section – 34

The Executive Director shall make provision for appropriate methods of settlement of:

(a) Disputes arising out of contracts and disputes of a private law character to which the UNEP is a party; and, in consultation with the Government,
(b) Disputes involving an official of the Environment Secretariat who, by reason of his official position, enjoys immunity, if such immunity has not been waived.

Section – 35

(a) Any dispute between UNEP and the Government concerning the interpretation or application of this Agreement or of any supplemental agreement, or any question affecting the headquarters seat or the relationship between the UNEP and the Government, which is not settled by negotiation or other agreed mode of settlement, shall be referred for final decision to a tribunal of three arbitrators: one to be chosen by the Executive Director, one to be chosen by the Minister for the time being responsible for Foreign Affairs of the Republic of Kenya, and the third, who shall be chairman of the tribunal, to be chosen by the first two arbitrators. Should the first two arbitrators fail to agree upon the third within six months following the appointment of the first two arbitrators, such third arbitrator shall be chosen by the President of the International Court of Justice at the request of the Secretary-General of the United Nations or the Government.

(b) The Secretary-General of the United Nations or the Government may ask the General Assembly to request of the International Court of Justice an advisory opinion on any legal question arising in the course of such proceedings. Pending the receipt of the opinion of the Court, an interim decision of the arbitral tribunal shall be observed by both parties. Thereafter, the arbitral tribunal shall render a final decision, having regard to the opinion of the Court.

Article XVI

General Provisions

Section – 36

The Republic of Kenya shall not incur by reason of the location of the headquarters seat of the UNEP within its territory and international responsibility for acts or omissions of the UNEP or of officials of the Environment Secretariat acting or abstaining from acting within the scope of their functions, other than the international responsibility which the Republic of Kenya would incur as a Member of the United Nations.

Section – 37

Without prejudice to the privileges and immunities accorded by this Agreement, it is the duty of all persons enjoying such privileges and immunities to respect the laws and regulations of the Republic of Kenya. They also have a duty not to interfere in the internal affairs of the Republic of Kenya.

Section – 38

(a) The Executive Director shall take every precaution to ensure that no abuse of a privilege or immunity conferred by this Agreement shall occur, and for this purpose shall establish such rules and regulations as may be deemed necessary and expedient for officials of the Environment Secretariat and for such other persons as may be appropriate.

(b) Should the Government consider that an abuse of a privilege or immunity conferred by this agreement has occurred, the Executive Director shall, upon request, consult with the appropriate Kenyan authorities to determine whether any such abuse has occurred. If such consultations fail to achieve a result satisfactory to the Executive Director and to the Government, the matter shall be determined in accordance with the procedure set out in section 35.

Section – 39

This Agreement shall apply irrespective of whether the Government maintains or does not maintain diplomatic relations with the State concerned and irrespective of whether the State concerned grants a similar privilege or immunity to diplomatic envoys or nationals of the Republic of Kenya.

Section – 40

Whenever this Agreement imposes obligations on the appropriate Kenyan authorities, the ultimate responsibility for the fulfilment of such obligations shall rest with the Government.

Section – 41

The provisions of this Agreement shall be complementary to the provisions of the General Convention. In so far as any provision of this convention relate to the same subject matter, the two provisions shall, wherever possible, be treated as complementary, so that both provisions shall be applicable and neither shall narrow the effect of the other.

Section – 42

This Agreement shall be construed in the light of its primary purpose of enabling the UNEP at its headquarters in the Republic of Kenya fully and efficiently to discharge its responsibilities and fulfil its purposes.

Section – 43

Consultations with respect to modification of this Agreement shall be entered into at the request of the United Nations or the Government. Any such modification shall be by mutual consent.

Section – 44

The UNEP and the Government may enter into such supplemental agreements as may be necessary.

Section – 45

This Agreement shall apply, *mutatis mutandis*, to such other offices of the United Nations as may in future be set up with the consent of the Government in the Republic of Kenya.

Section – 46

This Agreement shall cease to be in force:

(i) by mutual consent of the United Nations and the Government; or

(ii) if the permanent headquarters of the UNEP is removed from the territory of the Republic of Kenya, except for such provisions as may be applicable in connection with the orderly termination of the operations of the UNEP at its permanent headquarters in the Republic of Kenya and the disposal of its property therein.

Section – 47

This Agreement shall enter into force upon signature and shall replace any interim agreement hitherto governing the establishment and operation of the UNEP headquarters in the Republic of Kenya.

VI Agreement between the Secretariat of the Convention on Biological Diversity and the Government of Canada concerning the Headquarters of the Convention Secretariat*

WHEREAS the Second Meeting of the Conference of the Parties of the Convention on Biological Diversity accepted in decision 11/19 on 17 November 1995 in Jakarta the offer of Canada, as contained in document UNEP/CBD/COP2/Rev.1. and established under Article 24 of the Convention;

WHEREAS the Convention on the Privileges and Immunities of the United Nations to which Canada has been a party since 22 January 1948, applies to United Nations officials servicing the Secretariat;

NOTHING decision 1/4 contained in document UNEP/CRD/COP/1/17 of the Conference of the Parties of the Convention designating UNEP to carry out the functions of the Secretariat of the Convention;

NOTHING further the undertaking of the Government of Canada to ensure the availability of all the necessary facilities and conditions to enable the Secretariat of the Convention on Biological Diversity to perform its functions, including its scheduled programmes of work and any related activities;

* Headquarters Agreement between the Executive Director of UNEP (Elizabeth Dowdeswell) on behalf of the Secretariat of the Convention on Biological Diversity, and the representative of the Government of Canada (Robert Fowler) for the Government of Canada on 25 October 1996 in New York (on file with the author).

DESIRING, therefore, to conclude an Agreement regulating matters resulting from the establishment in Montreal, Canada of the Headquarters of the Secretariat of the Convention on Biological Diversity;

THE SECRETARIAT OF THE CONVENTION ON BIOLOGICAL DIVERSITY AND THE GOVERNMENT OF CANADA, here in after referred to as the "Parties"

HAVE AGREED as follows:

Article 1

Definitions

In this Agreement:

(a) "Convention" means the Convention on Biological Diversity cane at Rio de Janeiro on 5 June, 1992 and entered into force on 29 December 1993;
(b) "Executive Secretary" means the Official of the Secretariat who is the Head of the Secretariat, in conformity with decision 1/4 of the Conference of the Parties contained in document UNEP/CBD/COP/1/17;
(c) "Experts on missions" means persons, other than Officials of the Secretariat, performing missions at the request of and on behalf of the Secretariat;
(d) "General Convention" means the Convention on Privileges and Immunities of the United Nations adopted by the General Assembly of the United Nations on 13 February 1946, to which Canada is a Party;
(e) "Government" means the Government of Canada;
(f) "Premises of the Secretariat" means the buildings or part of buildings occupied permanently or temporarily by the Secretariat or by meetings convened in Canada by the Secretariat;

(g) "Officials of the Secretariat" means United Nations officials assigned to service the Secretariat, irrespective of nationality, with the exception of those who are recruited locally and assigned to hourly rates;

(h) "Parties to the Convention" means States and regional economic integration organizations under Article 33 of the Convention that are parties to the Convention;

(i) "Representatives of Parties of the Convention" means persons charged by a state with the duty to act on its behalf on matters related to the Convention;

(j) "Secretariat" means the secretariat established by Article 24 of the Convention.

Article 2

Juridical Personality and Legal Capacity

1. The Secretariat shall possess juridical personality in Canada. It shall have the capacity to:
   (a) contract;
   (b) acquire and dispose of immovable and movable property; and
   (c) institute legal proceedings.
2. For the purposes of this Agreement, the Secretariat shall be represented by the Executive Secretary.

Article 3

Inviolability of the Premises of the Secretariat and Archives

1. The Premises of the Secretariat shall be inviolable. The competent Government authorities shall not enter the Premises of the Secretariat to perform official duties except with the consent of, and under conditions agreed to, by the Executive Secretary or, in

his or her absence, by a senior official of the Secretariat acting on his behalf. These provisions shall not prevent the reasonable application of fire or safety regulations.

2. The Government shall accord the Premises of the Secretariat the same protection as it gives to diplomatic missions in Canada.
3. The archives, documents and electronic media, in whatever form, of the Secretariat shall be inviolable at any time wherever located.
4. The Secretariat shall prevent the Premises of the Secretariat from becoming a refuge either for persons who are avoiding arrest or for persons who are endeavoring to avoid service of legal process.

Article 4

Property, Funds and Assets

1. The Secretariat, its property, funds and assets, including funds administered in furtherance of its constitutional function, wherever located and by whomsoever held, shall enjoy immunity from every form of legal process except insofar as in any particular case it has expressly waived its immunity, it being understood that the waiver shall not extend to any measure of execution of legal actions.
2. The property, funds and assets of the Secretariat, wherever located and by whomsoever held, shall be immune from search, requisition, confiscation, expropriation and any other form of interference, whether by executive, administrative, judicial, or legislative action.
3. The Secretariat may hold funds, gold and currencies of any kind and operate accounts in any currency. It shall be free to transfer its funds, gold and currencies within Canada and from Canada to any other country and to convert any currency held by it into any other currency.

Article 5

Exemption from Taxes and Duties

1. The Secretariat, its property, funds and assets shall be:
   (a) exempt from all direct taxes: it is understood, however, that the Secretariat will not claim exemption from taxes which are no more than charges for public utility services;
   (b) exempt from customs duties and prohibitions and restrictions on imports and exports in respect of articles imported or exported by the Secretariat for its official use. It is understood, however, that articles imported under such exemption will not be sold in Canada except under conditions agreed with the Government of Canada;
   (c) exempt from customs duties and prohibitions and restrictions on imports and exports or sale in respect of its publications and other Secretariat educational and information materials.
2. While the Secretariat will not, as a general rule, claim exemption from excise duties and from taxes on the sale of movable and immovable property which form part of the price to be paid, nevertheless when the Secretariat is making important purchases for official use of property on which such duties and taxes have been charged or are chargeable, the Government of Canada will make appropriate administrative arrangements for the remission or return of the account of duty or tax.

Article 6

Communications Facilities

1. The Secretariat shall enjoy in Canada for its official communications, treatment not less favourable than that accorded by the

Government of Canada to any other Government including diplomatic missions in matters of establishment and operation, priorities, tariffs, charges on mail and cablegrams and on teleprinter, facsimile, telephone and other communications, as well as rates for information to the press and radio. No censorship shall be applied to the official correspondence and other official communications of the Secretariat.

2. The Secretariat shall have the right to use codes and to dispatch and receive its correspondence by courier or in bags, which shall have the same immunities and privileges as diplomatic couriers and bags.
3. The facilities provided for in this Article may, to the extent necessary for efficient operation, be established and operated outside the Premises of the Secretariat in the territory of Canada with the consent of the Government of Canada.

Article 7

Conference and Meeting Facilities

1. Meetings of the Conference of the Parties established under Article 23 of the Convention; meetings of the Subsidiary Body on Scientific, Technical and Technology Advice established under Article 25 thereof and such other Subsidiary bodies as the Conference of the Parties may establish may, at the decision of each of the bodies, be held at the seat of the Secretariat, or at any other venue in Canada.
2. The Government of Canada shall, when requested by the Secretariat, make every effort to facilitate the access of the Secretariat to conference and meeting facilities available in Canada, particularly those facilities belonging to institutions with which the Government has headquarters agreements.

Article 8

Access to the Premises of the Secretariat

1. The competent Canadian authorities shall not impose any impediments to transit to or from the Premises of the Secretariat of representatives of Parties to the Convention, observers, experts on missions, or other persons invited by the Secretariat thereto on official business.
2. Visas, where required, for persons referred to in paragraph 1, shall be issued by the Government free of charge and as promptly as possible.
3. The provisions of paragraphs 1 and 2 shall also apply, as appropriate, to the spouses and relatives dependent on the persons referred to in those paragraphs.
4. Except as provided above and in the relevant provisions of this Agreement, the Government retains full control and authority over the entry of persons or property into the territory of Canada and the conditions under which persons may remain or reside therein.

Article 9

Interruption of Public Services

In case of interruption or threatened interruption of public services, including communications and transportation, the Government will consider the needs of the Secretariat as being of equal importance with the similar needs of its essential agencies and attempt to ensure that the work of the Secretariat is not prejudiced.

Article 10

Privileges and Immunities for Representatives of Parties to the Convention

The representatives of Parties to the Conventions attending the Conference of the Parties meetings, or meetings of the subsidiary duties and other consultative meetings on programme implementation organized by the Secretariat shall, while discharging their duties in Canada and during their journeys to and from meetings, enjoy the following privileges and immunities:

(a) immunity from personal arrest or detention and from seizure of personal baggage, and immunity from legal process of every kind in respect of words spoken or written and all acts performed in their official capacity;
(b) inviolability of all papers, documents and electronic media;
(c) the right to use codes and to receive and send papers or correspondence by courier or in sealed bags;
(d) exemption in respect of themselves and their spouses and members of their family forming part of their households from immigration retractions, aliens registration or national service obligations;
(e) the same facilities, in respect of currency or currency exchange restrictions as are accorded to diplomatic agents;
(f) the same exemption from examination of personal baggage as accorded to diplomatic agents;
(g) such other privileges, immunities and facilities not inconsistent with the foregoing as diplomatic envoys enjoy, except that they shall have not right to claim exemption from customs duties on goods imported, otherwise than as part of their personal baggage, or from excise duties or sales taxes.

Article 11

Privileges and Immunities of Officials of the Secretariat

1. The Officials of the Secretariat shall enjoy in Canada the following privileges and immunities:
   (a) immunity from legal process in respect of words spoken or written and any act performed in their official capacity;
   (b) exemption from taxation on the salaries and emoluments paid to them by the Secretariats;
   (c) immunity for themselves, their spouses and relatives dependent on them from immigration restrictions and alien registration procedures.
   (d) immunity from national service obligations;
   (e) the same repatriation facilities in time of international crisis for themselves, their spouses and relatives dependent on them as are accorded to diplomatic agents;
   (f) the same privileges in respect of exchange facilities as accorded to officials of comparable rank forming part of diplomatic missions in Canada; and
   (g) the right to import free of duty their furniture and effects including motor vehicles, at the time of first entry into Canada, or in the case of former residents of Canada returning to Canada to resume residence in Canada after having been residents of another country, the right, subject to the applicable legislation, to import free of duty their furniture and effects, including motor vehicles, at the time of their return to Canada.
2. In addition to the immunities and privileges specified in paragraph 1 of this Article, the Executive Secretary, and his or her spouse and relatives dependent on him or her, unless they are Canadian citizens or are permanent residents in Canada as defined by applicable Canadian legislation, shall be accorded the same privileges,

immunities and facilities as are enjoyed by diplomatic agents and their families in Canada.

3. In addition to the immunities and privileges specified in paragraph 1, officials of the Secretariat belonging to senior categories of grade P-4 and above, their spouses and relatives dependent on them, unless they are Canadian citizens or are permanent residents in Canada as defined by applicable Canadian legislation shall be accorded the privileges, immunities and facilities as are granted to diplomatic agents of comparable rank in Canada.

Article 12

Privileges and Immunities of Experts on Missions

The Government of Canada undertakes to grant to Experts on Missions for the Secretariat, the privileges and immunities and facilities set out in Article VI of the General Convention.

Article 13

Employment of Dependents

Dependents of Officials of the Secretariat shall upon application, receive authorization for employment in Canada.

Article 14

Waiver of Immunity

1. The privileges and immunities of Officials of the Secretariat and of experts are accorded in the interest of the United Nations and not for the personal benefit of the individuals themselves.
2. The right and duty to waive the immunity referred to in paragraph 1, in any case, where it can be waived without prejudice

to the interests of the United Nations, shall lie with the Secretary General, of the United Nations.

Article 15

Respect of the Laws and Regulation of Canada

1. Without prejudice to their privileges and immunities, it is the duty of all persons enjoying such privileges and immunities to respect the laws and regulations of Canada. They also have a duty not to interfere in the internal affairs of Canada.
2. The Secretariat shall cooperate at all times with the appropriate authorities of Canada to facilitate the proper administration of justice, secure the observance of police regulations and avoid the occurrence of any abuse in connection with the privileges, immunities and facilities referred to in this Agreement.

Article 16

Notification

No person shall be accepted as a representative of a Party to the Convention, an Official or the Secretariat or an Expert on Mission for the purpose of Articles 10, 11 and 12 respectively, unless and until his or her name and status have been duly notified to the Minister of Foreign Affairs of Canada.

Article 17

Identity Card and United Nations Laissez – Passer

1. The Government of Canada shall provide all officials of the Secretariat as well as their dependents with an identity card certifying their status under this Agreement.
2. The Government of Canada shall recognize and accept United Nations laissez-passers held by officials of the Secretariat as valid

travel documents. Visas, where required, shall be granted free of charge and as promptly as possible.

Article 18

Settlement of Disputes

1. Any dispute concerning the interpretation or implementation of this Agreement that is not settled by negotiation or other agreed method of settlement shall, at the request of either Party, be referred to a tribunal of three arbitrators, one to be appointed by the Minister of Foreign Affairs of Canada, one to be appointed by the Executive Secretary and the third to be appointed by the two arbitrators. If, within thirty days of the request for arbitration or if, within fifteen days of the appointment of two arbitrators, the third arbitrator has not been appointed, either Party may request the President of the International Court of Justice to appoint an arbitrator.
2. The procedure of arbitration shall be determined by the arbitrators, and the expenses of the arbitration shall be borne by the Parties as assessed by the arbitrators. The arbitral award shall contain a statement of the reasons on which it is based and shall be accepted by the parties as the final adjudication of the dispute.
3. The Secretariat shall take the measures necessary for ensuring the proper settlement of disputes arising out of contracts or other disputes of a private law character to which the Secretariat is a party.

Article 19

Final Provisions

1. When a provision of this Agreement and a provision of the General Convention deal with the same subject, both provisions shall

be considered complementary. Whenever possible, both of them shall be applied and neither shall restrict the force of the other.

2. This Agreement shall apply, mutatis mutandis, to such other bodies of the Convention on Biological Diversity as may in future be set up in Canada by the Conference of the Parties with the consent of the Government of Canada.
3. This Agreement shall enter into force upon signature.
4. This Agreement may be amended by mutual consent at any time at the request of either Party.
5. This Agreement shall continue in effect indefinitely.
6. This Agreement shall cease to be in force if the Secretariat is relocated from the territory of Canada, except for such provisions as may be applicable in connection with the orderly termination of the operations of the Secretariat in Canada and the disposition of its property therein.

IN WITNESS WHEREOF the undersigned, duly authorized to that effect, have signed this Agreement.

DONE at New York this 25th day of October 1996, and at ________, this ________ day of ________ 1996, in duplicate in the English and the French languages, each version being equally authentic.

Appendix VII Agreement between the Federal Republic of Germany and the United Nations concerning the Headquarters of the United Nations Volunteers Programme*

The Federal Republic of Germany and the United Nations

Whereas the Executive Board of the United Nations Development Programme, by its decision 95/2 of 10 January 1995, endorsed the proposal of the Secretary-General to accept the offer of the Government of the Federal Republic of Germany to relocate the headquarters of the United Nations Volunteers Programme to Bonn;

Whereas paragraph 1 of article 105 of the Charter of the United Nations provides that "the Organisation shall enjoy in the territory of each of its Members such privileges and immunities as are necessary for the fulfilment of its purposes";

Whereas the Federal Republic of Germany is a party since 5 November 1980 to the Convention on the Privileges and Immunities of the United Nations;

* Headquarters Agreement between the Permanent Representative of Germany in New York (Tono Eitel) for the Federal Republic of Germany and Administrator of United Nations Development Program (James Gustave Speth) for the United Nations, signed in New York on 10 November 1995 (on file with the author).

Whereas the Federal Republic of Germany agrees to ensure the availability of all necessary facilities to enable the United Nations Volunteers Programme to perform its functions, including its scheduled programmes of work and any related activities;

Desiring to conclude an Agreement regulating matters arising from the establishment of and necessary for the effective discharge of the functions of the United Nations Volunteers Programme in the Federal Republic of Germany;

Have agreed as follows:

Article 1

Definitions

For the purpose of the present Agreement, the following definitions shall apply:

(a) "the Parties" means the United Nations and the Federal Republic of Germany;
(b) "the United Nations" means an international organization established under the Charter of the United Nations;
(c) "the Secretary-General" means the Secretary-General of the United Nations;
(d) "the UNV" or "the Programme" means the United Nations Volunteers Programme, a subsidiary organ within the terms of Article 22 of the Charter of the United Nations, established in 1970 by General Assembly resolution 2659 (XXV) of 7 December 1970;
(e) "the Executive Coordinator" means the Executive Coordinator of the United Nations Volunteers Programme;
(f) "the host country" means the Federal Republic of Germany;
(g) "the Government" means the Government of the Federal Republic of Germany;
(h) "the competent authorities" means Bund (federal), Länder (state), or local authorities under the laws, regulations and customs of the Federal Republic of Germany;

(i) "the Headquarters district" means the premises, being the building and structures, equipment and other installations and facilities, as well as the surrounding grounds, as specified in the Supplementary Agreement between the United Nations and the Federal Republic of Germany; and any other premises occupied and used by the United Nations in the Federal Republic of Germany, in accordance with this Agreement, or any other supplementary agreement with the Government;

(j) "the representatives of Members" means the representatives of Member States of the United Nations and other States participating in the United Nations Development Programme;

(k) "officials of the Programme" means the Executive Coordinator and all members of the staff of the United Nations Volunteers Programme, irrespective of nationality, with the exception of those who are locally recruited and assigned to hourly rates as provided for in United Nations General Assembly resolution 76(1) of 7 December 1946;

(l) "UN Volunteers" means persons with professional and technical qualifications, other than officials of the Programme, engaged on volunteer terms and conditions by the United Nations Volunteers Programme to provide services within the framework of programmes and projects of the United Nations;

(m) "experts on missions" means persons, other than officials and UN Volunteers, undertaking missions for the United Nations and coming within the scope of Articles VI and VII of the Convention on the Privileges and Immunities of the United Nations;

(n) "Offices of the United Nations" means and includes subsidiary bodies and organizational units of the United Nations;

(o) "the Vienna Convention" means the Vienna Convention on Diplomatic Relations done at Vienna on 18 April 1961, to which the Federal Republic of Germany acceded on 11 November 1964 and which came into force with respect to the Federal Republic of Germany on 11 December 1964;

(p) "the General Convention" means the Convention on the Privileges and Immunities of the United Nations adopted by the

General Assembly of the United Nations on 13 February 1946, to which the Federal Republic of Germany acceded on 5 November 1980.

Article 2

Purpose and Scope of the Agreement

This agreement shall regulate matters relating to or arising out of the establishment and the proper functioning of the UNV in and from the Federal Republic of Germany.

Article 3

Juridical Personality and Legal Capacity

1. The United Nations, acting through the UNV, a subsidiary organ of the United Nations, shall possess in the host country full juridical personality and the capacity:
   (a) to contract;
   (b) to acquire and dispose of movable and immovable property;
   (c) to institute legal proceedings.
2. For the purpose of this Article, the UNV shall be represented by the Executive Coordinator.

Article 4

Application of the General and Vienna Conventions and of the Agreement

1. The General and Vienna Conventions shall apply to the Headquarters district, the United Nations, including UNV, its property, funds and assets, and to persons referred to in this Agreement, as appropriate.

2. This Agreement shall also apply *mutatis mutandis* to such other Offices of the United Nations as may be located in the Federal Republic of Germany with the consent of the Government.
3. This Agreement may also be made applicable *mutatis mutandis* to other intergovernmental entities, institutionally linked to the United Nations, by agreement among such entities, the Government and the United Nations.

Article 5

Inviolability of the Headquarters District

1. The Headquarters district shall be inviolable. The competent authorities shall not enter the Headquarters district to perform any official duty, except with express consent, or at the request of, the Executive Coordinator. Judicial actions and the service or execution of legal process, including the seizure of private property, cannot be enforced in the Headquarters district except with the consent of and in accordance with conditions approved by the Executive Coordinator.
2. The competent authorities shall take whatever action may be necessary to ensure the UNV shall not be dispossessed of all or any part of the Headquarters district without the express consent of the United Nations. The property, funds and assets of the UNV, wherever located and by whomsoever held, shall be immune from search, seizure, requisition, confiscation, expropriation and any other form of interference, whether by executive, administrative, judicial or legislative action.
3. In case of fire or other emergency requiring prompt protective action, or in the event that the competent authorities have reasonable cause to believe that such an emergency has occurred or is about to occur in the Headquarters district, the consent of the Executive Coordinator or her/his representative to any necessary

entry into the Headquarters districts shall be presumed if neither of them can be reached in time.

4. Subject to paragraphs 1, 2 and 3 above, the competent authorities shall take the necessary action to protect the Headquarters district against fire or other emergency.
5. The UNV may expel or exclude persons from the Headquarters district for violation of its regulations.
6. Without prejudice to the provisions of this Agreement, the General Convention and the Vienna Convention, the United Nations shall not allow the Headquarters district to become a refuge from justice for persons against whom a penal judgment had been made or who are pursued *flagrante delicto*, or against whom a warrant of arrest or an order of extradition, expulsion or deportation has been issued by the competent authorities.
7. Any location in or outside Bonn which may be used temporarily for meetings by the United Nations and other entities referred to in Article 4 above, shall be deemed, with the concurrence of the Government, to be included in the Headquarters district for the duration of such meetings.

Article 6

Law and Authority in the Headquarters District

1. The Headquarters district shall be under the authority and control of the United Nations, as provided in this Agreement.
2. Except as otherwise provided in this Agreement, in the General Convention, or in regulations established by the United Nations applicable to the UNV, the laws and regulations of the host country shall apply in the Headquarters district.
3. The United Nations shall have the power to make regulations to be operative throughout the Headquarters district for the purpose of establishing therein the conditions in all respects necessary for the full execution of its functions. The UNV shall promptly inform the

competent authorities of regulations thus enacted in accordance with this paragraph. No Bund (federal), Lander (state) or local law or regulation of the Federal Republic of Germany which is inconsistent with a regulation of the United Nations authorized by this paragraph shall, to the extent of such inconsistency, be applicable within the Headquarters district.

4. Any dispute between the United Nations and the host country, as to whether a regulation of the United Nations is authorized by this Article, or as to whether a law or regulation of the host country is inconsistent with any regulation of the United Nations authorized by this Article, shall be promptly settled by the procedure set out in Article 26. Pending such settlement, the regulation of the United Nations shall apply and the law or regulation of the host country shall be inapplicable in the Headquarters district to the extent that the United Nations claims it to be inconsistent with its regulation.

Article 7

Inviolability of Archives and All Documents of the UNV

All documents, materials and archives, in whatever form, which are made available belonging to or used by the UNV, wherever located in the host country and by whomsoever held, shall be inviolable.

Article 8

Protection of the Headquarters District and Its Vicinity

1. The competent authorities shall exercise due diligence to ensure the security and protection of the Headquarters district and to ensure that the operations of the UNV are not impaired by the intrusion of persons or groups of persons from outside the Headquarters district or by disturbances in its immediate vicinity an

shall provide to the Headquarters district the appropriate protection as may be required.

2. If so requested by the Executive Coordinator, the competent authorities shall provide adequate police force necessary for the preservation of law and order in the Headquarters district or in its immediate vicinity, and for the removal of persons therefrom.

Article 9

Funds, Assets and Other Property

1. The UNV, its funds, assets and other property, wherever located and by whomsoever held, shall enjoy immunity from every form of legal process, except insofar as in any particular case the United Nations has expressly waived the immunity. It is understood, however, that no waiver of immunity shall extend to any measure of execution.
2. The property and assets of the UNV shall be exempt from restrictions, regulations, controls and moratoria of any nature.
3. Without being restricted by financial controls, regulations or moratoria of any kind, the UNV:
   (a) may hold and use funds, gold or negotiable instruments of any kind and maintain and operate accounts in any currency and convert any currency held by it into any other currency;
   (b) shall be free to transfer its funds, gold or currency from one country to another, or within the host country, to the United Nations or any other agency.

Article 10

Exemption from Taxes, Duties, Import and Export Restrictions

1. In pursuance of Section 7(a) of Article II of the General Convention, the UNV, its assets, income and other property shall be

exempt from all direct taxes. The direct taxes shall, in particular, include, but not be limited to:

(a) income tax (Einkommensteuer);
(b) corporation tax (Korperschaftsteuer);
(c) trade tax (Gewerbesteuer);
(d) property tax (Vermogenssteuer);
(e) land tax (Grundsteuer);
(f) land transfer tax (Grunderwerbsteuer);
(g) motor vehicle tax (Kraftfahrzeugsteuer);
(h) insurance tax (Versicherungsteuer).

2. In pursuance of Section 8 of Article II of the General convention, the UNV shall be exempt from all indirect taxes including value added tax/turnover tax (Umsatzsteuer) and excise duties which from part of the price of important purchases intended for the official use of the UNV. However it is understood that exemption from mineral oil tax included in the price of petrol, diesel and heating oil and value added tax/turnover tax (Umsatzsteuer) shall take the form of a refund of these taxes to the UNV under the conditions agreed upon with the Government. If the Government enters into an agreement with another international organization setting out a different procedure than that referred to above, this new procedure may also be applicable to the UNV by mutual consent of the parties.
3. The UNV, its funds, assets and other property shall be exempt from all customs duties, prohibitions and restrictions in respect of articles imported or exported by the UNV for its official use, including motor vehicles. It is understood, however, that articles imported or purchased under such an exemption shall not be sold in the Federal Republic of Germany except under the conditions agreed upon with the Government.
4. The exemptions referred to in paragraphs 1 to 3 shall be applied in accordance with the formal requirements of the host country. The requirements, however, shall not affect the general principle laid

down in this article. It is understood, however, that the UNV shall not claim exemption from taxes and duties which are, in fact, no more than charges for public utility services.

5. The UNV shall also be exempt from all customs duties, prohibitions and restrictions on imports and exports in respect of its publications, audio-visual materials, etc.

Article 11

Public and Other Service for the Headquarters District

The Government shall assist the UNV in securing, on fair conditions and upon request of the Executive Coordinator, the public and other services needed by the UNV under the terms and conditions set out in the Supplementary Agreement.

Article 12

Communications Facilities

1. The UNV shall enjoy, in respect of its official communications and correspondence, treatment not less favourable than that accorded by the Government to any diplomatic mission in matters of establishment and operation, priorities, tariffs, charges on, but not limited to, mail and cablegrams and on teleprinter, facsimile, telephone, electronic data and other communications, as well as rates for information to the press and radio.
2. The official communications and correspondence of the UNV shall be inviolable. No censorship shall be applied to the official correspondence and other official communications of the UNV.
3. The UNV shall have the right to use codes and to dispatch and receive its correspondence by courier or in bags, which shall have the same immunities and privileges as diplomatic couriers and bags.

4. The UNV shall have the right to operate radio and other telecommunications equipment on United Nations registered frequencies and those assigned to it by the Government, between its offices, within and outside the Federal Republic of Germany.

Article 13

Privileges and Immunities of the Representatives of Members

1. The representatives of Members who reside in the Federal Republic of Germany and who do not have German nationality or permanent residence status in the Federal Republic of Germany shall enjoy the same privileges and immunities, exemptions and facilities as are accorded to diplomats of comparable rank of diplomatic missions accredited to the Federal Republic of Germany in accordance with the Vienna Convention.
2. The representatives of Members who are not resident in the Federal Republic of Germany shall, in the discharge of their duties and while exercising their functions, enjoy privileges and immunities as described in Article IV of the General Convention.

Article 14

Privileges, Immunities and Facilities of Officials of the UNV

1. The officials of the Programme shall, regardless of their nationality, be accorded the privileges and immunities as provided for in Articles V and VII of the General Convention. They shall *inter alia:*
   (a) enjoy immunity from legal process in respect of words spoken or written and all acts performed by them in their official capacity. Such immunity shall continue to be accorded after termination of employment with the UNV;
   (b) enjoy exemption from taxation on the salaries and emoluments paid to them by the UNV;

(c) enjoy immunity from national service obligations;
(d) enjoy immunity, together with spouses and relatives dependent on them, from immigration restrictions and alien registration;
(e) be accorded the same privileges in respect of exchange facilities as are accorded to the members of comparable rank of the diplomatic missions established in the host country;
(f) be given, together with spouses and relatives dependent on them, the same repatriation facilities in time of international crisis as diplomatic agents;
(g) have the right to import free of duties and taxes, except payments for services, their furniture and effects at the time of first taking up their post in the host country.

2. In addition to the provisions of paragraph 1 above, the Executive Coordinator and other officials of P-5 level and above who do not have German nationality or permanent residence status in the host country shall be accorded the privileges, immunities, exemptions and facilities as are accorded by the Government to members of comparable rank of the diplomatic staff of missions accredited to the Government. The name of the Executive Coordinator shall be included in the diplomatic list.
3. The privileges and immunities are granted to officials of the UNV in the interests of the United Nations and not for their personal benefit. The right and the duty to waive the immunity in any particular case, where it can be waived without prejudice to the interests of the United Nations, shall lie with the Secretary-General.

Article 15

UN Volunteers

1. The UN Volunteers shall be granted privileges, immunities and facilities under Sections 17, 18, 20 and 21 of Article V, and Article VII of the General Convention.

2. The privileges and immunities are granted to UN Volunteers in the interests of the United Nations and not for their personal benefit. The right and the duty to waive the immunity in any particular case, where it can be waived without prejudice to the interests of the United Nations, shall lie with the Secretary-General.

Article 16

Experts on Missions

1. Experts on missions shall be granted the privileges, immunities and facilities as specified in Articles VI and VII of the General Convention.
2. Experts on missions may be accorded such additional privileges, immunities and facilities as may be agreed upon between the Parties.
3. The privileges and immunities are granted to experts on missions in the interests of the United Nations and not for their personal benefit. The right and the duty to waive the immunity of any expert, in any case where it can be waived without prejudice to the interests of the United Nations, shall lie with the Secretary-General.

Article 17

Personnel Recruited Locally and Assigned to Hourly Rates

1. Personnel recruited by the UNV locally and assigned to hourly rates, shall be accorded immunity from legal process in respect of words spoken or written and acts performed by them in their capacity for the UNV. Such immunity shall continue to be accorded after termination of employment with the UNV. They shall also be accorded such other facilities as may be necessary for the independent exercise of their functions for the UNV. The

terms and conditions of their employment shall be in accordance with the relevant United Nations resolutions, regulations, rules and policies.

2. The immunity from legal process shall be accorded to personnel recruited locally and assigned to hourly rates in the duty to waive the immunity of any such individuals, in any case where it can be waived without prejudice to the interests of the United Nations, shall lie with the Secretary-General.

Article 18

United Nations Laissez-Passer and Certificate

1. The Government shall recognize and accept the United Nations laissez-passer issued by the United Nations as a valid travel document equivalent to a passport.
2. In accordance with the provision of Section 26 of the General Convention, the Government shall recognize and accept the United Nations certificate issued to persons travelling on the business of the United Nations.
3. The Government further agrees to issue any required visas on the United Nations laissez-passer.

Article 19

Co-operation with the Competent Authorities

1. Without prejudice to their privileges and immunities, it is the duty of all persons enjoying such privileges and immunities to respect the laws and regulations of the host country. They also have a duty not to interfere in the internal affairs of the host country.
2. The United Nations shall co-operate at all times with the competent authorities to facilitate the proper administration of justice,

secure the observance of police regulations and avoid the occurrence of any abuse in connection with the facilities, privileges and immunities accorded to officials of the UNV referred to in Article 14, and the persons referred to in Articles 15, 16 and 17.

3. If the Government considers that there has been an abuse of the privileges or immunities conferred by this agreement, consultations will be held between the competent authorities and the Executive Coordinator to determine whether any such abuse has occurred and, if so, to attempt to ensure that no repetition occurs. If such consultations fail to achieve a result satisfactory to the Government and to the United Nations, either Party may submit the question as to whether such an abuse has occurred for resolution in accordance with the provisions on settlement of disputes under Article 26.

Article 20

Notification

The Executive Coordinator shall notify the Government of the names and categories of persons referred to in this Agreement and of any change in their status.

Article 21

Entry Into, Exit From, Movement and Sojourn in the Host Country

All persons referred to in this Agreement as notified, and persons invited on official business, by the Executive Coordinator shall have the right of unimpeded entry into, exit from, free movement and sojourn within the host country. They shall be granted facilities for speedy travel. Visas, entry permits or licenses, where required, shall be granted free of charge and as promptly as possible. The same facilities shall be extended to UNV candidates, if such is requested by the Executive Coordinator. No activity performed by persons referred to above in their official capacity with respect to the UNV shall constitute a reason for preventing their entry into or departure from the territory of the host country or for requiring them to leave such territory.

Article 22

Identification Cards

1. At the request of the Executive Coordinator, the Government shall issue identification cards to persons referred to in this Agreement certifying their status under this Agreement.
2. Upon demand of an authorized official of the Government, persons referred to in paragraph 1 above, shall be required to present, but not to surrender, their identification cards.

Article 23

Flag, Emblem and Markings

The United Nations shall be entitled to display its flag, emblem and markings on the Headquarters district and on vehicles used for official purposes.

Article 24

Social Security

1. The Parties agree that, due to the fact that officials of the United Nations are subject to the United Nations Staff Regulations and Rules, including Article VI thereof which establishes a comprehensive social security scheme, the United Nations and its officials, irrespective of nationality, shall be exempt from the laws of the Federal Republic of Germany on mandatory coverage and

compulsory contributions to the social security schemes of the Federal Republic of Germany during their employment with the United Nations.

2. The provisions of paragraph 1 above shall apply *mutatis mutandis* to the members of the family forming part of the household of persons referred to in paragraph 1 above, unless they are employed or self-employed in the host country or receive German social security benefits.

Article 25

Access to the Labour Market for Family Members and Issuance of Visas and Residence Permits to Household Employees

1. Spouses of officials of the Programme whose duty station is in the Federal Republic of Germany and their children forming part of their household who are under 21 years of age or economically dependent, shall not require a work permit.
2. The Government undertakes to issue visas and residence permits, where required, to household employees of officials of the Programme as speedily as possible; no work permit will be required in such cases.

Article 26

Settlement of Disputes

1. The United Nations shall make provisions for appropriate modes of settlement of:
   (a) disputes arising out of contracts and other disputes of a private law character to which the UNV is a party;
   (b) disputes involving an official of the UNV who, by reason of his or her official position, enjoys immunity, if such immunity has not been waived.

2. Any dispute between the Parties concerning the interpretation or application of this Agreement or the regulations of the UNV, which cannot be settled amicably, shall be submitted, at the request of either Party to the dispute, to an arbitral tribunal, composed of three members. Each Party shall appoint one arbitrator and two arbitrators thus appointed shall together appoint a third arbitrator as their chairman. If one of the Parties fails to appoint its arbitrator and has not proceeded to do so within two months after an invitation from the other Party to make such an appointment, the other Party may request the President of the International Court of Justice to make the necessary appointment. If the two arbitrators are unable to reach agreement, in the two months following their appointment, on the choice of the third arbitrator, either Party may invite the President of the International Court of Justice to make the necessary appointment. The Parties shall draw up a special agreement determining their subject of the dispute. Failing the conclusion of such an agreement within a period of two months from the date on which arbitration was requested, the dispute may be brought before the arbitral tribunal upon application of either Party. Unless the Parties decide otherwise, the arbitral tribunal shall determine its own procedure. The expenses of the arbitration shall be borne by the Parties as assessed by the arbitrators. The arbitral tribunal shall reach its decision by a majority of votes on the basis of the applicable rules of international law. In the absence of such rules, it shall decide *ex aquo et bono*. The decision shall be final and binding on the Parties to the dispute, even if rendered in default of the Parties to the dispute.

Article 27

Final Provisions

1. The provisions of this Agreement shall be complementary to the provisions of the General Convention and the Vienna Convention,

the latter Convention only insofar as it is relevant for the diplomatic privileges, immunities and facilities accorded to the appropriate categories of persons referred to in this Agreement. Insofar as any provision of this Agreement and any provisions of the General Convention relate to the same subject matter, each of these provisions shall be applicable and neither shall narrow the effect of the other.

2. The present Agreement shall cease to be in force six months after either of the Parties gives notice in writing to the other of its decision to terminate the Agreement. The Agreement shall, however, remain in force for such an additional period as might be necessary for the orderly cessation of the UNV's activities in the Federal Republic of Germany and the disposition of its property therein, and the resolution of any disputes between the Parties.
3. This Agreement may be amended by mutual consent at any time at the request of either Party.
4. The provisions of this Agreement shall be applied provisionally as from the date of signature, as appropriate, pending the fulfilment of the formal requirements for its entry into force referred to in paragraph 5 below.
5. This Agreement shall enter into force on the day following the date of receipt of the last of the notifications by which the Parties will have informed each other of the completion of their respective formal requirements.

Done at New York, on 10 November 1995, in duplicate in the English and the German languages, both texts being equally authentic.

The Permanent Representative of Germany to the United Nations

New York, 10 November 1995

Mr. Administrator,

I have the honour to refer, on the occasion of the signing of the Agreement between the Federal Republic of Germany and the United Nations concerning the Headquarters of the United Nations Volunteers Programme (hereinafter referred to as "the Agreement"), to the discussions held between the representatives of the Government of the Federal Republic of Germany and the representatives of the United Nations concerning the interpretation of certain provision of the Agreement and to confirm the following understandings:

1. Regulations of the United Nations under paragraph 3 Article 6 of the Agreement

   It is the understanding of the Parties that the regulations to be issued by the United Nations under paragraph 3 of Article 6 will be those necessary for the conduct of its operations and activities in the execution of its mandate and to establish conditions necessary for the exercise of its functions and fulfilment of its purposes.
2. Turnover and mineral oil tax
   (a) It is the understanding of the Parties that the Federal Finance Office of the Federal Republic of Germany, in pursuance of paragraph 2 of Article 10 of the Agreement, shall, on request, reimburse to the UNV the amount of value added tax/turnover tax (Umsatzsteuer) paid in respect of supplies and services purchased from a taxable person for official use of the UNV, provided that the tax has been separately identified in the invoice. If the reimbursed value added tax/turnover tax (Umsatzsteuer) is subsequently reduced as a result of a review of the originally paid price for the supplies and services in question, the UNV shall inform the Federal Finance Office of such a reduction in price and shall subsequently return the balance of the previously reimbursed tax.
   (b) Likewise the Federal Finance Office, in pursuance of paragraph 2 of Article 10 of the Agreement, shall, on request, also reimburse to the UNV the mineral oil tax for petrol, diesel and heating oil included in the price of purchases intended for official use of the UNV provided that the tax exceeds 50 Deutsche Mark per invoice in the aggregate.

3. Goods and services transactions
   (a) It is the understanding of the Parties that if goods purchased in the European Union or imported from outside of the European Union by the UNV for its official use, for which the UNV was granted exemption from value added tax/turnover tax (Umsatzsteuer) or import turnover tax (Einfuhrumsatzsteuer) in accordance with Section 7(b) or Section 8 of Article II of the General Convention or paragraphs 2 and 3 of Article 10 of the Agreement, are sold, given away or otherwise disposed of to taxable persons, who have the full right of deduction, international organizations entitled to tax exemption, or to other entitled to tax exempt status benefiting entities, no value added tax/turnover tax (Umsatzsteuer) shall be paid. If goods referred to above are sold, given away or otherwise disposed of to persons and entities other than those referred to above, the part of the value added tax/turnover tax (Umsatzsteuer) which corresponds to the sale price or the current market value of such good, as appropriate, shall be payable to the Federal Finance Office, as provided in paragraph 4 of Article 10 of the Agreement. It is further the understanding of the Parties that the amount of the tax due shall be determined on the basis of the tax rate applicable on the actual date of the transaction in question.
   (b) The goods imported exempt from customs duties under the terms of Section 7(b) of Article II of the General Convention or paragraph 3 of Article 10 of the Agreement shall not be sold in the Federal Republic of Germany except with the consent of the Government and subject to the payment of the applicable customs duties.
4. Motor vehicles

   It is the understanding of the Parties that the expression "furniture and effects" referred to in paragraph 1 (g) of Article 14 of the Agreement shall include motor vehicles in the possession and use of officials at least six months before their first taking up their post in Germany. This shall also apply to leased vehicles if the officials prove by means of a leasing agreement that said agreement was made at least six months before their first taking up their post in Germany. Furniture and effects may be brought into Germany over a period of 12 months from the date on which the officials first take up their post. This may be done in stages within that period. The six month requirement referred to above shall exceptionally be waived until six months after the formal relocation of UNV Headquarters to Bonn, Germany.

5. Officials of P- 4 level

   It is the understanding of the Parties that in well-founded individual cases, the Federal Republic of Germany shall, on request, grant to officials of P-4 level whose functions justify it the same privileges, immunities and facilities as accorded to officials of P-5 level and above in accordance with paragraph 2 of Article 14 of the Agreement. Requests on the matter shall be submitted by the Executive Coordinator to the Federal Foreign Office.

6. UN Volunteers at Headquarters

   It is the understanding of the Parties that United Nations Volunteers may only be invited to UNV Headquarters in Germany for limited periods of time, normally not exceeding eight weeks, for the purposes of briefing, debriefing, training, or for annual leave purposes, and would not be used to perform ordinary staff functions at Headquarters.

7. Laissez-passer for UN Volunteers

   It is the understanding of the Parties that UN Volunteers will be issued with United Nations laissez-passer.

8. General Consultations

   It is the understanding of the Parties that if the Government enters into any agreement with an intergovernmental organization containing terms and conditions more favourable than those extended to the United Nations under the present Agreement, either Party may ask for consultations as to whether such terms and conditions could be extended to the United Nations.

9. UNV Retirees

   Following retirement from active service with the UNV, after a number of years of UN service in Bonn and Geneva, officials of the UNV and members of their family forming part of their households (spouses, unmarried children under age 21 and other relatives dependent on them) shall, upon application, be issued with a residence permit, insofar as they are in a position to support themselves, including payment of health and care insurance contributions, in accordance with applicable German legislation.

   If the United Nations agrees to the understandings contained in paragraph 1-9 above, this Note and your affirmative reply in writing shall constitute an Agreement between the Federal Republic of Germany and the United Nations regarding the above-referenced understandings which shall enter into force in accordance with Article 27 of the Headquarters Agreement.

Please accept, Mr. Administrator, the assurances of my highest consideration.

Tono Eitel

Mr. James Gustave Speth
Administrator of United Nations
Development Programme
1 United Nations Plaza
New York, N.Y. 10017

UNDP

November 1995

The Administrator,
United Nations Development Programme

Excellency,

I have the honour to acknowledge receipt of your Note of 10 November 1995, in which you confirm the understandings concerning the interpretation of certain provisions of the Agreement between the United Nations and the Federal Republic of Germany concerning the Headquarters of the United Nations Volunteers Programme signed on 10 November 1995, which reads as follows:

(*Es folgt der Text der einleitenden deutschan Note*)

In accordance with your request, I wish to confirm, on behalf of the United Nations, that the understandings set out in your Note fully correspond to the views of the United Nations on the subject, and that this exchange of Notes shall constitute an Agreement between the United Nations and the Federal Republic of Germany regarding the above referenced understandings which shall enter into force in accordance with Article 27 of the Headquarters Agreement.

Please accept, Excellency, the assurances of my highest consideration

James Gustave Speth

His Excellency

Prof. Tono Eitel
Permanent Representative of Germany to the United Nations
NewYork

Permanent Representative of Germany to the United Nations New York
(Translation)

Text of the unilateral German statement re Article 8 of the Headquarters Agreement to be made on the occasion of the exchange of the communications regarding the fulfillment of the formal requirements for the entry into force of the Agreement

Excellency,

In connection with today's communication that the requirements for the entry into force of the Agreement of 10 November 1995 between the Federal Republic of Germany and the United Nations concerning the Headquarters of the United Nations Volunteers Programme have been fulfilled on the part of the Federal Republic of Germany, I have the honour to make the following statement on behalf of the Federal Republic of Germany:

"With regard to the obligations undertaken by the Federal Republic of Germany under International Law and under this Agreement, I would like to draw your attention to the following:

According to Article 8 of the Basic Law of the Federal Republic of Germany, all Germans have the right to assemble peacefully and unarmed without prior notification or permission. Under the Act on Public Assemblies and Provisions' (Assembly Act), everyone has the right to hold public assemblies and processions and to participate therein. The participants have in principle the right to choose the venue of the assembly in public areas. An assembly may therefore only be prohibited or dissolved if it directly endangers public safety or order.

It is thus clear that the right to assemble cannot be exercised on the United Nations premises, which is not a public area."

Accept, Excellency, the assurances of my highest consideration.

Appendix VIII Agreement among the United Nations, the Government of the Federal Republic of Germany, and the Secretariat of the United Nations Framework Convention on Climate Change concerning the Headquarters of the Convention Secretariat*

Whereas the first session of the Conference of the Parties of the UNFCCC, by its decision 16/CP. 1 of 7 April 1995, decided to accept the offer of the Federal Republic of Germany to host the Convention secretariat;

Whereas the Conference of the Parties to the United Nations Framework Convention on Climate Change, in its decision 14/CP. 1 of 7 April 1995, further decided that "the Convention secretariat shall be institutionally linked to the United Nations, while not being fully integrated in the work programme and management structure of any particular department or programme [of the United Nations]";

Whereas the General Assembly, by its resolution 50/115 of 16 February 1996, endorsed the institutional linkage between the Convention secretariat and the United Nations; as adopted by the Conference of the Parties;

* Headquarters Agreement among the United Nations, the Government of the Federal Republic of Germany, and the Secretariat of the United Nations Framework Convention on Climate Change, signed in Bonn on 20 June 1996 (on file with the author).

Whereas Article 4 paragraph 3, of the Agreement between the United Nations and the Federal Republic of Germany concerning the Headquarters of the United Nations Volunteers Programme concluded on 10 November 1995 provides that it "may also be made applicable, mutatis mutandis, to other intergovernmental entities, institutionally linked to the United Nations, by agreement among such entities, the Government and the United Nations";

Whereas Article 4 paragraph 2 of the Agreement between the United Nations and the Government of the Federal Republic of Germany concerning the Occupancy and Use of the United Nations Premises in Bonn concluded on 13 February 1996, inter alia, provides that "[t]he United Nations shall make available appropriate space in the Premises to the secretariat of the United Nations Framework Convention on Climate Change taking into account the offer of the Government to establish the headquarters of its secretariat in Germany . . . ",

Whereas the United Nations acknowledges that the offer of the Federal Republic of Germany to provide premises in Bonn to the secretariat of the United Nations Framework Convention on Climate Change, free of rent and on a permanent basis, has been accepted by the Conference of the Parties to that Convention;

Whereas the Convention secretariat and the Government of the Federal Republic of Germany intend to make appropriate arrangements specifying the particular elements contained in the latter's offer to host the Convention secretariat;

Whereas the offer of the Federal Republic of Germany, as contained in documents A/AC.237/Misc.45, A/AC.237-79/Add.4 and A/AC.237/91, inter alia, expresses the interest of the Government of the Federal Republic of Germany in concluding an agreement to host the secretariat of the United Nations Framework Convention on Climate Change, that would ensure the availability of all the necessary facilities in the Federal Republic of Germany to enable the Convention secretariat to perform its functions;

Whereas the Subsidiary Body for Implementation of the Convention, at its second session held at Geneva, Switzerland, in conclusions adopted at its 6th meeting on 8 March 1996, requested that "the Executive Secretary after consulting its Chairman and Officers to enter into an appropriate agreement required for the effective discharge of the secretariat's functions in the Federal Republic of Germany, that applies to the Convention secretariat, mutatis mutandis, the terms of the Agreement signed on 10 November 1995 by the United Nations and the Federal Republic of Germany regarding the Headquarters of the United Nations Volunteers Programme" (document FCCC/SBI/1996/9, paragraph 66(c));

Whereas, in the same conclusions the Subsidiary Body for Implementation also concluded that the agreement referred to above should, in particular, reflect that in the host country the Convention secretariat should possess such legal capacity and enjoy such privileges and immunities as are necessary for the effective discharge of its functions under the Convention, and that the representatives of the Parties and Observer States to the Convention as well as officials of the Convention secretariat should similarly enjoy such privileges and immunities as are necessary for the independent exercise of their functions under the Convention;

Desiring to conclude an Agreement regulating matters arising from the applicability, mutatis mutandis, of the Agreement between the United Nations and the Federal Republic of Germany concerning the Headquarters of the United Nations Volunteers Programme to the secretariat of the United Nations Framework Convention on Climate Change-

Have agreed as follows:

Article 1

Definitions

For the purpose of the present Agreement, the following definitions shall apply:

(A) "the UNV Headquarters Agreement" means the Agreement between the United Nations and the Federal Republic of Germany concerning the Headquarters of the United Nations Volunteers Programme concluded on 10 November 1995, and the Exchange of Notes of the same date between the Administrator of the United Nations Development Programme and the Permanent Representative of Germany to the United Nations concerning the interpretation of certain provisions of the Agreement (the Agreement and Exchange of Notes are appended in the Annex);

(B) "the Convention" means the United Nations Framework Convention on Climate Change adopted at New York on 9 May 1992;

(C) "the Conference of the Parties" means the Conference of the Parties to the Convention, the supreme body of the Convention, under Article 7 thereof,

(D) "the Convention secretariat" means the secretariat established body established under Article 8 of the Convention;

(E) "the Subsidiary Body for Implementation" means the subsidiary body established under Article 10 of the Convention;

(F) "the Executive Secretary" means the head of the Convention secretariat appointed by the Secretary-General of the United Nations, after consultation with the Conference of the Parties through its Bureau (decision 14/CP.1, paragraph 7);

(G) "Officials of the Convention secretariat" means the Executive Secretary and all members of the staff of the Convention secretariat, irrespective of nationality, with the exception of those who are locally recruited and assigned to hourly rates;

(H) "Headquarters" means the premises made available to, occupied and used by the Convention secretariat in accordance with this Agreement or any other supplementary Agreement with the Government of the Federal Republic of Germany.

Article 2

Purpose and Scope of the Agreement

This Agreement shall regulate matters relating to or arising out of the applicability, mutatis mutandis, of the UNV Headquarters Agreement to the Convention secretariat.

Article 3

Application of the UNV Headquarters Agreement

(1) The UNV Headquarters Agreement shall be applicable, mutatis mutandis, to the Convention secretariat in accordance with the provisions of the present Agreement.

(2) Without prejudice to the provisions in paragraph 1 above, for the purposes of the present Agreement the references to:

(A) "the United Nations", in Article 19 paragraph 2, Article 23, and with respect to Article 26 paragraph 1 (a), of the UNV Headquarters Agreement, shall be deemed to mean the Convention secretariat or the Conference of the Parties, as appropriate;

(B) "the UNV", in Article 5 paragraph 2, and in Articles 7, 8, 9, 10, 11, 12, 14, 17, 21 and 26 of the UNV Headquarters Agreement, shall be deemed to mean the Convention secretariat;

(C) "the Executive Coordinator", in Articles 8, 11, 14, 19 paragraph 3, and in Articles 20, 21 and 22 of the UNV Headquarters Agreement, shall be deemed to mean the Executive Secretary;

(D) "the representatives of Members", throughout the UNV Headquarters Agreement, shall be deemed to include the representatives of Parties and of observer States to the Convention;

(E) "officials of the Programme" or "officials", throughout the UNV Headquarters Agreement, shall be deemed to mean officials of the Convention secretariat;

(F) "persons", in Articles 20 and 21 of the UNV Headquarters Agreement, shall be deemed to include all persons referred to in the present Agreement, including interns of the Convention secretariat;

(G) "the Party" or "Parties", in Article 19 paragraph 3, and in Articles 24 and 26 paragraph 2, of the UNV Headquarters Agreement, shall be deemed to mean the Parties under the present Agreement,

(H) "the Headquarters district", throughout the UNV Headquarters Agreement, shall be deemed to mean the Headquarters of the Convention secretariat.

(3) Without prejudice to the provisions in Article 21 of the UNV Headquarters Agreement, arrangements shall also be made to ensure that visas, entry permits or licenses, where required for persons entering the host country on official business of the Convention, are delivered at the port of entry to the Federal Republic of Germany, to those persons who were unable to obtain them elsewhere prior to their arrival.

Article 4

Legal Capacity

(1) The Convention secretariat shall posses in the host country the legal capacity:

(A) to contract;

(B) to acquire and dispose of movable and immovable property;

(C) to institute legal proceedings.

(2) For the purpose of this Article, the Convention secretariat shall be represented by the Executive Secretary.

Article 5

Immunity of Persons on Official Business of the Convention

Without prejudice to the pertinent provisions of the UNV Headquarters Agreement, all persons invited to participate in the official business of the Convention shall enjoy immunity from legal process in respect of words spoken or written and all acts performed by them in their official capacity. Such immunity shall continue to be accorded after termination of their business. They shall also be accorded inviolability for all papers and documents.

Article 6

Final Provisions

(1) The provisions of this Agreement shall be complementary to the provisions of the UNV Headquarters Agreement. Insofar as any provision of this Agreement and any provisions of the UNV Headquarters Agreement relate to the same subject matter, each of these provisions shall be applicable and neither shall narrow the effect of the other.

(2) This Agreement may be amended by mutual consent at any time at the request of any Party to the present Agreement.

(3) The present Agreement shall cease to be in force twelve months after any of the Parties gives notice in writing to the others of its decision to terminate the Agreement. This Agreement shall, however, remain in force for such an additional period as might be necessary for the orderly cessation of activities of the Convention secretariat in the Federal Republic of Germany and the

disposition of its property therein, and the resolution of any dispute between the Parties to the present Agreement.

(4) Any dispute between the Parties concerning the interpretation or application of this Agreement, which cannot be settled amicably, shall be resolved in accordance with the procedures under Article 26 paragraph 2, of the UNV Headquarters Agreement.

(5) The provisions of the Agreement shall be applied provisionally as from the date of signature, as appropriate, pending the fulfilment of the formal requirements for its entry into force referred to in paragraph 6 below.

(6) This Agreement shall enter into force on the day following the date of receipt of the last of the notifications by which the Parties will have informed each other of the completion of their respective formal requirements.

Done in Bonn, on 20 June 1996, in triplicate, in the German and the English languages, both texts being equally authentic.

Appendix IX Agreement between the United Nations, the Government of the Federal Republic of Germany, and the Secretariat of the United Nations Convention to Combat Desertification concerning the Headquarters of the Convention Permanent Secretariat*

The United Nations, the Government of the Federal Republic of Germany and the Secretariat of the United Nations Convention to Combat Desertification in Those Countries Experiencing Serious Drought and/or Desertification, Particularly in Africa (UNCCD),

Whereas the first session of the Conference of the Parties to the UNCCD (CCD/COP) by its decision 5/COP.1 of 10 October 1997, decided to accept the offer of the Government of the Federal Republic of Germany to host the Secretariat of the United Nations Convention to Combat Desertification (CCD Secretariat);

Whereas the CCD/COP, in paragraphs 3 and 4 of decision 3/COP.1 of 10 October 1997, further decided to accept the offer of the Secretary-General of the United Nations on the institutional linkage between the CCD Secretariat and the United Nations;

* Headquarters Agreement between the United Nations, the Government of the Federal Republic of Germany, and the Secretariat of the United Nations Convention to Combat Desertification, signed in Bonn on 18 August 1998 (on file with the author).

Whereas the General Assembly, by its resolution 52/198 of 18 December 1997, endorsed the institutional linkage between the CCD Secretariat and United Nations, as adopted by the CCD/COP in its decision 3/COP.1;

Whereas Article 4 paragraph 3 of the UNV Headquarters Agreement provides that it "may also be made applicable, mutatis mutandis, to other intergovernmental entities, institutionally linked to the United Nations, by agreement among such entities, the Government and the United Nations";

Whereas Article 4 paragraph 2 of the Agreement between the United Nations and the Government of the Federal Republic of Germany concerning the Occupancy and Use of the United Nations Premises in Bonn concluded on 13 February 1996, inter alia, provides that "(t)he United Nations shall make available appropriate space in the Premises to the secretariat of the United Nations Framework Convention on Climate Change … as well as, subject to availability of space, to other intergovernmental entities institutionally linked to the United Nations";

Whereas the United Nations acknowledges that the offer of the Government of the Federal Republic of Germany to provide, inter alia, premises in Bonn to the CCD Secretariat, free of rent and on a permanent basis, has been accepted by the CCD/COP;

Whereas the CCD Secretariat and the Government of the Federal Republic of Germany intent to make appropriate arrangements specifying the particular elements contained in the latter's offer to host the CCD Secretariat;

Whereas the offer of the Government of the Federal Republic of Germany, as contained in documents A/AC.241/54/Add.2 and A/AC.241/63, *inter alia*, expresses the interest of the Government of the Federal Republic of Germany in concluding an agreement to host the CCD Secretariat that would ensure the availability of all the necessary facilities in the Federal Republic of Germany to enable the CCD Secretariat to perform its functions;

Whereas the CCD/COP, at its first session held at Rome, Italy in decision 5/COP.1 "encourages the Executive Secretary as a matter of urgency to negotiate a headquarters agreement in an appropriate manner with the Government of the Federal Republic of Germany in accordance with its offer, and upon such terms and conditions as are appropriate and necessary, in consultation with the Secretary-General, and to submit it to the Conference of the Parties for adoption at a subsequent session";

Whereas, in the same decision, the CCD/COP also stresses that with a view to enabling the CCD Secretariat to effectively discharge its functions under the UNCCD, such an agreement should, in particular, reflect the following:

(A) the CCD Secretariat should possess in the host country such legal capacity as is necessary for the effective discharge of its functions under the UNCCD, in particular to contract, to acquire and dispose of movable and immovable property and to institute legal proceedings;
(B) the CCD Secretariat should enjoy in the territory of the host country such privileges and immunities as are necessary for the effective discharge of its functions under the UNCCD;
(C) the representatives of the Parties and Observer States (and regional economic integration organizations) to the UNCCD as well as the officials of the CCD Secretariat should similarly enjoy such privileges and immunities as are necessary for the independent exercise of their functions under the UNCCD;

Whereas the Secretariat's functions referred to in Article 23 of UNCCD are being carried out on an interim basis by the secretariat (referred to as "interim secretariat" in Article 1(e) in this agreement) established by the General Assembly of the United Nations in its Resolution 47/188 of 22 December 1992 and continued by virtue of Decision 4/COP.1 of 10 October 1997 and Resolution 52/198 of 18 December 1997 of the General Assembly of the United Nations;

Desiring to conclude an Agreement regulating matters rising from the applicability, mutatis mutandis, of the UNV Headquarters Agreement to the CCD Secretariat;

Have agreed as follows:

Article 1

Definitions

For the purpose of the present Agreement, the following definitions shall apply:

(A) "the UNV Headquarters Agreement" means the Agreement between the United Nations and the Federal Republic of Germany concerning the Headquarters of the United Nations Volunteers Programme concluded on 10 November 1995, and the Exchange of Notes of the same date between the Administrator of the United Nations Development Programme and the Permanent Representative of Germany to the United Nations concerning the interpretation of certain provisions of the Agreement (the Agreement and Exchange of Notes are appended in the Annex);

(B) "the UNCCD" means the United Nations Convention to Combat Desertification in Those Countries Experiencing Serious Drought and/or Desertification, Particularly in Africa adopted at Paris, France on 17 June 1994;

(C) "the CCD/COP" means the Conference of the Parties to the UNCCD, the supreme body of the Convention, under Article 22 thereof;

(D) "the CCD Secretariat" means the Permanent Secretariat established under Article 23 of the UNCCD;

(E) "the Executive Secretary" means the head of the CCD Secretariat appointed by the Secretary-General of the United Nations, after consultation with the Conference of the Parties through its Bureau (decision 4/COP.1, paragraph 4), or, until such appointment takes effect, the head of the interim secretariat;

(F) "Officials of the CCD Secretariat" means the Executive Secretary and all members of the staff of the CCD Secretariat, irrespective of nationality, with the exception of those who are locally recruited and assigned to hourly rates;

(G) "Headquarters" means the premises made available to, occupied and used by the CCD Secretariat in accordance with this Agreement or any other supplementary Agreement with the Government of the Federal Republic of Germany.

Article 2

Purpose and Scope of the Agreement

This Agreement shall regulate matters relating to or arising out of the applicability, mutatis mutandis, of the UNV Headquarters Agreement to the CCD Secretariat.

Article 3

Application of the UNV Headquarters Agreements

1. The UNV Headquarters Agreement shall be applicable, mutatis mutandis, to the CCD Secretariat in accordance with the provisions of the present Agreement.
2. Without prejudice to the provisions in paragraph 1 above, for the purposes of the present Agreement the references to:
   (A) "the United Nations", in Article 1 (m), in Article 4 paragraph 1, in Article 19 paragraph 2, in Article 23 and Article 26 paragraph 1 (a), of the UNV Headquarters Agreement, shall be deemed to mean the CCD Secretariat or CCD/COP,

as appropriate; and, with respect to Article 19 paragraph 3 of the same Agreement, shall be deemed to mean the United Nations and the CCD Secretariat;

(B) "the UNV" in Article 5 paragraph 2, and in Articles 7, 8, 9, 10, 11, 12, 14, 17, 21 and 26 of the UNV Headquarters Agreement, shall be deemed to mean the CCD Secretariat;

(C) "the Executive Coordinator", in Articles 8, 11, 14, 19 paragraph 3, and in Articles 20, 21 and 22 of the UNV Headquarters Agreement, shall be deemed to mean the Executive Secretary;

(D) "the representatives of Members", throughout the UNV Headquarters Agreement, shall be deemed to include the representatives of Parties and of Observer States (and regional economic integration organizations) to the UNCCD;

(E) "officials", "officials of the UNV" or "officials of the Programme", throughout the UNV Headquarters Agreement, shall be deemed to mean officials of the CCD Secretariat;

(F) "persons", in Articles 20 and 21 of the UNV Headquarters Agreement, shall be deemed to include all persons referred to in the present Agreement, including interns of the CCD Secretariat;

(G) "the Party" or "Parties", in Article 19 paragraph 3, and in Articles 24 and 26 paragraph 2, of the UNV Headquarters Agreement, shall be deemed to mean the Parties under the present Agreement;

(H) "the Headquarters district", throughout the UNV Headquarters Agreement, shall be deemed to mean the Headquarters of the CCD Secretariat.

3. Without prejudice to the provisions in Article 21 of the UNV Headquarters Agreement, arrangements shall also be made to ensure that visas, entry permits or licenses, where required for persons entering the host country on official business of the UNCCD, are delivered at the port of entry to the Federal Republic of

Germany, to those persons who were unable to obtain them elsewhere prior to their arrival.

Article 4

Legal Capacity

1. The CCD Secretariat shall possess in the host country the legal capacity:
   (A) to contract;
   (B) to acquire and dispose of movable and immovable property;
   (C) to institute legal proceedings.
2. For the purpose of this Article, the CCD Secretariat shall be represented by the Executive Secretary.

Article 5

Immunity of Persons on Official Business of the Convention

Without prejudice to the pertinent provisions of the UNV Headquarters Agreement, all persons invited to participate in the official business of the UNCCD shall enjoy immunity from legal process in respect of words spoken or written and all acts performed by them in their official capacity. Such immunity shall continue to be accorded after termination of their business. They shall also be accorded inviolability for all papers and documents.

Article 6

Final Provisions

1. The previsions of this Agreement shall be complementary to the provisions of the UNV Headquarters Agreement. Insofar as

any provision of this Agreement and any provision of the UNV Headquarters Agreement relate to the same subject matter, each of these provisions shall be applicable and neither shall narrow the effect of the other.

2. This Agreement may be amended by mutual consent at any time at the request of any Party to the present Agreement.
3. The present Agreement shall cease to be in force twelve months after any of the Parties gives notice in writing to the others of its decision to terminate the Agreement. This Agreement shall, however, remain in force for such an additional period as might be necessary for the orderly cessation of activities of the CCD Secretariat in the Federal Republic of Germany and the disposition of its property therein, and the resolution of any dispute between the Parties to the present Agreement.
4. (A) Any bilateral dispute between any two of the Parties concerning the interpretation or application of this Agreement or the regulations of the UNV which cannot be settled amicably shall be submitted, at the request of either Party to the dispute, to an arbitral tribunal, composed of three members. Each Party shall appoint one arbitrator and the two arbitrators thus appointed shall together appoint a third arbitrator as their chairman. If one of the Parties fails to appoint its arbitrator and has not proceeded to do so within two months after an invitation from the other Party to make such an appointment, the other Party may request the President of the International Court of Justice to make the necessary appointment. If the two arbitrators are unable to reach agreement, in the two months following their appointment, on the choice of the third arbitrator, either Party may invite the President of the International Court of Justice to make the necessary appointment.

   (B) Any dispute amongst the three Parties concerning the interpretation or application of this Agreement or the regulations of the UNV which cannot be settled amicably shall be submitted, at the request of any Party to the dispute, to an arbitral tribunal, composed of five members. Each Party shall appoint one arbitrator and the three arbitrators thus appointed shall together appoint fourth and fifth arbitrators and the first three shall jointly designate either the fourth or the fifth arbitrator as Chairman of the arbitral tribunal. If any of the Parties fails to appoint its arbitrator and has not proceeded to do so within two months after an invitation from another party to make such an appointment, such other Party may request the President of the International Court of Justice to make any necessary appointments. If the three arbitrators are unable to reach agreement, in the two months following their appointment, on the choice of the fourth or fifth arbitrator or designation of the Chairman, any Party may invite the President of the International Court of Justice to make any necessary appointments or designation.

(C) The Parties shall draw up a special agreement determining the subject of the dispute. Failing the conclusion of such an agreement within a period of two months from the date on which arbitration was requested, the dispute may be brought before the arbitral tribunal upon the application of any Party. Unless the Parties decide otherwise, the arbitral tribunal shall determine its own procedure. The expenses of the arbitration shall be borne by the Parties as assessed by the arbitrators. The arbitral tribunal shall reach its decision by a majority of votes on the basis of the applicable rules of international law. In the absence of such rules, it shall decide *ex aequo et bono*. The decision shall be final and binding on the Parties to the dispute, even if rendered in default of one or two of the Parties to the dispute.

5. The provisions of this Agreement shall be applied provisionally as from the date of signature, as appropriate, pending the fulfilment of the formal requirements for its entry into force referred to in paragraph 6 below.

6. This Agreement shall enter into force on the day following the date of receipt of the last of the notifications by which the Parties will have informed each other of the completion of their respective formal requirements.

Done in Bonn, on 18 August 1998, in triplicate, in the German and the English languages, both texts being equally authentic.

Appendix X Agreement among the Government of the Federal Republic of Germany, the United Nations, and the Secretariat of the Convention on the Conservation of Migratory Species of Wild Animals concerning the Headquarters of the Convention Secretariat*

The Government of the Federal Republic of Germany the United Nations and the Secretariat of the Convention on the Conservation of Migratory Species of Wild Animals,

Whereas the United Nations Environment Programme (UNEP) provides secretariat services for the Secretariat of the Convention on the Conservation of Migratory Species of Wild Animals (CMS), in accordance with Article IX of the Convention,

Whereas the Government of the Federal Republic of Germany has a special responsibility towards the Convention and its Secretariat, in view

* Headquarters Agreement among the representatives of Government of the Federal Republic of Germany (Julius Georg Luy and Jurgen Trittin) for the Government of the Federal Republic of Germany, Deputive Executive Director UNEP (Shafqat Kakakhel) for the United Nations, and Executive Secretary UNEP/CMS (Amulf Muller-Helmbrecht) for the Secretariat of the Convention on the Conservation of Migratory Species of Wild Animals in Bonn on 18 September 2002 (on file with the author).

of its role in the Convention's early development and its present function as Depositary,

Whereas paragraph 2 of Article 4 of the Agreement between the Federal Republic of Germany and the United Nations concerning the Headquarters of the United Nations Volunteers Programme concluded on 10 November 1995 provides that it "shall also apply *mutatis mutandis* to such other Offices of the United Nations as may be located in the Federal Republic of Germany with the consent of the Government",

Whereas paragraph 3 of Article 4 of the Agreement between the Federal Republic of Germany and the United Nations concerning the Headquarters of the United Nations Volunteers Programme concluded on 10 November 1995 provides that it "may also be made applicable *mutatis mutandis* to other inter-governmental entities, institutionally linked to the United Nations, by agreement among such entities, the Government and the United Nations,"

Whereas paragraph 2 of Article 4 of the Agreement between the Government of the Federal Republic of Germany and the United Nations concerning the Occupancy and Use of the United Nations Premises in Bonn concluded on 13 February 1996 *inter alia* provides that "the United Nations shall make available appropriate space in the Premises…, subject to the availability of space, to other inter-governmental entities institutionally linked to the United Nations," and

Desiring to conclude an Agreement regulating matters arising from the applicability *mutatis mutandis* of the Agreement concluded on 10 November 1995 between the Federal Republic of Germany and the United nations concerning the Headquarters of the United Nations Volunteers Programme to the Secretariat of the Convention on the Conservation of Migratory Species of Wild Animals,

Have agreed as follows:

Article 1

Definitions

For the purpose of the present Agreement, the following definitions shall apply:

(a) "the UNV Headquarters Agreement" means the Agreement between the Federal Republic of Germany and the United nations concerning the Headquarters of the United Nations Volunteers Programme concluded on 10 November 1995, and the Exchange of Notes of the same date between the Administrator of the United Nations Development Programme and the Permanent Representative of Germany to the United Nations concerning the interpretation of certain provisions of the Agreement. The Agreement and Exchange of Notes are appended in the Annex;
(b) "the Convention" means the Convention on the Conservation of Migratory Species of Wild Animals, adopted in Bonn on 23 June 1979;
(c) "the Conference of the Parties" means the Conference of the Parties to the Convention, the decision-making organ of the Convention, under Article VII thereof;
(d) "the Convention Secretariat" means the Secretariat established under Article IX of the Convention;
(e) "Executive Secretary" means the Head of the Convention Secretariat;
(f) "Officials of the Convention Secretariat" means the Executive Secretary and all members of the staff of the Convention Secretariat, irrespective of nationality, with the exception of those who are recruited locally and assigned to hourly rates; and
(g) "Headquarters" means the premises made available to, occupied and used by the Convention Secretariat in accordance with

this Agreement or any other supplementary Agreement with the Government of the Federal Republic of Germany.

Article 2

Purpose and Scope of the Agreement

(1) This Agreement shall regulate matters relating to or arising out of the applicability *mutatis mutandis* of the UNV Headquarters Agreement of the Convention Secretariat.

(2) Subject to the consent of the competent bodies of Agreements concluded under Article IV of the Convention, this Agreement shall apply *mutatis mutandis* to Secretariat of such Agreements which have been administratively integrated within the Convention Secretariat and are institutionally linked to the United Nations by agreement among such Secretariats, the Convention Secretariat and the United Nations.

Article 3

Application of the UNV Headquarters Agreement

(1) The UNV Headquarters Agreement shall be applicable *mutatis mutandis* to the Convention Secretariat in accordance with the provisions of the present Agreement.

(2) Without prejudice to the provisions in paragraph 1 above, for the purposes of the present Agreement the references to:

(a) "the United Nations," in Article 1 (m), in Article 4 paragraph 1, in Article 19 paragraph 2, in Article 23 and with respect to paragraph 1 (a) of Article 26 of the UNV Headquarters Agreement, shall be deemed to mean the Convention Secretariat or the Conference of the Parties; and with respect to Article 19 paragraph 3 of the same Agreement shall be deemed to mean the United Nations and the Convention Secretariat;

(b) "the UNV", in Article 5 paragraph 2 and in Articles 7, 8, 9, 10, 11, 12, 14, 17, 19, 21 and 26 of the UNV Headquarters Agreement, shall be deemed to mean the Convention Secretariat;

(c) "the Executive Coordinator," in Articles 8, 11, 14, 19 paragraph 3, and in Articles 20, 21 and 22 of the UNV Headquarters Agreement, shall be deemed to mean the Executive Secretary;

(d) "the representatives of Members," throughout the UNV Headquarters Agreement, shall be deemed to comprise the representatives of Parties and observer States to the Convention;

(e) "officials," "officials of the UNV" or "officials of the Programme," throughout the UNV Headquarters Agreement, shall be deemed to include officials o the Convention Secretariat;

(f) "persons," in Articles 20 and 21 of the UNV Headquarters Agreement, shall be deemed to include all persons referred to in the present Agreement, including interns of the Convention Secretariat;

(g) "Party" or "Parties," in Article 19 paragraph 3, and in Articles 24 and 26 paragraph 2 of the UNV Headquarters Agreement, shall be deemed to mean the Parties under the present Agreement; and

(h) "Headquarters district," throughout the UNV Headquarters Agreement, shall be deemed to mean the Headquarters of the Convention Secretariat.

(3) Without prejudice to the provisions in Article 21 of the UNV Headquarters Agreement, arrangements shall also be made to ensure that visas, entry permits or licenses, where required for persons entering the host country on official business of the Convention, are delivered at the port of entry to the Federal Republic of Germany, to those persons who were unable to obtain them elsewhere prior to their arrival.

Article 4

Legal Capacity

(1) The Convention Secretariat shall possess in the host country the legal capacity to;
   (a) contract;
   (b) acquire and dispose of movable and immovable property; and
   (c) institute legal proceedings.

(2) For the purpose of this Article, the Convention Secretariat shall be represented by the Executive Secretary.

Article 5

Tenure

Without prejudice to paragraph 2 of Article 4 of the Agreement between the Government of the Federal Republic of Germany and the United Nations concerning the Occupancy and Use of the United Nations Premises in Bonn concluded on 13 February 1996, the Convention Secretariat shall be guaranteed permanent and rent-free tenure of sufficient space for it to carry out its work in a satisfactory manner, so long as its operations remain based in the Federal Republic of Germany, subject to the availability of space to other intergovernmental entities, institutionally linked to the United Nations.

Article 6

Immunity of Persons on Official Business of the Convention

Without prejudice to the pertinent provisions of the UNV Headquarters Agreement, all persons invited to the Headquarters on official business of the Convention shall enjoy immunity from legal process in respect of words spoken or written and all acts performed by them in their official capacity. Such immunity shall continue to be accorded after termination of their business. They shall also be accorded inviolability for all papers and documents.

Article 7

Final Provisions

(1) The provisions of this Agreement shall be complementary to the provisions of the UNV Headquarters Agreement. Insofar as any provision of this Agreement and any provision of the UNV Headquarters Agreement relate to the same subject matter, each of these provisions shall be applicable and neither shall narrow the effect of the other.

(2) This Agreement may be amended by mutual consent at the request of either party to the present Agreement

(3) The present Agreement shall cease to be in force twelve months after any of the Parties gives notice in writing to the others of its decision to terminate the Agreement. This agreement shall, however, remain in force for such an additional period as might be necessary for the orderly cessation of activities of the Convention Secretariat in the Federal Republic of Germany and the disposition of their property therein, and the resolution of any dispute among the Parties to the present Agreement.

(4) Any bilateral dispute between any two of the Parties concerning the interpretation of this Agreement or the regulations of the UNV, which cannot be settled amicably, shall be submitted, at the request of either Party to the dispute, to an arbitral tribunal composed of three members. Each Party to the dispute shall appoint one arbitrator and the two arbitrators thus appointed shall together appoint a third arbitrator as their Chairman. If one of the Parties fails to appoint its arbitrator and has not proceeded

to do so within two months after an invitation from the other Party to make such an appointment, the other Party may request the President of the International Court of Justice to make the necessary appointment. If the two arbitrators are unable to reach agreement, in the two months following their appointment, on the choice of the third arbitrator, either Party may invite the President of the International Court of Justice to make the necessary appointment.

(5) Any dispute amongst the three Parties concerning the interpretation or application of this Agreement or the regulations of the UNV, which cannot be settled amicably, shall be submitted, at the request of any Party to the dispute, to an arbitral tribunal composed of five members. Each Party shall appoint one arbitrator and the three arbitrators thus appointed shall together appoint fourth and fifth arbitrators and the first three shall jointly designate either the fourth or the fifth arbitrator as Chairman of the arbitral tribunal. If any of the Parties fails to appoint its arbitrator and has not proceeded to do so within two months after an invitation from another Party to make such an appointment, such other Party may request the President of the International Court of Justice to make the necessary appointment. If the three arbitrators are unable to reach agreement, in the two months following their appointment, on the choice of the fourth or fifth arbitrator or designation of the Chairman, any Party may invite the President of the International Court of Justice to make the necessary appointment or designation.

(6) The Parties shall draw up a special agreement determining the subject of the dispute. Failing conclusion of such an agreement within the period of two months from the date on which arbitration was requested, the dispute may be brought before the arbitral tribunal upon the application of any Party. Unless the Parties decide otherwise, the arbitral tribunal shall determine its own procedure. The expenses of the arbitration shall be borne by

the parties to the dispute as assessed by the arbitrators. The arbitral tribunal shall reach its decision by a majority of votes on the basis of the applicable rule of international law. In the absence of such rules, it shall decide *ex aequo et bono*. The decision shall be final and binding on all Parties to the dispute, even if rendered in default of one or two of the Parties to the dispute.

(7) The provisions of this Agreement shall be applied provisionally, as from the date of signature, as appropriate, until its entry into force referred to in paragraph 9 below.

(8) The headquarters agreement concluded between the Government of the Federal Republic of Germany and the United Nations Environment Programme by an exchange of letters dated 30 November and 17 December 1984, as amended by an exchange of letters dated 15 and 24 August 1989, shall expire upon entry into force of this Agreement, except paragraph 1 of the former agreement which shall remain applicable.

(9) This Agreement shall enter into force on the day following the date of receipt of the last of the notifications by which the Parties will have informed each other of the completion of their respective formal requirements.

Done in Bonn, on 18 September 2002, in triplicate, in the German and the English languages, both texts being equally authentic.

Index

For EU product safety concerns, contact us at Calle de José Abascal, 56–1°, 28003 Madrid, Spain or eugpsr@cambridge.org.

www.ingramcontent.com/pod-product-compliance
Lightning Source LLC
LaVergne TN
LVHW011528200926
848484LV00001B/186
* 9 7 8 0 5 2 1 8 8 3 2 8 3 *